The Legal Epic

The Legal Epic

Paradise Lost and the Early Modern Law

ALISON A. CHAPMAN

The University of Chicago Press ✻ *Chicago and London*

The University of Chicago Press, Chicago 60637
The University of Chicago Press, Ltd., London

Published 2017
Printed in the United States of America

26 25 24 23 22 21 20 19 18 17 1 2 3 4 5

ISBN-13: 978-0-226-43513-8 (cloth)
ISBN-13: 978-0-226-43527-5 (e-book)
DOI: 10.7208/chicago/9780226435275.001.0001

Library of Congress Cataloging-in-Publication Data

Names: Chapman, Alison A., author.
Title: The legal epic : Paradise Lost and the early modern law / Alison A. Chapman.
Description: Chicago ; London : The University of Chicago Press, 2017. |
Includes bibliographical references and index.
Identifiers: LCCN 2016028709 | ISBN 9780226435138 (cloth : alk. paper) | ISBN 9780226435275 (e-book)
Subjects: LCSH: Milton, John, 1608–1674. Paradise lost. | Milton, John, 1608–1674—Knowledge—Law. | Law in literature. | Religion and law. | Law and literature—England.
Classification: LCC PR3562 .C54 2017 | DDC 821.4—dc23
LC record available at https://lccn.loc.gov/2016028709

♾ This paper meets the requirements of ANSI/NISO Z39.48-1992 (Permanence of Paper).

Contents

Acknowledgments vii

On Texts xi

1. Introduction *1*
2. Law and Religion in Milton's World *35*
3. The Traitors of Heaven and Earth *65*
4. The Arch-Felon *97*
5. The Sole Propriety of Adam and Eve *125*
6. Acts of Possession *151*
7. The Mortal Sentence *184*
8. Begging Pardon *214*
9. Conclusion *244*

Bibliography 253

Index 277

Acknowledgments

This book took its genesis in the strangest of circumstances. In 2004 I received an invitation from a group of inmates at a maximum-security men's prison in central Alabama to come teach them *Paradise Lost*. I have chronicled the story of this extraordinary experience in an essay where I explore how Milton's language of inner liberty translated into a maximum-security setting.[1] What I did not discuss in that essay is that the inmates and I also had conversations about the way law works, about its relation to morality and justice. Those conversations sprang organically from the text of *Paradise Lost*, and they started me thinking about the idea that *Paradise Lost* was a deeply legal text. For a long time I assumed that it was deeply legal only in a symbolic or structural way, meaning that I assumed this Edenic story could not really have law in it because law was for later, fallen societies. I did not know enough at that point to see how and where law had worked its way into the poem. As I have learned more over the intervening years, I have developed a much expanded sense of the law's presence in *Paradise Lost*, and the ideas that emerged in my prison conversations have been either discarded or revised out of all recognition.

1. Chapman, "Milton's Captive Audience." I wish also to draw attention to the work of Sarah Higginbotham, a scholar of early modern literature and founder of the Georgia State Prison Initiative based at Phillips State Prison in Buford, Georgia.

Yet, however far this book has traveled from its point of origin, I am grateful that it began in a dingy cinderblock room deep inside the William E. Donaldson Correctional Facility. I extend my thanks to Dr. Deborah Marshall and Dr. Kathy Allen, the dedicated prison psychologists who made my regular visits both possible and safe, and to my inmate students for their honesty, their intelligence, and—what surprised me most in that setting—their kindness.

While the inmates planted the seed of this book, others have provided the circumstances that allowed it to grow. Ben Darlow generously offered his expertise as a legal historian and importantly refined my understanding of technical legal matters, ranging from the history of strict liability to the changing early modern relationship between case law and statutory law. Rebecca Ann Bach commented on the entire manuscript with her characteristic intelligence and cogency; I remain—as ever—in her debt. At a crucial juncture in the revision process, Mary C. Fenton provided support and a generous critical vision that allowed the argument to take an important stride forward. I also want to thank the anonymous readers, whose suggestions have strengthened the argument and given extra precision to my discussion of the law. I am grateful for Danny Siegel's and Jeanene Skillen's incisive comments on chapter 3. A Lindsey Young Fellowship from the University of Tennessee's Medieval and Renaissance Consortium enabled me to write the majority of chapter 7, and a sabbatical granted by the University of Alabama at Birmingham allowed me to complete the whole book. An earlier version of chapter 6, "Begging Pardon," appeared as "Satan's Pardon: The Forms of Judicial Mercy in *Paradise Lost*," *Milton Studies* 55 (2014): 177–206, and I offer my thanks to the journal for permission to print it, as revised, here. I could not have written this book without database resources funded by the Department of English at the University of Alabama at Birmingham under the leadership of Peter Bellis, and without the efforts of Eddie Luster at Mervyn Sterne Library.

Most importantly, this book has been made possible by my husband, Gordon. He has cared for our three splendid sons and was unstintingly supportive as I retreated for long hours into the world of seventeenth-century jurisprudence. I dedicate this book to him.

On Texts

In quoting from Milton's prose, I have used *Complete Prose Works of John Milton*, edited by Don M. Wolfe, 8 vols. (New Haven, CT: Yale University Press, 1953–82), abbreviated as *CPW* and cited parenthetically in the text by volume and page number. All quotes from Milton's poetry come from *The Complete Poetry and Essential Prose of John Milton*, edited by William Kerrigan, John Rumrich, and Stephen M. Fallon (New York: Modern Library, 2007) and are cited parenthetically in the text. I refer to the shorter poems by line number and to *Paradise Lost* by book and line number. The abbreviation *LR* refers to *The Life Records of John Milton*, edited by J. Milton French, 5 vols. (New Brunswick, NJ: Rutgers University Press, 1949).

When quoting from early modern works, I have modernized typography (e.g., changing *u* to *v* and *i* to *j*) and expanded abbreviations (e.g., changing *&* to *and*). When longer passages are italicized in early modern works, I have altered these to regular font, but I have retained the italics on other occasions. I have preserved original spellings and capitalizations except for titles, where I have followed modern rules about capitalizing all principal words. When citing early modern works, I have used page numbers except when they do not seem reliable, in which case I have opted for signature numbers. Translations are my own unless otherwise noted.

1

Introduction

Reflecting on the fundamental ideological orientations that impelled the French Revolution as opposed to the English Civil War, Matthew Arnold once observed succinctly, "1789 asked of a thing, Is it rational? 1642 asked of a thing, Is it legal?" Arnold's insight about seventeenth-century England's profoundly legal turn of mind has been reinforced by subsequent studies of the period. For example, Deborah Shuger writes that law occupies "the troubled center of the Renaissance episteme," and she calls it "the characteristic discipline of the late Renaissance, in much the same way that logic is the characteristic discipline of the Middle Ages."[1] We see this intense preoccupation with law in many of the period's major literary works. Authors like Sir Thomas More, Edmund Spenser, William Shakespeare, Ben Jonson, and John Donne all show both an interest in broad legal ideas and a familiarity with the technical nuts and bolts of legal justice.[2] In a nutshell, this book argues that we should add John

1. Arnold, "Function of Criticism," 15; Shuger, *Renaissance Bible*, 51, 52.

2. The scholarship on literature and law in the early modern period is too large to be adequately treated in a note. I have been most influenced by Hutson, *Invention of*

Milton to the list of early modern writers who had a detailed understanding of and interest in the law and who used his works to raise searching questions about the law's proper function. Although Milton's view of the law is my subject broadly speaking, I do not attempt here to provide a comprehensive study of Milton's comments about law and the just relations that law was supposed to ensure. Such a study lies beyond my present scope, given the various forms of legal justice in the period (constitutional, international, mercantile, criminal, civil, equitable, etc.), the many different legal systems with which Milton was familiar (common law, Roman law, canon law, brehon law, Anglo-Dutch law, etc.), and the sheer volume of his writings. Instead, as my title indicates, *The Legal Epic* concentrates on *Paradise Lost*. I argue that *Paradise Lost* sits at the apex of the early modern period's long fascination with law and judicial processes and that if we do not understand the links that the early modern period drew between law and religion, we cannot see the way law works in Milton's poem to help "justify the ways of God to men" (1.26).

Paradise Lost is saturated with legal terms. Examples include "patrimony," "realty," "injunction," "prohibition," "arch-felon," "grand thief," "allegations," "fact," "sentence," "devolved," "equal," "verdict," "evidence," "partner," "proof," "propriety," "crime," "contempt," "trespass," "collateral," "act of grace," "possession," "devise," and many more. When Milton uses these and other legal terms, he points both to general ideas of legality and to ways in which real early modern laws worked.[3] An excerpt from book 10 shows

Suspicion; Cormack, *Power to Do Justice*; and Wilson, *Theaters of Intention*. For other focused discussions of how Donne, Spenser, and Jonson, respectively, use legal terms and ideas, see Kneidel, *Donne and Legal Culture*; Zurcher, *Spenser's Legal Language*; and Wilson, "Jonson and the Law of Contract." In my reading, Milton uses literature to represent the origins of law. In this way my work is different from—but by no means inconsistent with—volumes like Beecher et al., *Taking Exception to the Law*; and Kezar, *Solon and Thespis*, which also trace the various relationships between early modern literature and law.

3. Legal historian A. W. B. Simpson warns against any effort to pin down when early modern words function in a generic as opposed to a specifically legal use: "It is futile to attempt to prise apart the ordinary use [of a word] from the legal use; they are

this legal precision at work. When the fallen angels drop to their bellies and turn into snakes, Milton calls them "accessories" to Satan's "riot" (10.520, 521). In doing so, he makes a set of exact legal discriminations. Since the fallen angels were confined to Hell while Satan roamed free, Milton means the word "accessories" in a specifically common law sense. Whereas a code like Roman law generally defined accessories as those who actually assisted in the commission of a crime, common law had a broader definition.[4] As the early modern common lawyer John Brydall explains, an accessory after the fact was "he, that receiveth, favoureth, aideth, or comforteteth [*sic*] any Man, that had done any murder or other felony, whereof he hath knowledge," even if he himself was not present at the crime's commission.[5] In book 10 Milton shows the fallen angels providing this kind of felonious favor, aid, and comfort to Satan, for, having heard the story of his success in Eden, they attempt to give him their "universal shout and high applause," an acclaim that turns to hissing (10.505). In the next sentence, Milton calls them "accessories," so he is applying this label with a lawyerly precision, as soon as possible after they clear the statutory bar.[6] When he convicts the fallen angels of abetting the specific crime of "riot," Milton also alludes to contemporary legal norms. Unlike our modern association of riot with large, violent crowds, an early modern riot occurred when "three or more do an unlawful Act."[7] The detail of three persons was

dovetailed together in so complicated a way that separation will distort both." Simpson, *Legal Theory and Legal History*, 346.

4. On the Roman law's definition of accessories, see Campbell, *Compendium of Roman Law*, 180.

5. Brydall, *Laws of England*, 125.

6. It is unclear whether the fallen angels would also qualify under common law as accessories before the fact. As Brydall explains, an accessory before the fact "is he that commandeth or procureth an other to commit felony, and is not there present himself, when the other doth it." *Laws of England*, 124. Lawyers for the defense would argue that since the other angels were Satan's inferiors, they could neither "command" nor "procure" Satan's crime. Lawyers for the prosecution, however, would argue that the fallen angels do indeed "procure" Satan's felony during the council in Hell.

7. Brydall, *Laws of England*, 101.

foundational to riot's legal definition, appearing consistently in early modern legal works.[8] By the time he enters Hell in book 10, Satan has recently collaborated with Sin and Death. As a result, when he addresses his followers, he is newly guilty of the three-personed crime of riot, and the fallen angels can be accurately called accessories to riot. (Early modern riots typically targeted either enclosures or food stores, and so Milton provides a dark parody: Sin and Death will breach Eden's "enclosure green" and Death will "stuff [his] maw" with Eden's riches [4.133; 10.601].)[9] These legal terms allow Milton to make two theological points. First, the fallen angels have earlier fantasized about being "exempt" from "Heav'n's high jurisdiction," but since riot and being an accessory to felony were both domestic crimes, Milton uses the law to remind readers that even in the heart of Hell, the fallen angels live under God's domestic jurisdiction (2.318, 319).[10] Second, the logic of the common law helps justify the punishments meted out to the fallen angels. In Brydall's words, any criminal accessory "shall be punished and shall have Judgement of life and member, as well as the principal," and so Milton applies a basic principle of English common law when he shows Satan's punishment being transmitted to his followers.[11]

A similarly informed use of early modern legal practices and ideas is evident at many of the poem's key junctures. For instance, when God and the Son make provision in book 3 for Adam and Eve's salvation, Milton shows both the theological virtue of mercy

8. For example, see Thomas Blount, *Nomo-Lexicon*, Llllv; Rastell, *Difficult and Obscure Words*, 168v.

9. For more on the origins and nature of early modern riots, see Sharp, *In Contempt of All Authority*; Manning, *Village Revolts*; and Walter, *Crowds and Popular Politics*.

10. By stressing the domestic law vocabulary in this passage, I offer a counter to Julie Stone Peters's argument that the bridge-over-Chaos scene reflects developing ideas of international law. Whereas Peters reads the actions of Satan/Sin/Death and God in the context of relations between different sovereign states, I would argue that Milton's use of a term like "riot" is meant to overturn any illusion of legal sovereignty. See her "'Bridge over Chaos.'"

11. Brydall, *Laws of England*, 125.

and an accurate version of early modern pardoning protocols. When God elevates the Son in book 5, we see Milton's anti-trinitarian beliefs, and we also see a reflection of the two-stage process that constituted early modern legislating. When he calls Satan a "grand thief," Milton assumes that readers will know the difference between petty and grand larceny (4.192), and when Abdiel refers to Satan as one who has lost not only "faith" but also "realty," Milton alludes to the fact that under common law, breaking faith with one's lord had historically resulted in the forfeiture of one's real estate (6.115). Likewise, when Adam refuses to relinquish his "bond" in Eve, readers are tacitly asked to remember the crucial role that sealed bonds played in early modern finance (9.956). In these and many other passages in *Paradise Lost*, Milton uses early modern legal principles, cases, and statutes to help readers make sense of God and God's plans for a wayward humanity.

The Paradise Within and Without

Seeing the role that law plays in *Paradise Lost* has the potential to change our thinking about the poem in two main ways. First, legal ideas support Milton's stated goal: to "assert eternal providence" and to "justify the ways of God to men" (1.25, 26).[12] The verb "to assert" evolved from a Roman legal practice (*ad* + *serĕre*) whereby a man either claimed or set free a slave by formally placing his hand on the slave's head.[13] Milton's goal to "justify" has a similar set of jurisprudential resonances. While Milton scholars have typically read the verb "to justify" in its moral/theological sense of "to confer or assure righteousness," it also had a range of specifically juridical meanings in Milton's day that sprang from its etymological root in *jure*. For example,

12. My argument about Milton's attempt to justify God is generally indebted to Danielson, *Milton's Good God*; and Donnelly, *Milton's Scriptural Reasoning*.

13. "Assert," v., etymology, *OED Online*.

"to justify" could mean "to corroborate, prove, verify," "to try as a judge," "to make lawful," and "to offer a defense that the act [in question] was lawful."[14] When he says his goal is to "justify" God, Milton signals that at one level, he will be providing a legal defense. He thereby invites his readers to judge the ways of God not only according to reason and conscience but also according to widespread ideas about legal justice. In *Doctrine and Discipline of Divorce*, Milton writes that God "binds himself like a just lawgiver to his own prescriptions, gives himself to be understood by men, judges and is judg'd, measures and is commensurate to right reason" (*CPW* 2:292). As I explain in chapter 2, for Milton and his contemporaries, the category of God's "prescriptions" was an elastic one that also included human law, and so God "binds himself" to the principles of both the Law and the law, divine law as well as temporal law. This act of self-binding means that God also wants to be "measure[d]" against these complementary sets of principles. God invites human beings to judge him, applying not only the yardstick of reason and conscience but also the yardstick of the law, which was—at least in theory—itself another expression of God's nature and his will for humanity. For example, when Death calls Satan a "traitor angel" who has "conjured" against God, and when the epic voice describes wedded love as a form of "sole propriety" (2.689, 693; 4.751), Milton draws on contemporary ideas about how the law works, and in each case, legal principles cooperate with theological ones to show that God's justice runs a comprehensible course.[15]

14. "Justify," v., defs. 1b, 3a, 4a, 6d, 7a, *OED Online*.

15. Peter C. Herman, in "'Whose Fault,'" uses developments in contributory negligence to make the opposite point: that God is to blame for his failure to contain Satan. While I agree with Herman's warrant that law is an important context for thinking about the poem, his discussion of contributory negligence is misleading. The early modern period lacked the modern distinction between actions in tort and in contract, and ideas of negligence were primarily worked out in relationship to transfers of property. For example, most early landmark cases relate to the duties of common carriers. As a result, contributory negligence was primarily a commercial issue, and the law of torts remained underdeveloped before the nineteenth century.

As a result, while fallen Adam complains, "Inexplicable/[God's] justice seems" (10.754–55), God's justice is not as wholly inexplicable as Adam claims, for Milton has taken pains to describe many aspects of it in terms of widely known legal principles and procedures. Adam himself offers a good example. Not long after he laments the unfathomable nature of God's justice, he and Eve conform to one of the most basic early modern assumptions about judicial pardons: they are careful to beg pardon in the same place where they were sentenced. At this point in *Paradise Lost*, as in so many others, Milton aligns the operations of human temporal justice and those of divine justice. Ironically, given his professed hostility to Milton's God, critic William Empson calls inadvertent attention to one of these law-Law alignments. Criticizing God for his professed inability in book 3 to remit Adam and Eve's penalty, Empson claims that God's rationale is "no part of English justice, because the prerogative of mercy has long been a fundamental power of the Crown."[16] But in reasoning by judicial analogy, Empson oversimplifies the early modern period's judicial terrain. While he is correct that the Crown had the authority to issue pardons, English juridical tradition also put careful restrictions on the nature and extent of pardons. Admittedly, English monarchs often ignored these restrictions, but the later Stuarts' insistence on their rights to issue dispensations at will was a major cause of their overthrow in 1688. As a result, when God scrupulously limits his pardoning power, he acts like a law-abiding monarch should and not like Empson's divine hypocrite.

By suggesting that Milton uses law in *Paradise Lost* to help explain God's ways, I part company from those critics who stress the inscrutability of Milton's God. For instance, Victoria Silver argues that God in *Paradise Lost* is perplexing and contradictory, and Stanley Fish claims that since human beings must simply obey, God's comprehensibility is beside the point.[17] In contrast, I emphasize the way law helps readers of *Paradise Lost* build a

16. Empson, *Milton's God*, 19.
17. Silver, *Imperfect Sense*; Fish, *How Milton Works*.

conceptual bridge between Heaven and Earth, using what they know of temporal law to understand, even if only partially, the operations of God and the practices of a distant Edenic world. My argument also pushes back against those critics who see Milton as embracing a position of conflicted ambivalence.[18] However, I am not suggesting that Milton had no doubts about God's justice. While *Paradise Lost*'s legal allusions help untie—or at least loosen—many of the knots in this poem, other knots remain fastened tight (How could Satan be "self-tempted" [3.130]? Why is the Son's sacrifice necessary for humanity's salvation? Why is Adam's guilt visited upon his offspring? Etc.). Rather than arguing that the law works as a universal solvent for the stubborn problem of God, my claim is that if we read *Paradise Lost* on the lookout for its moments of incertitude and divine impenetrability, we can miss the ways in which law helps to create rational order and stability. Continuing in *Doctrine and Discipline of Divorce* his exploration of the legality of God's ways, Milton writes, "God indeed in some wayes of his providence, is high and secret past finding out." However, "in the delivery and execution of his Law, . . . [he] hath plain anough reveal'd himself" (*CPW* 2:297–98). God's nature is beyond human comprehension. God's laws, however, are not. And since for Natural Law devotees like Milton, human laws and divine laws are part of the same cosmic fabric, human laws can help explain why God does what he does. This seems important to Milton because a God of law is a predictable God, one who works in perfectly consistent ways at every point between Alpha and Omega, and so the law provides Milton with a defense against the seemingly arbitrary God of Calvinist theology.[19]

18. Herman and Sauer's edited collection *New Milton Criticism* provides a good representative sample of readings that resist the orthodox Milton proposed by critics like C. S. Lewis and Fish. Other works that emphasize Milton's conflicted stance include Wittreich, "Milton's Transgressive Maneuvers"; Rumrich, *Milton Unbound*; Herman, *Destabilizing Milton*; Michael Bryson, *Tyranny of Heaven*; and Fallon, *Milton's Peculiar Grace*.

19. I am indebted to John Stachniewski's point that by justifying God, Milton is reacting against the Calvinist idea that God "should not be brought to the bar of human

Second, while on the one hand the presence of law in *Paradise Lost* points the reader's attention upward toward the justice of God, on the other hand it points outward toward the public sphere, much as the two tables of the Decalogue were intended to foster both individual righteousness and a just, stable social order. This outward-looking orientation of the law in *Paradise Lost* reflects Milton's changing views of legal systems vis-à-vis ecclesiastical ones. In his earlier works, Milton often pairs law and religion as the twin pillars supporting the nation. For example, in *Prolusion* 7, he describes the uncouth state of human beings when "they had no religion to guide them, no laws or law-courts" (*CPW* 1:299). He opens *Doctrine and Discipline of Divorce* with a complaint about custom, which he calls "the common climer into every chaire, where either Religion is preach't, or Law reported" (*CPW* 2:223). In *Areopagitica*, he refers to the Romans learning their "Religion and law," the two fundamental systems that ordered their society (*CPW* 2:497). And in *Tenure of Kings and Magistrates*, he writes that God gave humanity the twin gifts of "Justice and Religion," using "Justice" here as a synonym for "temporal Law" (*CPW* 3:222). All of these works were written in the 1640s, when Milton still believed that organized religion could create social cohesion. However, this optimism about religion soon waned. In later works, such as *Considerations Touching the Likeliest Means to Remove Hirelings Out of the Church* and *A Treatise of Civil Power*, he ardently rejects a social model in which the church serves as a weight-bearing structural member of society, in the manner of the Church of England. As he advises Cromwell in *A Second Defense*, "I would have you remove all power from the church" (*CPW* 4:678).

When religion goes inward, as Milton fervently believed it should, the just rule of law becomes all the more important as a means to organize social relations and protect the commonwealth.

justice," although whereas he reads "the bar of human justice" as meaning the verdict of reason and conscience, I regard it also as encompassing the temporal law. Stachniewski, *Persecutory Imagination*, 333.

Milton agreed with classical theorists such as Aristotle, Plato, Cicero, and Epicurus on the critical importance of legal justice in upholding human societies. In *The Judgment of Martin Bucer*, he writes, "Wee have need of civil laws," and in *Prolusion* 7 he claims that no culture can be happy that is not "firmly based on laws" (*CPW* 2:443, 1:299). Law helps bring social cohesion, and unlike religion, it has the advantage, from Milton's standpoint, of not telling men and women what to believe and of leaving them the management of their own hearts (although England's laws sometimes strayed across these dividing lines, as Milton complains in his anti-Erastian *A Treatise of Civil Power*). We see a breath of Milton's emerging preference for civil law over civil religion in *Tenure of Kings and Magistrates*, when, having claimed that justice (by which he means legal justice) and religion are "from the same God," Milton adds that "works of justice [are] offtimes more acceptable" (*CPW* 3:222).

While few people in the seventeenth century would have agreed with the medieval jurist Henri de Bracton that jus and lex were actual synonyms, most people felt that God had intended them to be. When the Natural Law mandates of jus slipped out of alignment with the positive law mandates of lex, it was the job of good men to try to push them back together again. The robust seventeenth-century movement for law reform recognized both the temporal law's failings and its divine potential. Indeed, the movement's pervasively religious language shows that law reform was regarded as an expression of Christian piety.[20] Milton's arguments in *Areopagitica* and *Doctrine and Discipline of Divorce* indicate that he had no illusions that the law was perfect. But he also wrote both of these works to change the law, addressing

20. Bracton, *Laws and Customs of England*, 2:22. Similarly, in Roman law "a *ius* was taken to be something objective, right, and discoverable, and in this sense it remained as a kind of synonym for 'law' throughout the history of Latin as an effective language": Tuck, *Natural Rights Theories*, 8. The seventeenth-century movement to reform the laws has been well chronicled by Veall, *Popular Movement for Law Reform*; and Prall, *Agitation for Law Reform*.

Areopagitica to the "High Court of Parliament" and the second edition of *Doctrine* to the "Judges and Lawgivers" of Parliament (*CPW* 2:486, 227). His impulse to reform the law also appears in five of the six political works he wrote on the eve of the Restoration. While he says virtually nothing in these works about religious observance, he offers concrete suggestions in each one for improving England's legal system, an indication of how the law underpins the hopes he still holds out for the nation's future.[21]

In *Paradise Lost* Milton shows that the rule of law is already beginning to grow in the soil of Paradise, and so even as human beings fall—indeed, even before they have fallen—laws are already springing up that will help to mitigate the effects of sin and create the conditions for stable societies. This does not mean that *Paradise Lost* provides a blueprint for a legal code or that Milton wants a single, monolithic set of rules that would govern all social arrangements. Nor does he think that all human actions should be subject to law. Indeed, Milton's commitment to the rule of law is simultaneously a commitment to limiting the rule of law, and we might think of law as forming the flip side of Milton's profound attachment to Christian liberty: in order to leave good men as free as possible to make choices about matters such as what to believe, whom to marry, and what to read, Milton supports a carefully circumscribed rule of law that provides order and stability in the social sphere. In *Paradise Lost* Milton imaginatively peers back into the earliest moments of human history and sees resident there prototypical ideas of legal justice, ideas that despite the ravages of sin could allow cultures to develop and could create the conditions for men and women to lead quiet, productive lives. In Joanna Picciotto's study of the way early modern experimentalism informs *Paradise Lost*, she writes, "The recovery of paradise and the reformation of public life were not separate things: the release of paradise from its idolatrous

21. A fuller discussion of Milton's comments about law in these works can be found in Chapman, "Milton and Legal Reform."

identification with the first garden was to create the conditions for the emergence of a productive public."[22] In Picciotto's view, Milton expects readers of his poem to emerge with a sense not simply of what was irrevocably lost in the fall but also of those habits of mind by which aspects of Eden might be recreated on Earth. My argument offers something of a legal corollary.[23] If temporal laws should reflect divine laws (as the early modern period as a whole believed), and if the source of all law is a deity whose operations are at least partly accessible by human reason (as Natural Law proponents like Milton believed), then a society that respects the rule of law and faithfully works to reform laws and judicial systems when they inevitably fail to do justice can help recover at least some of God's original plan for humanity.[24]

Chapter Summaries

In the remainder of this introductory chapter, I sketch in Milton's personal knowledge of the law, and then, as an example of my method in later chapters, I consider in more detail how early modern ideas of law can shed light on one of *Paradise Lost*'s great textual cruxes: the famous appeal to a "fit audience." In chapter 2 I contrast modern and early modern assumptions about the nature and origin of the law, to answer the question of why the presence of law in *Paradise Lost* has so generally escaped notice. From a modern point of view, law "cannot" be in the poem, since Milton describes a world before the establishment of civil

22. Picciotto, *Labors of Innocence*, 401.

23. Although he does not discuss law, John Rogers's *Matter of Revolution* provides an important foundation for my own argument. Rogers shows that the seventeenth century used basic ideas about the nature of the cosmos as a way to reorganize political and social relations, and so his claim runs parallel to my own study of how Milton thought temporal law should be made consistent with Natural Law.

24. By focusing on the way in which *Paradise Lost* looks outward as well as inward, I am indebted to those scholars who have emphasized the poem's engagement with the social and political sphere. See especially Achinstein, *Milton and the Revolutionary Reader*; Knoppers, *Historicizing Milton*; Dobranski, *Milton, Authorship*; Nigel Smith, *Literature and Revolution in England*; and Worden, *Literature and Politics*.

societies; fortified with an idea of law as an imposition of the secular state, we can easily look right past terms such as "trespass," "injunction" and "collateral" (9.693, 10.13, 8.426). However, if we look with early modern eyes and think of the law as one manifestation of divine wisdom and reason, then those legal allusions spring into view. At the conclusion of chapter 2, I survey the different kinds of law that were operative in Milton's world and consider how and where Milton critics have touched on each of them.

The remaining chapters move in roughly sequential order through *Paradise Lost*, tracing the ways early modern legal ideas weave through Milton's depictions of pre- and postlapsarian life. I begin with a pair of chapters on the law's criminal side. Chapter 3 takes up that most heinous of early modern crimes: treason. Milton calls both Satan and Adam traitors, and I argue that *Paradise Lost* reflects a new, contemporary definition of treason that emphasized threats to the rule of law and de-emphasized assaults on the monarch's person. This changing idea of treason can help us see how Milton depicts Heaven as a legal as well as a social order and God himself as a deity committed to the rule of law. I turn in chapter 4 to crimes that ranked below treason in the early modern legal hierarchy. Milton describes Satan's progress through Eden in book 4 in terms of a series of legal offenses (trespassing, larceny, burglary, poaching, and murder), crimes that pressed heavily on the early modern imagination. I conclude chapter 4 by situating the criminal language applied to Satan in the context of a growing late-seventeenth- and eighteenth-century preoccupation with law and lawbreakers.

Chapters 5 and 6 move away from the criminal and toward the civil arm of the law. In those two chapters, I examine the role that contemporary ideas of legal ownership and property law play in *Paradise Lost*. Chapter 5 explores the legal vocabulary of property ownership that Milton applies to Adam and Eve's relationship both before and after the fall, situating it in the context of early modern legal debates. Milton first works to establish an unfallen idea of property rights, based in mutuality and freedom, and then he shows how sin mutates this erected idea of "sole propriety" into a sadly more familiar model (4.751), distinguished by individual possession and exclusion. Chapter 6 traces how ideas of legal ownership and specifically of contract law crowd into books 9 and 10 in the wake of sin. For example, Eve falls in part because Satan stirs in her the desire to own things, and I show that this same impulse toward ownership subsequently characterizes Adam's fallen language in book 10. Resisting the idea that sin simply creates law, I argue that, instead, sin leads to the misapplication or abuse of law.

Chapters 7 and 8 move away from substantive law and take up instead the implementation of the law in the form of legal justice. Relying on contemporary judicial and law enforcement practices and on popular Assize sermons, chapter 7 argues that Milton infuses well-known judicial norms into his account of the trial scene of Eden: the Son's judgment of Adam and Eve in book 10. The Son far exceeds any human judge, and yet by clothing this scene in the language of familiar judicial practices, Milton shows readers how they might do justice and mercy among themselves. The sentence passed by the Son in book 10 is mitigated in book 11 when Adam and Eve beg pardon, and chapter 8 looks at pardons in *Paradise Lost* in the context of the rising number of pardons in early modern England. When he depicts Adam and Eve's pardon and also Satan's repudiation of pardon, Milton is not only thinking theologically. He is also thinking about his own world and the ways in which pardons could help knit up or unravel different human communities.

In chapter 9, the conclusion, I suggest that Milton's attempt to find a nascent rule of law in Eden was made more urgent by the changing ideas of jurisprudence in his own world. Over the course of the early modern period, the basic conception of the law changed. The view of law as subordinate to the mandates of conscience and to larger, prior discourses such as philosophy, ethics, and theology slowly receded, pushed back by an emerging idea of the common law as an "empire of truth," a sovereign and oracular set of norms.[25] By so consistently coupling law with theology, Milton resists what we might think of as the idolatry of the law that was emerging in the late seventeenth century, an approach that helped to prop up England's moneyed classes. Instead, he repeatedly tries to anchor law in conscience and the will of God, to show how law should serve something greater than itself.

Ultimately, the law's role in *Paradise Lost* resembles the presecular political vision that Paul Stevens finds in the poem. Stevens explains this presecular politics by contrasting it to the worldview espoused by the Catholic theologian John Milbank, who characterizes the time between the fall of Adam and Eve and the Apocalypse as a period when "coercive justice, private property, and impaired natural reason must make shift to cope with the unredeemed effects of sinful humanity." Milton saw this same ribbon of time in a very different way, for, in Stevens's words, "God's grace is always there capable of repairing the ruin of our first parents, both saving souls and rebuilding the polis."[26] Whereas Stevens identifies politics and education as the arenas where God's grace moves in the social world, Milton equally feels the breath of God when he thinks about the law. Naturally, he was not blind to the law's failings. Like both politics and education, law was a two-edged knife: indispensable for vindicating the wrongly accused, helping the poor, and carving order out of chaos, and yet also likely to be wielded in the interests of greed and ambition. Laws enabled what Samuel Johnson called the "legal massacre" at places like Tyburn as men and women were executed in droves for petty property crimes, but laws also stabilized the social order and allowed men and women to raise their children, tend their shops, and peaceably socialize with their neighbors. The minister Luke Beaulieu, in the

25. Goodrich, "Ars bablativa," 44.

26. Stevens, "Pre-Secular Politics of *Paradise Lost*," 98. Stevens quotes on the same page from Milbank, *Theology and Social Theory*, 9.

published version of his 1684 Assize sermon, eloquently captures this divided nature of the law. He writes, "If there were no Laws, there would be no Transgression properly so called." Without law, there would be no gallows and no pillory. But then, Beaulieu adds, "neither would there be any peace." Although Beaulieu was a royalist, he and Milton seem to have had a shared view of the law. As I explore in chapter 3, the laws of God trigger Satan's rebellion, but Milton also sees them as the framework around which the heavenly polis coheres. Writing *Paradise Lost* after the tumultuous decades of the Civil War and Commonwealth, and concerned about the fate of the nation in the wake of the Restoration, Milton infused the principles of law into his poem not only in an attempt to understand the ways of God but also because the rule of law offered what Beaulieu calls "the Terms of peace amongst Men."[27]

The Legal Life of John Milton

All of the chapters in this book rest on the bedrock assumption that Milton knows his way around the early modern law and that when he uses words like "accessories" or "bond," he does so with a full appreciation of their technical legal meanings and associated jurisprudential contexts. Since Milton's familiarity with legal terms, procedures, theories, cases, and jurisdictions remains one of the least-explored areas of his biography, I offer here a compressed survey of his encounters with various forms of law and legal knowledge. Then I show how this personal familiarity with the law emerges at various points in his prose works.

Milton's father made a living as a scrivener. During previous centuries, this profession had been more confined to the drawing up of basic legal documents such as wills and bills of sale, but early modern scrivening had evolved rapidly to meet changing social needs. By Milton's day, most scriveners were performing services that today we would sort out severally to the work of estate

27. Johnson, *Rambler*, 45; Beaulieu, *Terms of Peace and Reconciliation*, 11, 9.

agents, trustees, stockbrokers, accountants, bankers, and solicitors.[28] It was almost impossible to be a successful scrivener—which John Milton Sr. evidently was, based on the estate he left—without having a good working knowledge of the law. Furthermore, both Milton and his father loaned money in a culture that still, on occasion, prosecuted excessive interest as the crime of usury. Milton writes in *Doctrine and Discipline of Divorce* that charging interest "so much as is permitted by the Magistrate, and demanded with common equity, is neither against the word of God, nor the rule of charity" (*CPW* 3:322). Although each man could determine with his own conscience what constituted "common equity" or fairness, he would have to check the printed compilations of English statutes to know how much was "permitted by the Magistrate."

Milton Sr.'s work in a quasi-legal capacity may have influenced his younger son, Christopher, to study law at the Inner Temple, one of the Inns of Court. Christopher enrolled in 1632, and he was called to the bar in 1640. During the Commonwealth, Christopher made his living primarily with debt composition, and in 1660 he was called to the bench of the Inner Temple, becoming one of its senior members. He went on to serve as a justice of the peace and deputy recorder in Suffolk and then, under James II, as a serjeant-at-law, a baron of the Exchequer, and, finally, a justice of the Common Pleas with an annual salary of £1000.[29] Since Christopher was a royalist and may later have become a Catholic, the fraternal relationship was probably neither an easy nor an uncomplicated one, and John Milton's derogatory comments about "law-puddering" and "lawyerlie mooting" seem in part like expressions of sibling rivalry (*Colasterion*, *CPW* 2:742; *Eikonoklastes*, *CPW* 3:403). That said, records from Chancery and other courts show that the two Milton brothers collaborated closely on legal matters throughout most of John Milton's life, and this collaboration probably provided him with a regularly

28. Coleman, "London Scriveners."
29. Campbell, "Milton, Sir Christopher."

updated knowledge of cases, statutes, and legal procedures.[30] Three of Christopher's four sons (Christopher Jr., Richard, and Thomas) followed their father into law and were also admitted to the Inner Temple.[31] Christopher Milton was also a friend of Richard Powell, John Milton's brother-in-law, who was "a major member of the Inner Temple," and Powell's son, also named Richard, also became a member of the Inner Temple. As a result, John Milton's brother, brother-in-law, and four nephews were all prominent lawyers.[32] Milton's sister, through her marriages, added to the number of legal officials in the family circle. Anne Milton's first husband was Edward Phillips, a senior clerk in the Court of Chancery, and her second husband was Thomas Agar, a prominent member of the Middle Temple. Agar had succeeded Edward Phillips in the Chancery position, and when Agar died, the position passed to Christopher Milton's lawyer son Thomas.[33] In short, Milton lived in a family network densely populated with men who made their living at the law.

Although Milton may well have considered joining the Inns of Court, he ultimately did not, and in *Ad patrem*, he thanks his father for not hurrying him off to the clamor of the law and what he calls the nation's badly kept statutes. As H. F. Fletcher points out, however, this was not the final, ringing renunciation that it sounds. A letter to Charles Diodati, written five years later, refers to Milton's plan of residing at the Inns of Court, and the idea of law as a career was not definitively ruled out until Milton went to the Continent in 1638.[34] After he returned from Italy and settled down to a life of reading and tutoring, he regularly socialized with men at Gray's Inn, and since Cambridge friends like Justinian Pagitt became lawyers, we can guess that Milton would have had continued contact with a legal milieu and le-

30. On the Chancery cases, see French, *Milton in Chancery*.

31. Shawcross, *Arms of the Family*, 24–29. See also Jones, "Itinerant Sibling," 89–90.

32. Shawcross, *Arms of the Family*, 43, 45.

33. On Agar's importance to Milton, see ibid., 47–72.

34. Fletcher, *Intellectual Development of John Milton*. See also *LR* 1:346.

gal thinking.[35] Milton writes of his experiences listening to the arguments—called moots—that the Inns of Court staged in order to instruct students, and a passage from *Of Education* offers specific suggestions for an improved form of legal education. Whether his knowledge of legal procedures was picked up from visits to the Inns, from books, from friends, or from working on Chancery cases with his brother (or, more likely, from a combination of all four), Milton had a solid competence. In *Milton in Chancery*, James French examines the detailed set of interrogatories that Milton drew up during the drawn-out litigation with John Cope, and he concludes that Milton displays a "thoroughly workmanlike" grasp of equity procedures and the case's central legal issues.[36] The range of his learning about the law and his able assistance of his brother in Chancery suits suggest that Milton was in that growing early modern group of "learned lay clients," men with enough competence in the law to manage their affairs and to direct their lawyers intelligently and efficiently.[37]

Milton's network of friends and esteemed colleagues was also full of lawyers (it would have been surprising had this not been the case, since common lawyers made up the bulk of the revolutionary Long Parliament). In 1638, as he passed through Paris, Milton made a special point to meet the famous Dutch jurist Hugo Grotius, the author of *De jure belli ac pacis*, a masterwork in Natural Law theory. In *Tetrachordon*, Milton calls Grotius "one of prime note among learned men," and in *Doctrine and Discipline of Divorce*, Grotius is "a man of these times, one of the best learned" (*CPW* 2:715, 2:238).[38] Closer to home, Milton had nothing but praise for the jurist and polymath John Selden, who had collaborated with Sir Edward Coke in drawing up the Petition of Right and who can justly be regarded as a sort of role

35. Edward Phillips records Milton's friendship with Gray's Inn men. See the reprint of Phillips's biography of Milton in Darbishire, *Early Lives of Milton*, 62.

36. French, *Milton in Chancery*, 136.

37. Barnes, "Inns of Court," 1056.

38. On the known details of this visit, see Campbell and Corns, *John Milton*, 105–7.

model for Milton.[39] In *Areopagitica* Milton lavishes praise on Selden's *De jure naturali et gentium*, another landmark work in Natural Law, and in *Doctrine and Discipline of Divorce* he calls Selden's book a "noble volume . . . worthy to be perus'd, whosoever studies to be a great man in wisdom, equity, and justice" (*CPW* 2:350). In Sonnet 21 he praises Coke for his legal writings, and he calls Coke that "great Lawyer" in *Brief Notes upon a Late Sermon* (*CPW* 7:483). Similarly, Sonnet 10 compliments Sir James Ley's work as Lord Chief Justice under Charles I. Milton was also a good friend of John Bradshaw, the judge who presided at Charles I's trial. Bradshaw had represented Milton in the 1647 Chancery case against Sir Robert Pye, and the two men may have been distantly related.[40] In his *Second Defense of the English People*, Milton offers the following encomium to Bradshaw: "He spent all his early years in diligent study of the laws of his country and then, a most effective lawyer and eloquent pleader, an alert defender of liberty and the people, he was employed in grave affairs of state and on several occasions served as an incorruptible judge" (*CPW* 4:638). Milton was also a good friend of the lawyer John Desborough, a man deeply involved in many of the contemporary efforts to reform England's laws, and he worked closely with Henry Marten and Bulstrode Whitelocke, jurists who attempted to reform England's oppressive debt laws and equity proceedings. While Milton was an avowed enemy of legalism and of legal corruption, he supported those who tried to uphold and advance what he saw as good laws.[41]

Milton was also clearly familiar with an array of written texts about the law, and his widow's inventory mentions eleven law books.[42] He owned classic works about law and legal theory such as Cicero's *De officiis*, Plato's *Laws*, Aristotle's *Ethics* and *Politics*,

39. Rosenblatt, *Renaissance England's Chief Rabbi*; Campbell and Corns, *John Milton*, 161.

40. Campbell and Corns, *John Milton*, 190.

41. For a more detailed discussion of Milton's thoughts on legal reform, see Chapman, "Milton and Legal Reform."

42. French, *Milton in Chancery*, 151.

Aquinas's *Summa*, and Hooker's *Laws of Ecclesiastical Polity*. He also owned most of the greatest hits of the English and Continental legal tradition: Justinian's *Institutes*, Bracton's *On the Laws and Customs of England*, the anonymous treatise known as *Fleta*, Horn's *Mirror for Justices*, Lambarde's *Archaeion*, Grotius's *De jure belli ac pacis*, Spelman's *Concilia ecclesiastica*, Selden's *De jure naturali*, Coke's *Institutes of the Laws of England*, Fitzherbert's *La nouvelle natura brevium*, and Smith's *De republica anglorum*.[43] Based on written references, Milton was also familiar with and might have owned Glanville's *Treatise on the Laws and Customs of the Kingdom of England*, Fortescue's *On the Laws and Governance of England*, Gratian's *Decretum*, Littleton's *Tenures*, and Thomas Powell's *The Attourneys Academy*, to which Milton refers in *Colasterion*. Judging from what he calls "this evidence and citation of laws" in *A Defense of the English People*, Milton had also read—or at least was generally familiar with—a range of other documentary material relating to English laws (*CPW* 4:494). Much of this material, such as the older plea rolls and yearbooks, was in held in manuscript collections, and common lawyers like Coke and Selden were increasingly mining these archives in search of precedents and then printing their findings in collections of statutes. Milton refers to "our records," the evidence of "our public records and legal scholars," "our most venerable documents," and "ancient evidence" (*CPW* 4:496, 497, 500, 505), and it is clear that he has read widely enough in printed and manuscript documents that he can cite statutes, such as the thirteenth-century Statute of Marlborough on liability for waste. When Salmasius cites laws from the reigns of Henry I and Edward IV, Milton retorts, "That either of these laws appears in our statute-books is so wholly untrue that in the years you speak of there were no laws at all passed by either of these kings" (*A Defense of the English People*, *CPW* 4:530). Milton is cross-checking Salmasius's claims against the legal authorities he has available, and he summarizes

43. Boswell, *Milton's Library*.

his sources as "divine law, the law of nations, and the statutes of my country" (*CPW* 4:507).

This range of reading helps account for Milton's passing expertise in various areas of law. Writings about the law form a significant section of his *Commonplace Book*, and whereas the law being examined in works like *A Defense of the English People* or *Tenure of Kings and Magistrates* is usually constitutional law, in the *Commonplace Book*, Milton also probes other legal matters, such as the common law division between grand and petty larceny and the legality of shore dwellers' appropriating shipwrecks.[44] His anticlerical and divorce tracts demonstrate his knowledge of canon law and the ecclesiastical courts, and the divorce tracts also show his familiarity with legal practices in places like Lutheran Germany. In his capacity as a licenser, Milton would have known statutes related to publishing, and as a translator of sensitive documents for Cromwell's government, he ranged across a variety of legal and quasi-legal matters. For example, his writings and translations for the Anglo-Dutch negotiations repeatedly turn to legal questions, as when he lays out the provisions for ownership of salvaged goods or when he stipulates that when citizens of one country harm citizens of another, "first justice [shall] be sought in the Ordinary course of Law" before the matter is appealed to a commission.[45]

Milton also regularly uses legal references to bolster his arguments and assumes that readers are perfectly capable of following him. For instance, he provides a detailed discussion of statutes and precedents in chapter 9 of his *First Defense of the English People*, and in his *Defense of Himself*, he refers with offhand ease to the Romano-canon two-witness rule and to Justinian's statutes about libel (*CPW* 4:713, 717, 726). His opponent in *Colasterion* had used common law scenarios about land ten-

44. See Ruth Mohl's excellent discussion in *Milton and His Commonplace Book*, 223–43.

45. Quoted in Miller, *Milton's Writings*, 178. On the range of Milton's experiences working for the Commonwealth and Protectorate governments, see also Robert Thomas Fallon, *Milton in Government*.

ure and inheritance to argue against Milton's divorce proposals, and in response, Milton systematically attacks these instances of reasoning improperly across juridical lines. H. F. Fletcher, in his 1956 study of the young Milton's intellectual development, glances briefly at Milton's legal learning and offers the following assessment: Milton has a "wide, fairly intensive, and highly sentient knowledge" of law, and "the more one reads Milton's works with the intention of discovering his references to legal matters, or seeks to find his awareness of such matters, the more striking is his extraordinary concern with them, as is also his constant use of legal material."[46] Fletcher even says that his greatest regret about limiting his study to Milton's pre-Cambridge years was that he was unable to explore the legal knowledge Milton displays as an adult.

Milton's extensive knowledge of the law means that even when he is not talking about the law per se, he often resorts to legal language and legally informed metaphors. This tendency is especially evident at the beginnings of works, as if the law helps him think his way into a subject. For example, in the opening of *Tetrachordon*, Milton refers to himself as "return'd, as to a famous and free Port, my self also bound by more then a maritime Law, to expose as freely what frautage [freight] I conceave to bring of no trifles" (*CPW* 2:578). He is the ship that has been trading overseas, and, obedient to the "maritime Law" that requires a manifold from all vessels entering a free port, he declares his metaphorical cargo by means of his introduction. Milton begins his *Apology against a Pamphlet* in a similar way. He alludes to the "law of *Solon*" that made it a crime to be a "cold neuter" (i.e., not to take sides) in questions of sedition against the state, and he argues by extension that a tepid neutrality would be equally culpable in "the cause of the Church" (*CPW* 1:868). A related legal gambit appears in the first sentence of *The Reason of Church Government*: "In the publishing of humane lawes, which for the most part aime not beyond the good of civill society, to set them

46. Fletcher, *Intellectual Development of John Milton*, 2:530–31.

barely forth to the people without reason or Preface, like a physical prescript, or only with threatnings, as it were a lordly command, in the judgement of *Plato* was thought to be done neither generously or wisely" (*CPW* 1:746).[47] Laws should be prefaced by the reasons for those laws. Remarkably, Milton then argues that Moses follows the same method: knowing "how vaine it was to write lawes to men whose hearts were not first season'd with the knowledge of God and his works," Moses wrote Genesis "as a prologue to his lawes" (*CPW* 1:747). Both the Pentateuch and the best human legal codes share the same organizational principle. In a famously autobiographical passage of his *Second Defense of the English People*, Milton writes, "I had so practiced myself from youth that I was above all things unable to disregard the laws of God and man" (*CPW* 4:622). Besides attesting to the links that Milton and his culture saw between temporal law and divine law (the subject of chapter 2), this statement also accurately captures what we might think of as Milton's deeply legal turn of mind.

In this respect Milton was very much a man of his time. It is hard to overstate the intense law-mindedness of the English during the early modern period, and especially during the seventeenth century. Historian Christopher W. Brooks offers the following succinct summary: "Ordinary people were in court more often, and knew more about 'law' (however defined) than they have at any time subsequently."[48] Veneration for the rule of law was fundamental to English identity, for the English saw their legal rights as distinguishing them from people of other nations, such as the French, who lacked the kinds of protections provided by the common law and the Magna Carta. This deeply embed-

47. In his *Commonplace Book*, Milton quotes Sarpi to the opposite effect: "The lawgiver who gives reasons for his laws diminishes his authority, because the subject attacks the reason given, and when he believes he has determined its meaning, he thinks also that he has taken the virtue from the precept" (*CPW* 1:424). As Mohl points out, Milton is here citing Sarpi as an example of an argument he would refute: Mohl, *Milton and His Commonplace Book*, 227.

48. Brooks, *Lawyers, Litigation and English Society*, 128. See also his "Law-Abiding and Litigious Society."

ded respect for the rule of law was combined with a national pugnacity about protecting legal rights. The English were notoriously litigious, and the percentage increase in early modern lawsuits easily outstripped the percentage growth in population. Furthermore, for men of middling fortune and above, the major milestones in an ordinary life increasingly involved legal documents: marriage contracts, wills, deeds, trusts, contracts, sealed bonds, and so forth.[49] The English obsession with the law is perhaps best epitomized in the debates leading up to the Civil War. In response to flashpoint events like ship money, the forced loan, and the Militia Ordinance, both parliamentary and royalist apologists tried to argue for the legality of their position. No one simply made a positivist case for actions, and such was the ideological power of the rule of law that even those trying to work around the law had to frame their actions in its terms.[50]

Milton's Fit Audience

I close this chapter by looking through a jurisprudential lens at Milton's famous address to a "fit audience" (7.31). Understanding both the judicial associations attached to the word "audience" and the deeply participatory nature of the early modern common law can provide a new understanding of the kind of active engagement that Milton expects from his readers.

The early modern period more or less took it for granted that "the completely virtuous man must be a judge, or at least a man of judgment."[51] Milton agreed, for he often structures his works so that his reader arrives at a prudent choice by means of a jurisprudential one. For instance, Milton wrote three works that he titled "defenses" (*A Defense of the English People*, *A Second Defense of the English People*, and *A Defense of Himself*), which participate

49. Sharpe, "People and the Law," 251–54.

50. For a thorough discussion of the role that ideas of law played in the months before the Civil War, see Sirluck, introduction to *Complete Prose Works*.

51. Stoner, *Common Law and Liberal Theory*, 18.

in the classical tradition of forensic argument. Milton adopts the role of the one presenting a case for the justice of a given action or person. In the process, he characterizes his readers as the metaphorical judges who will listen to the evidence he presents and render a verdict. While in some works Milton asks his readers to bring only reason and a native sense of right and wrong to bear on the issue at hand, in others he assumes that readers can make basic kinds of legal discriminations as well. Arguing in *Doctrine and Discipline of Divorce* against the idea that God simply permitted divorce without actually condoning it, Milton turns to the legal interpretation of silence: "Silence in the Law is consent, and consent is accessory" (*CPW* 2:291). As a result, we should not interpret instances of biblical silence on the subject of divorce as indicating God's disapproval, since this is not what silence means in a human court of law. Legally speaking, saying nothing is a form of saying yes. Milton follows this legal logic to its conclusion: if divorce is a "crime" and the Law is "silent or not active against" it, then we must conclude that the Bible is "accessory to its own conviction, it self judging," a position that Milton categorically rejects (*CPW* 2.291).

Tetrachordon provides another good example of how Milton assumes that readers are familiar with the rudiments of the law. This work was written in response to attacks on *Doctrine and Discipline of Divorce* and its author, such as the one leveled by the minister Herbert Palmer. Milton opens by depicting himself as the defendant in a calumny suit: "I shall therefore take license by the right of nature and that liberty wherein I was born, to defend myself publicly against a printed Calumny, and do willingly appeal to those Judges to whom I am accused" (*CPW* 2:580). Milton argues that Palmer is guilty not only under the law of common charity but also under the "Canon Law" (to which Palmer, as a minister, ought ostensibly to feel some allegiance), since canon law forbade the "naming or traducing of any person in the Pulpit" (*CPW* 2:580). When he imagines himself as a party to a "calumny" action, Milton is remarkably exact about the jurisdiction in question. The common law equivalent to calumny was defamation, but in a defamation case, the plaintiff had to demonstrate that the slur had resulted in monetary damage, clearly a legal bar that does not apply in the case of Palmer's attack on Milton. However, calumny, which was tried by the church courts, could include an injury to the plaintiff's dignity or reputation.[52] Milton claims that Palmer is guilty of calumny, and he characterizes himself as following the Romano-canon procedures by which calumny cases were tried: as the defendant, he "willingly appeal[s] to those Judges to whom I am accused" (an appeal to judges was a procedure in the ecclesiastical courts, but not in the common law system). Sharon Achinstein, in her discussion of this passage, argues that since *Tetrachordon* was not licensed, Milton's reference to the "license" given him by "right of nature" shows him making an extralegal appeal to conscience.[53] I bring another set of emphases, for I see Milton exuberantly bending the law to his own purposes rather than stepping outside it. He shows off his virtuoso ability to defend himself as nimbly in one imagined jurisdiction as in another. Perhaps more importantly, this passage—like so many of Milton's appeals to his readers—presumes a legally literate readership, one that can enjoy the agile wit of casting the same Parliament that had outlawed the criminal jurisdiction of the ecclesiastical courts as a panel of Romano-canon judges presented with a *calumnia* case.

Although at one level, Milton's idea of the "judicious Reader" (*Areopagitica*, CPW 2:512) is based on a similitude rather than an actual identity (readers perusing *Areopagitica* are merely analogous to those in a courtroom listening to evidence), the metaphor

52. Having distinguished between calumny (church courts) and defamation (common law courts), I must also allow that the gap between them was in practice sometimes very narrow. Lawyers on both sides of the fence modeled their practice on each other and sometimes even quoted each other's pleadings (Helmholz, *Canon Law and Ecclesiastical Jurisdiction*, 9–11; Gray, *Writ of Prohibition*, xli–xlii). The difficulty of drawing firm jurisdictional lines in this particular area of the law is amply illustrated by the complexity of Plucknett's discussion in *Concise History*, 483–502. I am indebted to one of the University of Chicago Press's anonymous readers for this point about the ways Milton draws on the different legal inflections of defamation versus calumny.

53. Achinstein, *Milton and the Revolutionary Reader*, 60.

works in part because of the way legal knowledge and legal experience had saturated England's social strata. In contrast to the situation on the Continent, a working knowledge of the law in England was by no means exclusive to lawyers and judges.[54] In a society without a standing police force and with a paucity of magistrates, legal actions required a high level of lay participation. When someone escaped from prison or when a crime was suspected, entire neighborhoods were expected to participate in the hue and cry, and communities could even be fined if a sufficient number of men did not turn out to hunt down the offender. While the state's role in prosecution expanded steadily in the period, a substantial portion of the work in ordinary criminal cases (collecting evidence, interviewing witnesses, presenting an argument in court, etc.) was still carried out by the victim or the victim's family, and even with the growth of a nationwide jail delivery process, the community still remained deeply involved in the arrest and the presentation of accusations.[55] Another important means of lay participation in the legal process was the jury. English civil law cases required one jury of twelve men, and significant criminal offenses (e.g., felony, burglary, arson, riot, etc.) required two: the grand jury, which evaluated the charges and drafted the accusation, and the petty jury, which heard the trial.[56] Other legal proceedings also involved public participation, and Milton's Quaker friend Thomas Ellwood, in his autobiography, writes of the Newgate jailer stopping carriages in the streets and hauling men inside to make up a coroner's inquest panel.[57] Cynthia Herrup estimates, in her study of crime and criminal accusations in early modern eastern Sussex, that almost 50 percent of the population of one parish had had personal experience with the criminal law, either as jurors, magistrates, apprehenders, con-

54. This point has been made eloquently by historical studies like Gaskill, *Crime and Mentalities*; and Shapiro, *Culture of Fact*.

55. Baker, "Criminal Courts and Procedure," 32.

56. Over the course of the early modern period, justices of the peace were increasingly given summary jurisdiction over minor crimes.

57. Ellwood, *History of the Life*, 182.

stables, sureties, or witnesses.[58] When we factor in exposure to the civil law not only through direct courtroom contact but also through legal instruments such as wills, deeds, and contracts, the percentage of men who had some experience with the legal system rises significantly.

Other indicators point to the broad diffusion of legal experience and knowledge. The English were "avid consumers of legal stories in oral and written form," and judges and sergeants often held "table cases" in which they debated points of law in taverns and public houses.[59] The early modern presses were also issuing an unprecedented number of legal books, and these works were not simply reaching an elite, London-based readership. The Yorkshire yeoman Adam Eyre recorded in his diary that he had read Dalton's *Country Justice* and that the work was a favorite among his neighbors.[60] There were guidebooks for justices of the peace, for constables, for juries, for clerks, and for attorneys. There were law dictionaries, compilations of statutes, descriptions of manorial courts, lists of the forms of action for journeyman solicitors, explanations of contract, works on forest law and Admiralty law, descriptions of mercantile law, and even guidebooks for getting through a stint in prison. Lorna Hutson and Luke Wilson have also persuasively connected the exploding early modern interest in the law to changes on the early modern English stage, for early modern plays such as *Othello*, *Hamlet*, *Bartholomew Fair*, and *Arden of Faversham* were both shaped by and dependent upon the profound popular involvement in the law and forms of legal reasoning. The highly participatory nature of the English common law means that we should be cautious about accepting Michel Foucault's vision of the law as mediating

58. Herrup, *Common Peace*, 194–95. Since Milton met the property qualifications for service at both the grand and the petty jury level, and since, unlike a majority of eligible jurors (especially those at the grand jury level), he was not prone to shirk public service, it is likely that he fell into the half of Englishmen who had served on at least one jury.

59. Cunningham, *Imaginary Betrayals*, 15–17.

60. Lawson, "Lawless Juries," 143.

the will of the authorities downward to the people.[61] Foucault was writing about a French Romano-canon system that put the administration of law into the hands of professional jurists. But as Hutson points out, when a London theater audience apprehended a cutpurse in their midst and tied him to a post onstage, or when that same audience watched Hamlet trying to solve the crime of his father's murder, we are not looking at the state enforcing law onto a passive populace.[62]

The broadly participatory nature of the English justice system and the wide diffusion of legal knowledge provide a context for understanding why Milton so frequently imagines his readers as jurors. When he tells readers of *Animadversions*, "Have patience therefore a little, and heare a Law case," he casts them in the role of the judge and/or jury about to hear a civil suit about land tenure (*CPW* 1:716). In *Doctrine and Discipline of Divorce*, he explains that he chose to write in English because he prefers to receive his "Countries judgement" before he "assay[s] the verdit of outlandish readers" (*CPW* 2:233). Milton plays on the fact that "country" in this context means both the people who occupy a given land and also a jury. When defendants in a lawsuit formally announced their desire to "put themselves on the country," they were pleading innocent and asking for trial by a jury of their peers.[63] In the opening of *An Apology against a Pamphlet*, he offers a similar kind of appeal to the reader-juror (another instance in which Milton begins a work by looking at his topic through a legal lens). Even though it is "lawfull" to rely on his God-given talents and "justice not to defraud of due esteeme" his many years of study, he worries nonetheless that readers might "sentenc[e]" his work simply on the basis of his youth. As a result, hoping to be "acquitted of presumption," he offers the reader evidence of the rightness of his cause (*CPW* 1:868–87).

61. Hutson, *Invention of Suspicion*; Wilson, *Theaters of Intention*; Foucault, *Discipline and Punish*.

62. Hutson, *Invention of Suspicion*, 64–68.

63. "Country," n., def. 7, *OED Online*.

The image of readers as jurors becomes even clearer when Milton turns to a discussion of his opponent's full title: *A Modest Confutation of a Slanderous and Scurrilous Libell, Entituled, Animadversions upon the Remonstrants Defense Against Smectymnuus*. He imagines his opponent as "sitting in the chaire of his Title page upon his poore cast adversaries both as a Judge and Party, and that before the jury of Readers can be impannell'd." Milton's complaint is that by using words like "slanderous" and "scurrilous libel" on the title page, his opponent has short-circuited the judicial process and convicted the Smectymnuuans before the trial. A book should allow "others . . . to judge of by reading, not the author to anticipate to himself by forestalling." The whole image is one of justice gone awry: before the jury (i.e., the readers) has even been assembled to examine the evidence (i.e., to read the book), a corrupt judge who is a "Party" to the action (i.e., allied with his opponent) has already rigged the verdict (*CPW* 1:876). This image of an unjust trial is contrasted to the true justice that would be done if a "jury of Readers" could be properly "impannell'd" and could try the case by reading it.

The most famous example of the reader-as-juror appears in *Areopagitica* when Milton refers to the injustice of a book's being sent before "a Jury ere it be borne to the World" (*CPW* 2:505). As Sauer points out, while the "identification of writers and readers as judges and juries is a rhetorical device with a long history," this kind of epithet "acquired new meaning at a time when structures of authority were subject to interrogation as never before."[64] Milton likens a book to the condition of a "peccant soul" subjected to judgment before even being born, and just as the human soul should be judged only at the end of the person's life, a book should be judged only after it has circulated (*CPW* 2:505). Instead of a prepress jury, Milton suggests that judgment is rightly executed by a later jury, the panel of readers who can examine a book's merits and demerits, and he echoes both John 7:51 ("Doth our law judge any man, before it hear him, and know

64. Sauer, *"Paper Contestations" and Textual Communities*, 21.

what he doeth?") and the fundamental common law principle that people could not be sentenced without a jury trial. Licensing is essentially a violation of due process.[65] The sense of books as defendants continues when he says that destroying a book can be "a kind of homicide" (*CPW* 2:493). Milton does not object to the killing of books; what he deplores is the killing of books outside the law. He allows that a book proven to be bad can be "justly burnt or sunk in the sea," and he writes that it is allowable to "confine, imprison and do sharpest justice" on those books that have been proved to be "malefactors" (*CPW* 2:505, 492). The difference between one kind of book-killing ("homicide") and the other (the "sharpest justice" that might burn or drown a book) is the intervening judicial process. Law turns homicide into justice, and the deliberations of mature readers, weighing the innocence or guilt of a book, are analogous to the deliberations of a jury in a courtroom. As Achinstein argues, Milton's jury reference in *Areopagitica* is part of his pervasive concern to fashion readers as active and capable participants in the public sphere.[66] A country that trusts its citizens to render fair and impartial verdicts on defendants in capital cases should also trust them to judge books properly.

This pervasive idea of the judicial reader makes its way into *Paradise Lost* when Milton imagines himself speaking to "fit audience . . . though few" (7.31). Since the modern sense of "audience" as readership was yet to emerge in Milton's day, his hope for a "fit audience" has typically been read in the sense provided by the *Oxford English Dictionary*, "the assembled listeners or spectators," an interpretation that highlights the oral traditions associated with epic.[67] But most of the seventeenth-century definitions of "audience" relate to a judicial gathering. An "audience" in Milton's day could mean "the action, practice, or fact of holding a judicial hearing"; "an assembly gathered for a formal

65. Bible quotations are from the King James Version unless otherwise noted.

66. Achinstein, *Milton and the Revolutionary Reader*, 61–62.

67. "Audience," n., def. 7a, *OED Online*.

(judicial) hearing or inquiry; a court"; and "a formal interview or hearing"; these juridical meanings had also given rise to ancillary usages of "audience" to designate a Spanish colonial court and the physical space of a courtroom.[68] Because of the deep classical and Renaissance humanist connections between rhetoric and law, a word like "audience" could slide easily from a broadly oratorical meaning to a more narrowly construed judicial one. Milton relies on both meanings of "audience" in a work like *Doctrine and Discipline of Divorce* when he asks his readers—the "Judges and Lawgivers" of Parliament—to give "free audience and generous construction" to his argument (*CPW* 2:225). Before roughly the end of the seventeenth century, the English did not distinguish in any categorical way between the judicial and legislative functions of government, and so Parliament was both the source of laws and a high court that interpreted those laws.[69] Thus, when Milton addresses the members of Parliament as "judges," he is not simply speaking metaphorically, since Parliament had served for centuries as the nation's highest court of appeals. Moreover, one of the common meanings of "construction" was an act of legal interpretation.[70] So when Milton asks for a "construction" from this "audience" of "judges," he invites them to assess his argument both in a generically evaluative way and in a more literally judicial way.[71]

At several points in *Paradise Lost*, Milton plucks at the specifically judicial overtones of "audience." In the epic debate of book 2, Beelzebub rose and "drew audience," and having secured a popular vote for his plan, he told the fallen angels, "Well have ye judged" (2.308, 390). When Milton writes that Satan's "bold discourse" in book 5 "without control/Had audience" (5.803–4), he means not only that the angels are listening to him but that

68. "Audience," n., defs. 1a, 1b, 3a, 5a, 5b, 6, *OED Online*.

69. On the history of Parliament's role as a legislative and/or judicial entity, see McIlwain, *High Court of Parliament*.

70. "Construction," n., defs. 9a, 9b, *OED Online*.

71. My claim is indebted to Frances E. Dolan's argument about the evidentiary burden placed on seventeenth-century readers. See her *True Relations*.

they are doing so in an informally judicial sense: they are both hearing and assessing. In the argument to book 10, the gathered angels in Hell who listen to and applaud Satan's actions on Earth are called his "audience" (10.arg.). When God explains his plan to renew humanity at the end times and to cast Sin and Death into Hell, the "heav'nly audience loud/Sung hallelujah" (10.641–42). Unlike the angelic audience that approves Satan's argument against "new laws," this angelic audience understands and approves God's justice. When Milton addresses his readers as a "fit audience," he imagines them not just as a body of attentive listener-readers who can understand and appreciate his poem. He also imagines an audience in its judicial sense, a group that will listen attentively in order then to judge carefully and impartially. He wants the kind of audience that will know why Beelzebub's angelic audience is wrong and why God's angelic audience is right. Moreover, readers are implicitly being asked to judge not only using reason and an innate sense of equity but also using related principles embedded in the law, principles that were widely diffused in the English cultural consciousness. These acts of judgment help the reader to create the spiritual conditions for the paradise within, and they also have a vital role in the social sphere. When Milton's fit audience respects the rule of law and also works diligently to remake the law when it strays from its divine original, they can also help create the conditions for justice to flourish on Earth.

2

Law and Religion in Milton's World

Two modern assumptions about the nature of law seem to have prevented readers from seeing the role that law plays in *Paradise Lost*. First, we moderns have a tendency to put the law into an isolated disciplinary silo. Legal historian Peter Goodrich refers to the modern "estrangement of the law" from disciplines such as literature, history, philosophy, and ethics, arguing that this estrangement—the belief that an entity known as "the law" speaks with a unified, dogmatic, sovereign voice—has resulted in a widespread "closure of the legal mind."[1] Second, we regard the law as primarily a technique of government, a coercive system of the secular state. As a result of these modern ideas of law, we have trouble recognizing the degree to which the early modern period still saw law as inextricably tied to other disciplines and as a normative system that pointed outside itself to God.

In the first two sections of this chapter, I explore these two modern assumptions about law, contrasting them with Milton's views. For example, writing in his *Commonplace Book*, Milton says that "Justinian, here and there, calls his laws oracles," referencing

1. Goodrich, *Law in the Courts*, vii.

a passage in Justinian's *Institutes* (the foundational text of Roman law) where he writes, "The wisdom of the law is its conception of divine and human things" (*CPW* 1:438).[2] At its best, the law shows both how mortal things work and how God's mind works; as an "oracle," it provides a peephole into the operations of Heaven. Since this claim could equally be made about the Bible, Milton is hardly writing as one who feels that law and theology can be productively held apart.

The third section of this chapter surveys existing scholarly studies of Milton and law, most of which are focused on his prose works. I use the three major systems of law operative in Milton's world—common law, equity, and Romano-canon law—as an organizing framework. This framework offers the advantages of allowing me to clarify jurisprudential terms and concepts that are used in later chapters and to explain Milton's growing commitment to statutory law. In the final section, I show how modern assumptions about law have informed studies of *Paradise Lost*. The work of lawyer and Milton critic Stanley Fish serves to show how those most expert in the law today can be unaware of how law functioned in an earlier world.

Rethinking the Early Modern Law

Aldo Schiavone, in his *Invention of Law in the West*, points to the sense of the law as "something entirely apart—a compact, impenetrable corpus." Around this separateness or isolation, an "extraordinary ideological discourse quickly took shape to recast it as 'independence' and 'neutrality'—of norms, procedures, judges—making it one of the underlying values of our civilization."[3] This sense of the law as a thing set apart has proved to be one of the law's most enduring strengths, since it is the precondition for an idea of impartial judgment. However, it comes at a price, for it

2. Ruth Mohl, translator of *Milton and His Commonplace Book*, provides this translation of Justinian in a note.

3. Schiavone, *The Invention of Law in the West*, 3–4.

makes us less likely to think about law in relationship to other disciplines.[4] For example, while seventeenth-century England was home to one of the great movements for law reform in the West, legal historians who study the period's profound jurisprudential transformations typically relate them to earlier and later legal practices and not to contemporaneous cultural movements.[5] The effect is to create what Barbara J. Shapiro calls a "legal-history ghetto."[6] Scholars in other disciplines similarly assume that law is a subject best left to lawyers. Seventeenth-century political ideas of the social contract were enabled by advancements in contract law, and natural philosophy borrowed its ideas of fact and evidence from the early modern courts; however, scholars who study early modern political transformations and the rise of empiricism often overlook the ways in which law contributed to cultural change.[7] In the literary sphere, Lorna Hutson, Bradin Cormack, Luke Wilson, and many others have traced the role that law plays in early modern poetry and drama, especially the plays of Shakespeare.[8] However, few of these discussions extend past the death of James I in 1625.[9] As a result, we are left with an underdeveloped sense of how later authors responded to and were shaped by contemporary jurisprudence. This crucial lacuna is all the more striking because some of the period's most important legal and judicial changes occurred during the Civil War, Commonwealth, and Restoration periods, including important refinements in contract

4. Berman, *Faith and Order*, 27.

5. Berman has provided definitive studies of the changing jurisprudence of the West in his two books *Law and Revolution* and *Law and Revolution: II*.

6. Shapiro, "Law and Science," 728.

7. The migration of fact from courts to laboratory is the argument of Shapiro, *Culture of Fact*.

8. Hutson, *Invention of Suspicion*; Cormack, *Power to Do Justice*; Wilson, *Theaters of Intention*.

9. In pointing out the dearth of criticism about literature and law under the later Stuarts, I must pointedly exempt Kahn, *Wayward Contracts*; and Dyson, *Staging Authority in Caroline England*. Although Kahn and Dyson have both shown how vibrant legal issues were in the period, they both regard law primarily within a political context, whereas I attempt to think about law in relationship to theology.

law, the codification of rules of evidence, and the use of defense counsel in criminal trials.

A debate between Goodrich and Fish centers on the issue of the law's disciplinary isolation, and Fish displays a typically modern reflex to erect a high fence around the law. As a legal historian, Goodrich has repeatedly called attention to the conceptual and historical connective tissue that binds law to systems like religion and ethics. For example, in *Reading the Law*, he argues that in "constructing the abstract world of law," the legal community has tended to forget the law's ties to other areas of human inquiry, and he calls for that community to be more aware of the philosophical bases of its practices. In his rebuttal of Goodrich, Fish says that jurists cannot also become "psychologists, or sociologists, or statisticians," and he strenuously defends the law's separation from other disciplines. In his words, "Law is not philosophy."[10] Fish's career as a Milton critic reflects this same divide between law and not-law, for he has written about Milton with one hand and about law with the other, thus tacitly reinforcing the assumption that they share no common ground. If asked to take sides in the Goodrich versus Fish debate, Milton would have decisively backed Goodrich. Over and over again, his writings demonstrate his view—shared by his entire culture—that law was not separate from other disciplines. For instance, quoting Cicero in *A Defense of the English People*, he writes that law is "nothing but that right reason derived from divine will which commands what is right and forbids what is wrong" (*CPW* 4:383). Whereas Fish claims, "Law is not philosophy," Milton in effect claims, "Law is simply a form of applied philosophy."

A second, related obstacle to understanding the early modern law is our own entrenched ideas about the law's origin. The modern idea of positive law—that is, law that has been handed down (literally "posited") by a sovereign legislative power—was developed by Jeremy Bentham and John Austin and later elaborated by thinkers like H. L. A. Hart. We also see this positivist idea

10. Goodrich, *Reading the Law*, 209; Fish, *Doing What Comes Naturally*, 397.

clearly in Max Weber's sociology of law, in which the state claims political power and then uses the law to protect its hegemony.[11] Perhaps more than anyone else, Weber has fostered the idea that law is created so that people with a monopoly on physical force can legitimate their rule and enforce their will. Thomas Hobbes has also been generally associated with an authoritarian idea of law, in which legal power flows downward from the sovereign. Repudiating the common law's claim that its authority derived from reason and custom, Hobbes writes, "A law is the Command of him, or them that have the Sovereign Power, given to those that be his or their Subjects, declaring Publicly, and plainly what every one of them may do, and what they must forbear to do."[12] Even those today who do not see the law as simply the expression of sovereign command still generally see it as a set of secular propositions that a society uses to govern itself. These arrangements are arbitrary in the sense that other arrangements could be substituted if the society in question deemed others to be preferable. As a result, law is primarily an expression of policy, and certain offenses are illegal not because they are intrinsically immoral but because society sees them as disruptive. We might compare in this regard the illegality of bigamy to the legality of adultery. One might argue that adultery is more immoral in that it involves a breach of trust, but only bigamy is outlawed, because it is seen as more erosive of the social order.

Deborah Shuger points out how readily our own ideas about the law can prevent us from accurately understanding how law worked in the early modern world. She shows that we have misunderstood censorship in the sixteenth and seventeenth centuries

11. So, for instance, law is guaranteed "by a staff of people" willing to exercise physical or psychological coercion, and the legal system is upheld by those possessed of "the strongest coercive power." Weber, *Economy and Society*, 34, 337. On the way in which Weber's vision of law has obscured the very different legal configurations of an earlier world, see Berman, *Faith and Order*, 239–50.

12. Hobbes, *Dialogue*, 71. David Dyzenhaus presents a cogent challenge to the traditional view of Hobbes as a positivist in his "Hobbes on Authority of Law." See also Lobban, "Hobbes and the Common Law."

because we have trouble imagining it as anything other than ideological control exercised by a repressive state. For most of the early modern period, however, censorship was more about communal civility, about keeping people from harming or defaming one another, than about repressing dangerous ideas.[13] Thus, Natural Law jurisprudence did not necessarily lend itself to a conservative political stance in the way that it does today. Shuger's work complements that of legal historians such as Harold J. Berman, John Witte Jr., and Goodrich, who have shown how profoundly legal practices and theological ideas animate one another. Witte argues that law and religion are best understood as a set of binoculars that show coordinated and overlapping visual fields.[14] For example, the belief that God punished sins had led to the presumption that breaking certain laws should result not in forced restitution (as is the case with torts) but rather in punishment, a presumption that regards criminal sentences as the corollary to spiritual penance. Similarly, the theological assumption that the sins of the father taint the sons helped to produce the legal practice of forfeiture, in which the felon's possessions became the property of either the landlord or the state, depending on the severity of the offense.[15] And the requirement that legal defendants had to plead either innocence or guilt in a quasi-confessional setting attests to

13. Shuger, *Censorship and Cultural Sensibility*. Marianne Constable, in her fascinating study of the mixed jury, explores the history and the implications of positivism as the primary conception of law in the Anglo-American world: Constable, *Law of the Other*.

14. See Berman's three books *Law and Revolution*; *Law and Revolution: II*; and *Faith and Order*. For the comment on law and religion as providing a binocular field of vision, see Witte, *God's Joust, God's Justice*, 4–5. Witte makes comparable arguments for the cross-pollination of law and religion in *Reformation of Rights* and *Law and Protestantism*. See also Brooks, *Law, Politics, and Society*, 208–20.

15. Baker, *Introduction to English Legal History*, 274. In the case of felony, the felon forfeited his chattels to the state. The state had the use of the felon's real properties for a year and a day, at which point they reverted to the landlord. In the case of treason, all goods and properties passed immediately to the Crown, although the monarch sometimes remitted this penalty in consideration of the traitor's family.

the "penitential character of the legal profession."[16] The works of George Herbert also show how deeply law suffused seventeenth-century religious practices. In his *Country Parson*, Herbert writes that the good parson "endures not that any of his Flock should go to Law; but in any Controversie, that they should resort to him as their Judge." Initially, this sounds like a rejection of law as a means of resolving disputes; however, Herbert does not mean that those who disagree should open their Bibles instead of their statute books. Rather, he means that the parson himself should have enough reading in "some initiatory treatises in the Law, with Daltons Justice of Peace, and the Abridgements of the Statutes, as also by discourse with men of that profession" that he can act as ad hoc legal counsel.[17]

As Goodrich explains about early attitudes toward the law, "the temporal law was moulded upon a spiritual regnancy, it was a shadow of a greater power, it mimicked a regnancy that ordered the soul and all its externalizations, including property and chattels." This idea provides the conceptual warrant for most of the major juristic texts of the late medieval and early modern period. In *On the Laws and Governance of England*, Sir John Fortescue writes, "Not only the laws of Deuteronomy, but also all human laws are sacred" and "To learn the laws, even though human ones, is to learn laws that are sacred and decreed of God." Fortescue even says that lawyers are like priests in that they teach "the art of the just and the good." Christopher St. German, in his influential *Doctor and Student*, a legal textbook reprinted frequently during the sixteenth and seventeenth centuries, expressed conventional wisdom when he wrote that "all other Laws are derived" from God's law and that "in Every Law of man well made is somewhat of the Law of Reason, and of the Law of God."[18] Of course, the

16. Goodrich, *Law in the Courts*, 126.

17. Herbert, *Works of George Herbert*, 259.

18. Goodrich, "Amici curiae," 27; Fortescue, *Laws and Governance of England*, 6–7; St. German, *Exact Abridgement*, B1v, B2v.

shared idea that the temporal law is rooted in the will of God did not prevent intense disagreements about the interpretation and application of the law. At John Lilburne's trial in 1649, Judge Jermyn told him, "You must know that the law of England is the law of God."[19] While defendant and judge both agreed on this opening premise, they had radically different ideas about how authority was delegated within the judicial system and about whether the order that had exiled Lilburne conflicted with the dictates of reason and conscience.

The deep links between religion and law did not mean that early modern men and women saw the law as above reproach or that the collected statutes and cases of English common law were regarded as an unsullied expression of God's perfect will. Indeed, the seventeenth century was characterized by escalating attacks on the manifest failings and corruptions of the laws and the judicial system. A comparison with contemporary views of the church can help us understand how the period could both revere law in the abstract and express righteous anger at the law as enacted and applied. Most people in early modern England would have agreed that the Protestant church was the bride of Christ. However, this view did not prevent—indeed, it enabled—vehement critiques of the ways in which the church had betrayed its divine mandate. So with the law. In *Doctrine and Discipline of Divorce*, Milton claims that law—and he here means all law, both divine and temporal—in its "integrity and faithfulnesse" sits "next to God" in "scepter'd royalty," a claim that makes law into the handmaiden of God (*CPW* 2:323). And yet works like *Areopagitica* show Milton's keen awareness of how law could become a tool of narrow-minded oppression. Just as Milton could castigate English Protestantism for its various failings and yet still see it as a manifestation of God's will, he saw clearly the often lamentable reality of the law and yet also asserted that law should be a perfect mirror of divine justice.

19. Quoted and discussed in Green, *Verdict according to Conscience*, 171.

Milton's Views of Law

Milton's prose writings provide us with textbook examples of the early modern tendency to link human laws and divine laws. In *Doctrine and Discipline of Divorce*, he writes, "All Ordinances are establisht in thir end; the end of Law is the vertu, is the righteousness of Law." The goal of law is not just social stability but "vertu." He continues, "The general end of every Ordinance, every severest, every divinest, eevn of Sabbath is the good of man, yea his temporal good not excluded" (*CPW* 2:623). Milton's reference to "every divinest [law], eevn of Sabbath" may lure us into thinking that he is talking only about the Mosaic Law, but his references to "all Ordinances" and "every Ordinance" indicate that he is thinking in the broadest terms about what laws do: they should all have the shared goal of "righteousness." This legal ecumenicism is also clear when he writes, "Yet all Law, and Gods Law especially grants every where to error easy remitments" (*CPW* 2:629). God's Law may be "especially" good at granting "remitments" in the case of error, but this flexibility is one that Milton decisively claims for "all Law" as well.

The tendency to mingle divine and temporal laws allows Milton to skip back and forth between biblical and later legal codes with a sometimes disorienting speed. For example, he examines the Roman law's provisions about "the setting free of a slave," and then he argues on that basis that it is much more becoming for "the Law of God to enact the restorement of a free born man from an unpurpos'd, and unworthy bondage" (i.e., a bad marriage). Similarly, he compares the laws of "that Civilian Emperour in his title of *Donations*" about recalling gifts to the "equity" of Moses, who similarly "permit[s] heer the giver to recall . . . the guift of himself from one who most injuriously and deceitfully uses him against the main ends and conditions of his giving himself" (*Doctrine and Discipline of Divorce*, *CPW* 2:626). In both cases, biblical law is bolstered by and interpreted through the precepts of temporal law. Arguing that the Mosaic Law attends to the needs of the wife, Milton considers "the rescript of

Antoninus in the Civil Law." He reasons that since this law gave release to servants "flying to refuge to the Emperours statue" to escape cruel masters, God, "who in his Law also is good to injur'd servants," similarly considers "the wrongs and miseries of a wife which is no servant" (ibid., 2:627). Noticing how frequently Milton thinks about temporal law when he is trying to grapple with the nature of spiritual freedom, Martin Dzelzainis writes, "The paradox which we need to grasp therefore is that, in the very act of defining Christian liberty as freedom from the law, Milton falls back on the conceptual framework of the Roman law of persons."[20] While Dzelzainis concentrates on the pairing of the Mosaic Law of divorce with Roman laws about slavery in this one treatise, his insight has a broad applicability, for Milton characteristically shuttles back and forth between law and Law when he is trying to think about the way God's mind works.

In these and other cases, Milton is not simply reasoning by analogy between discrete systems. For instance, one might argue that a given social institution (say, a university) would do well to regulate itself in the manner of another (the family, the democratic state, the corporate world, etc.) without positing an actual identification between the two. But in the case of Law and law, Milton insists on precisely this ideal identification. They are not separate things that resemble one another; they are instead parts of the same cosmic system. Milton opens *An Apology against a Pamphlet* by commenting that "the plain authority of Scripture" and "the reason of justice and equity" lead in the same direction (*CPW* 1:868). He offers a similarly unified vision of the law in *Eikonoklastes* when he says that those who, like King Charles, defy their own consciences will have little pity "whether at the barr of human, or Divine Justice," since these jurisdictions share "common grounds and verdicts" (*CPW* 3:430).

He develops this idea in more detail in *Doctrine and Discipline of Divorce*, when he argues against the idea that a "politick

20. Dzelzainis, "Liberty and the Law," 61.

Law . . . may regulate sin"—in other words, that a human law can allow and moderate sinful behavior, unlike a moral or divine law, which must forbid it. Milton here is fighting against Theodore Beza's argument that the function of the temporal law is simply to organize the polity, not to foster righteousness, a position that Milton calls Machiavellian. He writes: "The Judiciall law can serve no other end then to be the protector and champion of Religion and honest civility . . . and is but the arm of morall law, which can no more be separate from justice then justice from virtue: their office also in a different manner steers the same cours; the one teaches what is good by precept, the other unteaches what is bad by punishment" (*CPW* 2:322). Both forms of law steer "the same course" and should have precisely the same end in view. And he relies on this same fusion of religion and law when he argues in *A Defense of the English People* that since "the law is always considered the highest and ultimate power" and since—remarkably—the teachings of both reason and the Gospel "accord with . . . the laws of nations," the one who "wholeheartedly obeys the laws" is by implication doing the will of God (*CPW* 4:383).

We need to take this last statement—that obeying the law is necessarily a form of obeying God—with a grain of salt, since Milton is mounting a very specific argument in *A Defense* about the legality of the Civil War, the execution of Charles I, and parliamentary supremacy. In other works, he makes what looks like the opposite claim: that righteous men sometimes must defy the laws. For example, in *Tetrachordon* he writes, "Men of most renowned vertu have sometimes by transgressing most truly kept the law; and wisest Magistrates have permitted and dispenc't it" (*CPW* 2:588). And in *Eikonoklastes*, he writes: "That is not always best, which is most regular to writt'n Law. Great Worthies heertofore by disobeying Law, ofttimes have sav'd the Commonwealth: and the Law afterward by firme Decree hath approv'd that planetary motion, that unblamable exorbitancy in them" (*Eikonoklastes*, *CPW* 3:562). However, at these moments when he is most aware of the lapses—and indeed, the outright injustices—of the temporal law, Milton also uses Natural Law to preserve the law's sanctity. The Natural Law principle *lex iniusta non est lex* provided that unjust laws were not real laws at all. If regarded through a Natural Law prism, the defiance of the "writt'n Law" that Milton celebrates in *Eikonoklastes* is not, in fact, actual lawbreaking, since the rules being broken were not reasonable and just and therefore not truly laws to begin with.

Even when Milton wants to indicate how much greater laws made by God are than laws made by human beings, he ends up calling attention to the continuities between them. For example, in *Doctrine and Discipline of Divorce*, he extols the Mosaic Law allowing divorce as "this tenure and free-hold of mankind, this native and domestick Charter giv'n us by a greater Lord then that *Saxon* King the Confessor" (*CPW* 2:230). Although his argument rests on a contrast between the two legal systems, the fact that he describes God's words to his people in legal terms—as a new "tenure and free-hold" and as a charter that trumps the Magna Carta—undermines the very distinction he is trying to draw. As a lawgiver, God is immeasurably greater than Edward the Confessor, but Milton also situates God's words squarely within the same legal tradition that contains the twelfth-century *Leges Edwardi Confessori*. This blurring of Law and law similarly characterizes a passage in *Animadversions* where Milton provides what looks like a parable: one gardener, who represents England's good clergy, has tended a garden for years but is now threatened with eviction by a recent arrival, who represents England's bishops. Milton introduces this exemplum by telling the reader, "Have patience therefore a little, and heare a Law case" (*CPW* 1:716). The label "Law case" highlights the fact that many biblical parables—like the unevenly paid workers in the vineyard or the poor investment strategy of the servant who was given one talent—revolve around judicial questions (who should be paid? who should be punished?). When Milton tells a parable and yet calls it a "Law case," he undermines any clear distinction between moral and legal forms of judgment.

The Jurisdictional and Critical Field

While Milton had no doubt that true law should funnel God's justice to Earth, like most of his contemporaries he was not always sure how to bring this about. In various prose works, he frankly acknowledges the challenge of making human law into a better reflection of God's will. In the preface to the second edition of *Doctrine and Discipline of Divorce*, for example, he admits the difficulty of knowing "how far the territory and dominion extends of just and honest liberty." Since the law must not encroach into the "territory" of liberty, "as little must [the lawmaker] offer to bind that which God hath loos'n'd, as to loos'n that which he hath bound"—a hard task indeed. In *The Character of the Long Parliament*, Milton again takes up the delicate balance between too much law and too little, acknowledging the "happy skill" of those who know "what is grievance, and unjust to a People, and how to remove it wisely." Those who have this happy—and implicitly rare—skill know "what good Laws are wanting, and how to frame them substantially, that good Men may enjoy the freedom they merit, and the bad the Curb which they need" (*CPW* 5.1:448). A similar search for the right legislative middle ground also appears in a passage from *A Second Defense of the English People*. Addressing Cromwell and offering both praise and advice, Milton warns about those who "itch with a kind of lust to promulgate many laws, as versifiers itch to pour forth many poems," and he claims that "the greater the number, the worse in general is the quality of the laws" (*CPW* 4:678).[21] Accordingly, Milton tells Cromwell that he should "propose fewer new laws than you repeal old ones." Milton wants "only those laws that are essential" and not those that would "subject good men with bad to the same yoke, nor, while they take precautions against the wiles of the wicked, forbid also that which should be free for good men" (*CPW* 6:678–79). In his call for only

21. On the frequent admonitions in the period against being too quick to change the laws, see Burgess, *Politics of the Ancient Constitution*, 24–25.

those laws that are "essential" and in his critique of those who "itch . . . to promulgate many laws," we can hear the author of *Areopagitica* and the divorce tracts speaking, for the Licensing Order of 1643 and England's canon laws on marriage were, for Milton, precisely the kind of superfluous precepts that forbade "that which should be free for good men."

On the one hand, Milton seems wary about the "itch" to create new laws, and yet on the other he shows a mounting support for statutory law. To explain both the nature of this support and the resulting jurisprudential bind into which revolutionary events pushed Milton, I turn here to a brief overview of the period's jurisdictional complexities. This overview has two added benefits. First, it allows me to clarify juridical terms and concepts that come up in subsequent chapters. Second, it gives me a framework for describing the existing scholarship on Milton's legal references. While our modern world has its share of jurisdictional rivalries (e.g., the tensions between local, state, and federal law in the United States), these bear little comparison with the situation in early modern England, where different courts and different legal systems jostled, competed, and overlapped.[22] For instance, Sir Edward Coke counted sixteen separate legal systems or independent jurisdictions in England, ranging from dominant ones such as common law courts and prerogative courts down to more restricted juridical entities such as the Palatinates and England's forest courts.[23] While some scholars, including Victoria Silver and Leah S. Marcus, are well aware of the early modern jurisdictional patchwork, most of those who write about Milton and law project backward a modern idea of the law as a unified set of norms.[24] For example, John Shawcross, in his discussion "Milton and Legal

22. See, for instance, the discussion of early modern jurisdictional problems in Ford, "Law's Territory," although I would argue that the modern jurisdictional field is more conflicted than Ford allows.

23. For two other discussions of the period's jurisdictional complexities, see Cormack, *Power to Do Justice*; and Gray, *Writ of Prohibition*.

24. On Milton's awareness of specifically jurisdictional tensions, see Marcus, *Politics of Mirth*; and Silver, "'Taken Scandal Not a Given.'"

Matters," lumps together Milton's Chancery dealings, his allusions to legal conveyances, and his knowledge of contemporary restrictions on usury, without acknowledging that this discussion mingles equity, common law, and canon law.[25] Such an uncritical consolidation of different, independent jurisdictions under the heading of "the early modern law" is as problematic in its own way as would be a comparable mingling of Quakers, Puritans, and Church of England stalwarts under the label "Protestants." Just as Milton thought both about "the Church" writ large—that is, all of Christendom—as well as about subsets of "the Church" such as Presbyterianism, his legal outlook is variously panoramic and granular. At times, he considers law in its broadest sense, and at others he focuses on the way specific laws were defined and implemented by specific jurisdictions. In this section I explore first Milton's overarching philosophical commitment to Natural Law, and then I turn to the three jurisdictions to which Milton most often alludes in his prose works: Romano-canon law, common law, and equity.

Building on Cicero and the pre-Socratics, St. Thomas Aquinas had developed an idea of Natural Law as the moral reason implanted in human beings by God that allowed them to know the right thing to do and allowed societies to create laws that were themselves extensions of the overarching divine law. Protestant reformers like John Calvin had sidelined Natural Law on the grounds that the human ability to apprehend it had been hopelessly corrupted by the fall, but Natural Law experienced an upsurge in the seventeenth century. Its proponents—Milton included—discovered that it was a potent weapon in the fight for political and civil liberties.[26] Milton's commitment to Natural Law has been the subject of several fine critical discussions, although since Natural Law was a set of ideas rather than a set of applied rules, examining Milton's belief in Natural Law takes us

25. Shawcross, *Development of Milton's Thought*, 25–48.

26. On contemporary transformations occurring in the concept of Natural Law, see Kahn and Hutson's introduction to their *Rhetoric and Law*.

only partway toward understanding how he thought law should work in the world.[27] Most early modern jurists took it for granted that their legal code was in some way authorized by Natural Law (itself a remarkably slippery term put to a wide variety of sometimes contradictory purposes), but this shared commitment did not prevent intensely partisan debates about the use of the law any more than a shared belief in Jesus Christ created unity between Protestants and Catholics. The challenge for Milton, as for all Natural Law proponents, was to bridge the gap between asserting that law should reflect the mind of God and implementing that assertion in the form of real laws. Moreover, any one of the many operative legal systems in early modern England could be seen as an expression or a corruption of Natural Law principles.

The first of the three major legal systems with which Milton was most familiar was Romano-canon law. Beginning in the eleventh century, Justinian's newly rediscovered *Corpus juris civilis* was made into the basis of ecclesiastical law, and this ecclesiastical or canon law—systematized by Gratian and supplemented by papal decretals and the rulings of various provincial councils—enabled the Church's discrete institutional identity and eventually its medieval ascendency.[28] Elaborated and refined in the ecclesiastical sphere, these Romanist legal ideas were subsequently transmitted back to the secular states, and by the end of the sixteenth century, most European nations had adopted a version of law that was based on Justinian's legal code and was procedurally consistent with canon law. As a result, while Continental church courts and state courts had different jurisdictions, they all operated generally on the principles of Romano-canon law.[29] Some countries, how-

27. On Milton's commitment to Natural Law, see White, *Natural Law*, 216–51; Fulton, *Historical Milton*, 99–101, 143–73; Smith, "*Areopagitica*," 105–11; and Sauer, *Milton, Toleration, and Nationhood*, 74–94. For general discussions of Natural Law, see Tuck, *Natural Rights Theories*; Oakley, *Natural Law*; and Bobbio, *Hobbes and Natural Law Tradition*.

28. This story is eloquently told in Berman, *Law and Revolution*.

29. A note on terminology: this legal code is often referred to as "civil law" or "Civil

ever, were resistant to Romano-canon law. For instance, most of the Lutheran states adopted a legal code based on the writings of Johann of Schwarzenberg and Philip Melanchthon. In England, widespread prejudice against Catholicism had stiffened resistance to a legal system associated with Rome and the papacy, even though English common law and Roman law shared many core precepts. As a result, Romano-canon law was practiced only in England's ecclesiastical courts. These courts had jurisdiction only in the areas, such as family law and probate, where common law had little to say and only to the extent that Romano-canon law did not conflict with common law. Even with this restricted jurisdictional range, Romano-canon law was continually subject to encroachments from the common law courts.[30] Romano-canon law expanded its domestic purview somewhat in the seventeenth century with the increased reliance on prerogative courts such as the Star Chamber and the Council of Wales and the Marches. While these courts did not necessarily adhere to Romano-canon substantive law, they generally operated along Romano-canon lines.

Romano-canon law has tended to attract the most attention from Milton critics, and Martin Dzelzainis, Quentin Skinner, and others have argued for the influence of Justinian's *Institutes* on Milton's thinking.[31] In the absence of a broader corpus of work on Milton and law, these arguments, however persuasive in themselves, result in a very partial picture. Focusing only on Milton's knowledge of the *Corpus juris civilis* (the larger body of texts of which the *Institutes* is one part) suggests that he was more indebted to the legal texts and ideas that constituted law on the Continent than to the teeming, combative, and rapidly evolving

law"—hence the term "civilians" for Romano-canon lawyers in England. But since in later chapters I will be centrally concerned with differentiating between criminal and noncriminal offenses, I reserve the term "civil" to indicate laws that regulate relations between private individuals—contracts, negligence, debt, and so forth—as opposed to public, or "criminal," laws that protect the stability of the state.

30. Helmholz, *Roman Canon Law*.

31. E.g., Dzelzainis, "These Western Parts," "Liberty and the Law"; Skinner, "Milton and Slavery"; Nyquist, *Arbitrary Rule*.

world of contemporary English law. We need to know more about Milton's reliance on Roman ideas of law, but these discussions also need to be set in a larger legal and cultural framework. For example, England had its own set of *Institutes*, Coke's intentionally titled four-volume work on the common law, and the legal systems epitomized by the two different *Institutes*—Roman and English—had been engaged throughout the early modern period in a slow-motion struggle for dominance.[32] Without this larger framework, we risk misreading. For instance, the marginal farewell to Justinian's laws ("Justiniane vale") that Milton wrote in a copy of Ariosto's *Orlando Furioso* does not necessarily signal what one critic calls Milton's "formal and definitive renunciation of the study, practice, and even interest in law in favor of literary pursuits" any more than a farewell to Aquinas's *Summa* would necessarily be a rejection of theology.[33] Since Justinian's *Institutes* was the basis of law on the Continent, Milton's marginal note could mean simply that he had decided to forgo training as a civilian (Romano-canon) lawyer or as a diplomat. (Although it could conceivably mark his decision to forgo training at the Inns of Court, one would then expect him to bid farewell to a common law authority such as Coke or Glanville.) Moreover, since Milton continued to read Justinian and to cite the *Institutes* often in his *Commonplace Book*, this marginal note should not be read as evidence that Milton crisply renounced jurisprudential interests and turned instead to literary ones.

The heavyweight in the early modern English legal ring was the common law. Common law had two main components: custom (expressed in case law) and statutes.[34] Provoked by Charles

32. On the centrality of law to English nationhood and on Coke's calculated response to the threat represented by Justinian's *Institutes*, see Helgerson, *Forms of Nationhood*, 63–104.

33. Greenberg, "Law," 328.

34. Although the critical conversation about the ideological underpinnings of the early modern common law is too large to summarize in a single note, four primary voices are J. G. A. Pocock, Glenn Burgess, J. W. Tubbs, and J. P. Sommerville. Pocock

I's increasing use of the prerogative courts to support his Personal Rule, Coke, helped by junior colleagues such as Selden, increasingly proclaimed the antiquity and supremacy of the common law, and England's common lawyers were successful at creating an image of their legal system as the great guarantor of the Englishman's life, liberty, and property. Over the course of the seventeenth century, the common law steadily extended its jurisdiction. As Cormack points out, "while at the beginning of the Tudor period it was possible to imagine English law substantially in terms of interrelated spheres of judicial activity," by the end of the seventeenth century, the common law had become "the dominant source of juridical norms." Even though it was the dominant legal system in England, the common law has received relatively little consideration from Milton scholars, with the signal exceptions of Lynne Greenberg and Leah S. Marcus, who have persuasively established Milton's familiarity with common law terms and principles.[35]

The challenge facing any critic who wants to deal with the common law is that, unlike Romano-canon law, there is no central written text that sums up what "the law" says. As Judge Jermyn argued at Lilburne's trial, in a line of reasoning that may strike modern readers as strange, the common law's unwritten nature was the basis of its rational perfection: "It does not depend upon statutes, or written and declared words or lines. . . . Therefore I

famously postulated the existence of what he called the "common law mind," an insular commitment to the antiquity and purity of the common law. Burgess, Tubbs, and Sommerville have variously argued that Pocock's thesis is oversimplified. See Pocock, *Ancient Constitution and Feudal Law*; Burgess, *Politics of the Ancient Constitution*; Tubbs, *Common Law Mind*; Sommerville, "History and Theory."

35. Cormack, *Power to Do Justice*, 27; Greenberg, "Paradise Enclosed," "Law," "'Peal of Words.'" Marcus, in her "Justice for Margery Evans," writes about the Council of Wales and the Marches, which was a prerogative court, and her focus is on that court's common law jurisdiction, especially in felonies such as sexual assault. As of the writing of this book, Sarah Higginbotham's Georgia State University dissertation—on law and legal processes in seventeenth-century literature, including Milton—was not yet in the public domain, so I was unable to consult it.

say again, the law of England is pure primitive reason."[36] English archives contained lists of statutes dating back for centuries, but statutes were only one part of "the law." Furthermore, since there was no concern to build a coherent body of statutes, newer statutes were likely to contradict or duplicate older ones. There were mountains of legal yearbooks and plea rolls describing legal cases as far back as the twelfth century, but since the doctrine of precedent was not stabilized until later in the seventeenth century and stare decisis did not acquire its strict modern formulation until the nineteenth, this documentary material was not necessarily "the law" either. There were increasing numbers of printed legal textbooks, but these were more like users' manuals than formal statements of the law's contents. The early modern common law's unsystematic nature is epitomized by the first edition of Coke's commentary on Littleton's *Tenures*, the period's most comprehensive statement of the complexities of land law. Coke declined to provide either a table of contents or a functional index or even to organize the work in anything like a methodical fashion, because he wanted to discourage men from thinking that the law was a body of knowledge that one could just dip into.[37] Rather, it had to be "lived," and so readers interested in Coke's ideas of, say, fee tail or socage had to comb through more than four hundred pages of dense legal argumentation to cull out what they needed.

Finally we come to equity, the third major legal system in England. It is hard to speak of equity even as a legal system per se, since it was not based on either statutes or case law, and its goal was to provide remedies in situations that fell outside the cognizance of the law. England's main equity court was the Court of Chancery. Suitors in Chancery reported their grievances directly to

36. Quoted and discussed in Green, *Verdict according to Conscience*, 171. Helgerson discusses the written and unwritten nature of various forms of English law: *Forms of Nationhood*, 63–87.

37. Coke's first edition has a one-page table of chapter topics. The difficulty of navigating Coke's massive text must have provoked frustration among contemporary readers, for the printer of the second edition provided an alphabetical index that runs to sixty-four pages.

Chancery (as opposed to the highly formalized system of pleadings in common law), and then both parties appeared in court to answer questions. In equity's early days, the chancellor or his equity representatives decided cases on the basis of their subjective sense of the rightness of things, but by Milton's day, rules called "maxims of equity" had evolved that offered more objective guidelines. However, these were not laws in the sense of statutes. Equity was the system with which Milton had the most direct experience, since, as French demonstrates in *Milton in Chancery*, the poet, his brother, and his father were in and out of Chancery Court for years (although, as French notes, these equity cases frequently crisscrossed into other courts as well, so we cannot attach Milton's personal experience with litigation exclusively to any one judicature). Victoria Silver argues that in his later works Milton expresses a preference for equity over law, and he clearly liked the judicial flexibility that equity provided.[38] For example, it is hard to read about the 1637 *Milton vs. Duck* case and not sense Milton's frustration with the strictures of the common law. (In brief, since the names of plaintiffs and defendants on a common law writ had to be spelled exactly right—a single incorrect letter could cause the whole case to fail—and since the two Milton brothers had no access to Arthur Duck's will, they could not name the legatees. Thus they had no option but to abandon their common law suit and seek relief through equity.)[39] However, Milton's liking for equity should not be generalized into a claim that he thought that equity should replace law. England's equity courts were established to serve as a safety net for those cases that fell through the common law cracks. Virtually no one—including the Lord Chancellor, the head of Chancery—thought that more of the nation's rapidly increasing volume of lawsuits could be productively handled by the already beleaguered equity system.

In his prose writings, Milton draws from various jurisdictions, depending on the argument at hand. Rather than merely being

38. Silver, "'Taken Scandal Not a Given.'"

39. On the Duck suit, see French, *Milton in Chancery*, 62–67.

opportunistic and seizing on the legal system that offered the best support for his immediate claim, he seems to have agreed with early modern jurists such as Hooker and Bacon that the goals of true justice were best served when many jurisprudences cooperated together. The early modern mind-set could accommodate a pluralized and heterogeneous idea of legal justice far more readily than the modern one does. Because there was no common law of marriage or divorce, Milton relies in his divorce tracts on classical juristic texts such Plato's *Laws* or Cicero's *De Officiis* and on the heavy-hitters of the Romano-canon legal tradition. For example, in *Tetrachordon*, he devotes considerable space to discussing the laws of the Roman emperors Theodosius, Justinian, and Valentinian. However, in works like *Tenure of Kings and Magistrates* and *Eikonoklastes*, where the issues are constitutional ones, Milton resorts almost exclusively to the English common law. For example, in *Eikonoklastes*, Milton criticizes King Charles because he has not respected native English legal traditions, and he argues from old legal sources such as the laws of Edward III and the *Mirror for Justice*, a work purporting to contain England's earliest laws (*CPW* 3:398–99). At times, Milton seems to participate in the historical jurisprudence characteristic of jurists such as Coke, Selden, and Sir Matthew Hale.[40] In his *Defense of the English People*, he praises the English people for having adhered to their own laws: "They have laws, and followed them; laws which they got from their fathers and which are here the most excellent, whatever may be the case in the rest of the world" (*CPW* 4:533). The phrase "here the most excellent" echoes a core principle of humanist jurisprudence that laws should serve the needs of each nation. Developing this idea, Selden and Hale argued that a body of laws could not be evaluated in isolation from the people to whom it applied or from that people's history, a jurisprudential approach that made room for

40. Berman, "Origins of Historical Jurisprudence"; See Knafla, *Law and Politics*, 68–69, for a discussion of how this historical thinking characterized earlier European jurists.

the consent of the governed. Instead of simply asking about a law, "Is it rational?" (the litmus test applied by Natural Law) or "Was it duly posited by a sovereign authority?" (the positivist litmus test), one also had to ask, "Does it meet the unique needs of the people, and how has it evolved to match its particular historical context?" Historical jurisprudence admitted a wider national and regional variety than Natural Law did. As Hale wrote, laws are "to be accommodated to the Conditions, Exigencies and Conveniences of the People, for or by whom they are appointed, [and] as those Exigencies and Conveniences do insensibly grow upon the People, so many Times there grows insensibly a Variation of Laws, especially in a long Tract of Time."[41] When Milton argues that the common law is "most excellent" "here,"—that is, in England—and then adds "whatever may be the case in the rest of the world," he writes in the Coke-Selden-Hale vein, asserting that each country should build the legal system that best suits it and that regional and national variations are the natural result of historical evolution.

But Milton's support for Natural Law often pushed his legal views out of alignment with those of common law jurists. For instance, while Coke believed fervently in the consonance of common law and reason, he did not regard reason as an extralegal principle to which one could appeal over the head of the law. Instead, it was embodied in and expressed by the law itself.[42] Similarly, Hale opposed changing the death penalty for theft, because this sanction had become historically woven into the fabric of English law. For Coke and Hale, the history of a law was normative, but Milton did not agree. In the passage from *Defense* quoted just above, where he praises the English for respecting their own native legal traditions ("They have laws, and followed them; laws which they got from their fathers . . ."), Milton next claims that the English "cherish one law of great age, passed by

41. Hale, *History of the Common Law*, 39. For discussion of this passage, see Berman, *Law and Revolution: II*, 256.

42. A good account of Coke's legal thinking is provided by Boyer, *Sir Edward Coke*.

Nature herself, which makes all laws, all rights, all civil government depend not on the desire of kings but primarily on the well-being of the better citizens" (*CPW* 4:533). This sounds Cokean in its emphasis on the common law as the expression of reason, but by measuring the soundness of the law against some standard that is outside the law (the "well-being of the better citizens," the adjective "better" providing a hint of Milton's growing disaffection with the general populace), Milton makes the common law contingent in a way that Coke opposed. *Eikonoklastes* provides another example. Milton echoes Coke's celebration of the rationality of the common law when he refers to "the Law of *England*, which Lawyers say is the quintessence of reason and mature wisdom." However, on the same page, almost in the same breath, he appeals to "a better evidence then Rowles and Records, Reason." In claiming to supersede the "Rowles and Records" that comprised the history of common law decisions, Milton claims to supersede much of what made the common law what it was (*CPW* 3:409).[43] At times, he is openly dismissive of the common law's authority. In his *Tenure of Kings and Magistrates*, Milton claims that the "temporal Law both may and ought, though without a special Text or precedent, extend with like indifference the civil Sword, to the cutting off without exemption him [i.e., a king] that capitally offends" (*CPW* 3:222). The crucial phrase is "without a special Text or precedent." In other words, the "temporal Law" does not need an existing law—either one based on custom and case law ("precedent") or on statute ("special Text")—to execute a king. To be legal, it simply needs to be reasonable.

While Milton had a scholar's appreciation for the theoretical coherence of Justinian's *Institutes* and a patriot's allegiance to his native common law, both of these affinities were subordinated to his willingness to attack any legal system that he saw as unreasonable. For instance, when he writes that "bishops have no right to rule the church, much less do kings, whatever human laws

43. We see here what David Baker identifies as Milton's impatience with antiquarianism as an obstacle to reformation. See his "'Dealt with at His Weapon.'"

may say" (*Defense of the English People*, *CPW* 4:499), he is criticizing all those "human laws" that do not involve the consent of the governed. In *Of Reformation*, answering the objection that "the government of Episcopacy, is now so weav'd into the common Law" that it cannot safely be changed, Milton retorts, "In *Gods* name let it weave out againe; let not humain quillets keep back divine authority." While this sounds like a criticism just of the common law, Milton soon broadens his scope: "Tis not the common Law, nor the civil [i.e., Romano-canon law], but piety, and justice, that are our foundresses" (*CPW* 1:605). Milton is consistent in this appeal to that reasonableness that, in his view, forms the basis of all true law.

Ultimately, Milton's support for reasonableness made him a champion of Parliament's statutory law. Because the history of English legal cases and statutes did not provide clear precedents for the kinds of social and political changes he most believed in, and because Natural Law had no jurisdictional teeth (with the possible exception of equity, there was no "Court of Natural Law" handing down verdicts in seventeenth-century England), Milton celebrated the binding authority of new statutes. In answer to King Charles's argument that his coronation oath obliged him to uphold only existing laws and not new ones, Milton argues that "those [existing] Laws were not a sufficient remedy to all greevances, many were found to be greevances themselves," and he asks, "When did we loose that other part of our freedom to establish new?" (*Eikonoklastes*, *CPW* 3:463). In proclaiming the right of Parliament to make whatever new laws it sees fit, Milton drifts away from Coke's vision of the law as founded on tradition and custom, and where Coke de-emphasizes the power of legislation, Milton celebrates it. We see a similar support for the updating of statutory law at the beginning of *Tenure of Kings and Magistrates*. Milton refers approvingly to "those Worthies" who begin the "alteration of Lawes" in the wake of political upheavals, and he is scathing about those who prefer instead the "old entanglement" of unwritten legal traditions (*CPW* 2:192–93). Similarly, in *Eikonoklastes* he loosely equates law with statutory law when he writes, "What the Lawes of the Land are, a Parlament should know best, having both the life and death of Lawes in thir Lawgiving power" (*CPW* 3:451–52). Milton wants to have it two ways: to put "both the life and death of Lawes" in Parliament's control and yet to argue that laws can only truly be laws if they are rational. We see this uneasy fusion of law-as-reason and law-as-the-will-of-Parliament when he writes in *Eikonoklastes* that "law in a Free Nation hath bin ever public reason, the enacted reason of a Parlament" (*CPW* 3:360). The broad appeal to reason in the first part of the sentence narrows to the "enacted reason of a Parlament" in the second. The jurisprudential tension becomes more pronounced in *A Readie and Easie Way*, when Milton complains about those who would support parliamentary statutes "which for the most part are meer positive laws, neither natural nor moral," and claims that these statutes could "by any parliament . . . be at any time repealed" (*CPW* 7:413). "Natural and moral" laws have staying power; "meer positive laws" do not. The problem Milton faces, however, is that all statutory law lay in the keeping of Parliament. Here on the threshold of the Restoration, Milton worries that newer royalist statutes can undo older Commonwealth ones, "till all law be lost in the multitude of clashing statutes" (*CPW* 7:434). But since Milton had earlier argued for felling traditional case law trees to pave the way for more parliamentary statutes, the problem of "clashing statutes" is one whose conditions he himself had helped to create.

Not Seeing the Law in Paradise Lost

Because most critics who have explored Milton's view of the law focus on his prose tracts, we are left with very little sense of how his views of law impact his epic poem. In this final section, I look at three arguments about *Paradise Lost* to show how in each case modern assumptions have deflected attention away from the role that law plays in Milton's poem. In "Penal Theory in *Paradise Lost*," lawyer Jillisa Brittan and US appellate judge Richard Posner offer one of the only sustained legal readings of Milton's poem, for they relate the penal practices depicted in *Paradise Lost* to foundational Western ideas about law. However, Brittan and Posner then qualify the relevance of their argument in a way that casts modern assumptions about law into sharp relief: they apologize for providing a legal reading of what they term Milton's "cosmic prelegal society."[44] Since they think of law as what societies do, and since Milton depicts a world before the establishment of civil orders, Brittan and Posner have an uneasy sense of anachronistically applying the law where it does not belong. But for Milton, no society is "prelegal" in the way Brittan and Posner assume, and so their argument needs no apology. As a proponent of Natural Law, Milton believed that temporal law should reflect on the mortal plane the principles that God had coded into the nature of things. We moderns tend to think of scientific laws (e.g., the law of gravity, the law of gas diffusion, etc.) as being "discovered" in the sense that they were there all along. Conversely, we tend to think of statutory laws as being "made" in the sense that they are created from scratch by a legislating body. However, Natural Law proponents were more likely to see all good laws as being merely new discoveries—or perhaps new applications—of rational principles that had existed since the creation. Within the framework of Natural Law, it is no more anachronistic for Milton to infuse the principles of temporal law into *Paradise Lost* than it is for him to allude in his poem to the laws of motion or optics.

Jason Rosenblatt's wonderful *Torah and Law in "Paradise Lost"* is another example of how modern ideas can get in the way of a full appreciation of law's presence in the poem. Rosenblatt argues for the pervasiveness of law in Eden, but he is talking exclusively about Law with a capital "L," meaning divine Law and specifically Mosaic Law. In Rosenblatt's persuasive reading, Milton saw the Law of Eden—to abstain from the fruit, to be fruitful and multiply, and to tend the Garden—as containing within itself the entire Mosaic code. The Law takes on its Pauline, adversarial role only after the fall; before that point the Law of Eden—which is

44. Brittan and Posner, "Penal Theory in *Paradise Lost*," 1051.

a compressed form of the Mosaic Law—enabled righteousness. But having mounted a powerful argument for Milton's belief in "the complete unity of the law," Rosenblatt does not extend his argument to include temporal law.[45] In short, while he convincingly dismantles the conceptual bulkhead between the Edenic Law and the Mosaic Law, he leaves another bulkhead untouched: that between those normative rules authored by God and those authored by human legislators and jurists. Milton, however, doesn't just poke holes in this second bulkhead; he has trouble seeing the need for it in the first place. For example, in *Doctrine and Discipline of Divorce*, he writes, "The judicial law can serve to no other end then to be the protector and champion of Religion" (*CPW* 2:321). Here and elsewhere he uses the phrase "judicial law" to refer to England's temporal law, but at other points in the treatise, the same phrase refers to God's decrees in Exodus and Leviticus, a slippage that speaks eloquently of Milton's refusal to erect firm boundaries between what God declares legal and what human beings declare legal.

Finally, the work of Stanley Fish similarly illustrates what happens when we do not understand the law-religion linkage that was so pervasive in Milton's world. In his legal writings, Fish insists that law and religion belong in different sealed compartments, as when he refers to the "uncongeniality of theological discourse to the legal mind." This uncongeniality may generally characterize the modern world, but it is starkly at odds with the early modern one. Noting the frequency with which early modern jurists and theologians borrowed one another's terms and principles, Shuger points out that this cross-fertilization "would have been inconceivable had the aims and interests of the law differed in fundamental respects from those of Christian ethics."[46] The works of Sir Francis Bacon, Sir Matthew Hale, and Richard Hooker—three of the period's foremost jurists—amply illustrate Shuger's

45. Rosenblatt, *Torah and Law*, 3.

46. Fish, *Doing What Comes Naturally*, 399. See also similar claims in Fish, "Law Wishes to Have." Shuger, *Censorship and Cultural Sensibility*, 139.

point. Sir Francis Bacon wrote *Elements of the Common Law of England*, and he also wrote a collection of theological reflections known as *Sacred Meditations*. Sir Matthew Hale, arguably England's preeminent judge during the Civil War and Commonwealth periods, wrote both his landmark *A History of the Common Law of England* and *Contemplations, Moral and Divine*, which went through fifteen editions. Similarly, Richard Hooker's *Laws of Ecclesiastical Polity* is simultaneously a reflection on God's will for his church and an astute work of jurisprudence. The writings of these men categorically refute any attempt to draw the kinds of crisp law-religion dividing lines that Fish insists on.

Ironically, at the beginning of his iconic *Surprised by Sin*, Fish quotes from a text that epitomizes the law-religion connection that was so pervasive in the early modern period and that remains so absent in the modern one. On the first page of his preface, Fish likens Milton's project in *Paradise Lost* to that of contemporary devotional writers such as Richard Bernard, and he quotes from Bernard's *Isle of Man*: the goal of reading is to "shew how a man may come to a holy reformation and so happily recover himself."[47] Since Fish provides only the first part of Bernard's title and gives no citation or bibliography entry, a reader unfamiliar with Bernard's work will probably assume that it resembles the thousands of other Protestant devotional manuals of the period. However, Bernard's full title is follows: *The Isle of Man: or, the Legall Proceeding in Man-shire Against Sinne Wherein, by Way of a Continued Allegory, the Chief Malefactors Disturbing both Church and Commonwealth Are Detected and Attached: with Their Arraignment and Judicial Tryal According to the Laws of England*. Beginning with the premise that sin should be proceeded against "as heere we do against a lewd and wicked Malefactor, legally, according to the lawes of this Realme," Bernard provides an extended allegory in which every stage in the process of catching and convicting a criminal—including the testimony of informants, the hue and cry, the arrest, the presentation to the justice of the peace, the

47. Fish, *Surprised by Sin*, ix.

arraignment, the trial, and the sentencing—has a precise corollary in the conviction of sin.[48] Bernard is not merely providing a kind of elaborate metaphysical conceit in which unlike things are yoked together. To the contrary, his book springs from the assumption that the things in question—the trial of sin at the bar of divine justice and the trial of criminals in the earthly judicial system—are extensions of one another. Fish cites Bernard's work in support of his claim that reading *Paradise Lost* is an intensely inward business, effectively a private transaction between God and the human heart. However, *The Isle of Man* looks as much outward as inward. Bernard expects his readers to bring the structures of the judicial law inward to help arraign the soul, and these same readers are also expected to project the fruits of the spirit outward to sustain and reform the processes of human justice.

48. Bernard, *Isle of Man*, 2–3.

3

The Traitors of Heaven and Earth

Appropriately, my study of the law in Milton's poem begins with treason, the greatest of all early modern crimes. Treason is at the heart of *Paradise Lost*. In their confrontation outside the gates of Hell, Death calls Satan "that traitor angel" (2.689). In book 3 God says that Adam is guilty of "treason," and Adam himself admits the justice of this verdict when he says that he is to Satan "like [in] crime and doom" (3.207, 10.841). Given the absence of criticism about treason in *Paradise Lost*, scholars have implicitly read words like "traitor" and "treason" in a generic sense as indicating those who betray, rather than in a specifically legal sense as indicating those who break the law of treason. But Milton uses these terms with a full awareness of their legal implications. The law of treason was changing rapidly in the seventeenth century. Once defined almost exclusively as a personal attack on the monarch's person, treason was increasingly defined instead as an insult to the state and especially to the rule of law. In *Paradise Lost*, Milton consistently privileges the more recent interpretation of treason by showing that Satan's and Adam's greatest crime is their insult to the law, rather than their personal affront to or attack on God. This strategic emphasis on one kind of treason over another has important stakes for how Milton depicts God. By making Satan and Adam primarily traitors in the impersonal sense, Milton shows that God punishes insults to the law more than insults to himself; he is not a deity who respects persons, even—so to speak—divine persons. As I demonstrate in this chapter's concluding section, Milton's emphasis on treason as primarily an offense against the law forms the flip side of his depiction of Heaven. He suggests that the angelic polity is ordered and stabilized by a corpus of laws, and he invites readers to trace the continuities between these heavenly laws and core early modern ideas of legal justice.

Two Kinds of Treason

By the time Milton wrote his *Brief Notes upon a Late Sermon*, his last work of political prose, he, like most of his countrymen, had thought a lot about the law of treason.[1] Responding in this work to his royalist opponent's claim that the rule of kings was an intrinsic part of England's fundamental law, Milton writes, "In this land not only the late King and posteritie, but kingship it self hath bin abrogated by a law; which involves with as good reason the posteritie of a King forfeited to the people, as that Law heretofore of Treason against the King, attainted the children with the father" (*CPW* 7:479). Milton's logic is based on the fact that those convicted of treason were attainted. Their blood was held to be corrupted, and since the traitor was thus unable to transmit or inherit property, all his real and personal estate was forfeit. Milton argues that the judgment passed against Charles I—that he and his family should lose their "posteritie," that is, their claim

1. Treason was considered the worst of all crimes, and it is not an exaggeration to say that the early modern period was obsessed with it. See Lemon, *Treason by Words*; Cunningham, *Imaginary Betrayals*; and Breight "'Treason Doth Never Prosper.'" This chapter is also indebted to Sauer's discussion of the textual firestorms that erupted in the wake of Strafford's, Laud's, and Charles I's trials, firestorms that made the nature of treason and underlying questions of justice a subject of intense public interest. See her *"Paper Contestations" and Textual Communities*, 35–76.

on the throne of England—is no more unjust than the law that attainted traitors.[2] For my purposes, the crucial word in this passage is "heretofore." When Milton refers to the "Law heretofore of Treason," he indicates his familiarity with the contemporary shift in treason statutes.

Before roughly the early seventeenth century, treason was primarily defined as a personal crime against the monarch or the monarch's family, a legal interpretation that evolved out of a Germanic legal tradition in which the most heinous crimes were betrayals of personal trust and allegiance. The Treason Act of 1351 codified the common law offense of treason, and although Tudor and Stuart parliaments passed a variety of legislative acts that added to and clarified the scope of treason, this act remained the general basis of most treason trials in the period.[3] While the act encompassed a variety of offenses, such as counterfeiting the coinage of the realm or attacking one of the king's justices during the commission of his duty (since both coins and magistrates represented the king—coins literally bearing the king's image—both crimes qualified as personal assaults on the monarch), three primary offenses lay at its heart. Coke, in the beginning of his *Third Institutes*, offers a straightforward summary: (1) "When a man doth compasse, or imagine the death of our Lord the King," (2) "if a man doe levie warre against our Lord the King in his Realm," or (3) if a man is "adherent to the Kings enemies in his Realm, giving to them aide and comfort in the Realme or elsewhere."[4] The presence of "the king" in each of these definitions shows just how much treason was seen as a threat to the monarch's person. Milton

2. Milton's interest in attainder appears also in *On Christian Doctrine*, where he explains original sin by recourse to treason laws that similarly make descendants bear the penalty of a forebear's infamy (*CPW* 7.388).

3. John Bellamy provides a thorough discussion of treason legislation before the Stuarts in his *Tudor Law of Treason*. As Richard Firth Green argues, the 1351 Treason Act itself marked a change from even earlier ideas: from a betrayal of personal trust (i.e., a betrayal of anyone to whom the offender was bound by oath) to a crime that applied only to those in positions of political authority, primarily the king and his family. See his *Crisis of Truth*, 206–47.

4. Coke, *Third Part of the Institutes*, 2.

relies on this idea of treason in his early poem "In quintum novembris." He imagines a cave strewn with skeletons and impaled corpses, and the cave's main residents, the ones who skulk in the darkest recesses, are Murder (*Phoni*) and two-tongued Treason (*Prodotaeque bilinguis*) (141).[5] Not yet disillusioned with kingship at the writing of this poem, Milton folds together the political crime of treason and the personal crime of murder, and so treason is that which threatens the physical safety of James I, a monarch whom Milton terms "pius" and "Pacificusque" (1, 5).

Within a decade or so, Milton had moved beyond the idea of treason as a crime against the person of the monarch. This shift is evident in the "heretofore" of his *Brief Notes*, and it also appears in his antimonarchical arguments, particularly *Eikonoklastes* and *Tenure of Kings and Magistrates*, where he strenuously resists the idea that killing a king is treasonous by definition. Milton's awareness of what counted as treason was likely amplified in 1660, for the regicides were tried for treason under the traditional interpretation of the crime and then, per the customary legal penalties, hanged, drawn, and quartered. *Paradise Lost* shows the imprint of Milton's thinking about treason. For example, when God convicts Adam of "treason" (3.207), it is hard to reconcile this verdict with Coke's traditional definition, for Adam has not attempted to "levie warre," nor has he "compasse[d]" or even unambiguously "imagine[d]" the death of God. To the contrary, Adam commits a nonviolent act—eating a piece of fruit—in a garden an exceedingly long distance away from the person of his monarch. If brought to the bar under the 1351 Treason Act, Adam would most likely be charged with being "adherent to the Kings enemies in his Realm, giving to them aide and comfort in the Realme or elsewhere." This hypothetical charge raises the question of whether Adam knew that he was aiding and abetting Satan. Before he eats the fruit, Adam allows to himself that Eve has been beguiled by "some cursèd fraud/Of enemy" (9.904–5). Implicitly he knows that

5. On the influence of the Gunpowder Plot on Milton's poetry, see Revard, *War in Heaven*, 93–107.

in joining Eve, he is allying himself to an adversary. Did he know that the enemy in question was Satan? Certainly he should have known, based on Raphael's warnings, but Adam calls this enemy "yet unknown" (9.905). He does not appear to suspect the serpent of any deliberate malice, for when he tells Eve that the snake "gains to live as man," he characterizes it as a mere animal that has eaten from the Tree and thereby acquired speech (9.933). The upshot is that while Adam is not a victim of circumstances, neither is he deliberately aiding and abetting Satan in the same manner as the fallen angels rising in armed rebellion in book 5 or Sin opening the gates of Hell in book 2.[6] This is not to suggest that Adam is innocent of other, equally grave offenses, such as idolatry and the destruction of his children. Rather, my point is that he does not obviously commit the legal crime of treason as it had been understood for centuries in English practice.

Satan's guilt under the 1351 Treason Act is more patent than Adam's, springing into being in the middle of his confrontation with Abdiel in book 5. During the first part of his address to his assembled troops, Satan is more a sinner than a traitor in the legal sense. He initially argues to the angels that they should withdraw their allegiance from God and "cast off this yoke" of divine rule (5.786). He asks,

> Will ye submit your necks, and choose to bend
> The supple knee? Ye will not, if I trust
> To know ye right. (5.787–89)

At this moment, Satan is in murky legal waters. He has committed two actions that closely resemble the early modern crimes of diffidation (renouncing allegiance) and departing contemptuously from the realm, but while these were at times treated as treasonous, they were not central to the crime of treason in the same

6. Fine discriminations about intent were particularly irrelevant in cases of treason where the heinousness of the crime often swept away the protests of the accused about what they did and did not know or mean to do; as a late sixteenth-century judicial rule put it, in the case of treason, "there be noe Accessories but all [are] principals." Quoted and discussed in Manning, *Village Revolts*, 107.

manner as an action like levying war.[7] Even Satan's rallying of his troops does not unambiguously meet the treason bar. Coke writes that "a compassing or conspiracy to levy war, is no Treason, for there must be a levying of war *in facto*." There must be some "open fact," as when men assemble and arm a band with the express purpose "to depose the King, or take the King by force and strong hand."[8] Since Satan has theoretically assembled his angels in order to prepare for the Son's grand tour, his status as a traitor at this moment is ambiguous. Abdiel, for one, seems to feel that Satan has not yet crossed some important line in the legal sand. He tells Satan, "Tempt not these," suggesting that the other angels are still in the temptation stage and not yet in outright rebellion (5.846). He also urges Satan to go before God and repent "while pardon may be found in time besought" (5.848). By implication, Satan's crime is still incipient rather than full-blown, and he might be "in time" to receive a pardon from God.

Satan commits high treason in the following lines. Stung by Abdiel's reproof, he says that he and his followers will take offensive action:

> Our own right hand
> Shall teach us highest deeds, by proof to try
> Who is our equal: then thou shalt behold
> Whether by supplication we intend
> Address, and to begirt th'Almighty Throne
> Beseeching or besieging. (5.864–69)

Satan here commits a textbook form of personal treason, for, in Coke's terms, he has rallied his followers with the proclaimed intent to "depose the King, or take the King by force and strong hand." Since the 1351 Treason Act included any violent threat to the monarch's "eldest sonne and Heire," Satan's animus against the Son only compounds his crime.[9] Abdiel recognizes that Satan

7. Bellamy, *Tudor Law of Treason*, 26, 39.

8. Coke, *Third Part of the Institutes*, 9, 12.

9. As Revard argues, Satan's animus against the Son distinguishes Milton's account from that of other hexameral authors. Revard, *War in Heaven*, 210–11.

has just stepped across a criminal threshold. Whereas he previously urged Satan to seek a pardon, now he calls Satan "O alienate from God, O spirit accursed" (5.877). Satan has committed a capital crime, and his punishment is imminent. Indeed, Abdiel hastens to leave Satan's camp, "least the wrath [of God]/Impendent, raging into sudden flame/Distinguish not" between himself and all the other fallen angels who have chosen to share in Satan's "crime and punishment" (5.890–92, 881).

Impersonal Treason: Betraying the Law

While Satan and, to a lesser extent, Adam both commit the older form of personal treason, Milton shows them as comprehensively guiltier of the new interpretation of treason; this is clearly the legal yardstick that most interests him. By the middle of the seventeenth century, the law of treason had been expanded to encompass crimes against the state.[10] This change began with the Reformation and was accelerated by the Elizabethan conquest of Ireland, for these circumstances put new pressures on existing treason statutes. English Catholics who covertly celebrated mass or Irish men and women who defied English authority in their own land could not readily be construed as having threatened the sovereign's person. Accordingly, English jurists developed a more elastic interpretation of treason. Relying on the Roman law idea of *laesa maiestas*, or an injury to majesty, common lawyers expanded on the idea that treason could include attacks on the juristic fiction of the king in the abstract. By applying the political idea of the king's two bodies to the legal sphere, lawyers could construe as treason as any action that threatened the sovereignty and stability of the realm, whether or not that act presented a direct danger to the king.[11] For example, the civil lawyer John Cowell, in his 1607 *The Interpreter*, one of the first comprehensive legal dictionaries published in England, writes that treason "signifieth

10. This section is heavily indebted to D. Alan Orr's monograph *Treason and the State*.
11. The definitive study of this doctrine remains Kantorowicz, *King's Two Bodies*.

an offence committed against the amplitude and majestie of the commonwealth" and that high treason was "an offence done against the securitie of the commonwealth, or the King's most excellent Majestie."[12] Even though he was a royalist who tended toward absolutism, Cowell puts the safety of the commonwealth first and emphasizes it twice, while the "securitie" of the monarch appears second. The tendency to see treason as an offense against the state increased during the middle decades of the seventeenth century, and it lay at the heart of the treason trials of the Earl of Strafford, Archbishop William Laud, and Charles I. The king could hardly be charged with having criminally threatened his own safety, and Strafford and Laud had devoted their careers to furthering Charles I's Personal Rule. Instead, prosecutors charged all three with having treasonously undermined the integrity of the state; such arguments would have been legally and ideologically impossible a century before.

Milton champions this same interpretation of treason in his political works. In *Eikonoklastes*, he sounds much like Cowell when he writes that Strafford is guilty of "treason against the Commonwealth" and that Charles I's alliances with the Irish and the Scots were "no less then manifest Treason against the Commonwealth" (CPW 3:375, 378). Milton gives sustained attention to the subject of treason in chapter 12 of *A Defense of the English People*. His opponent, Salmasius, had argued that English law admitted only the personal form of treason. A king, by definition, could not be considered a traitor, nor could treason be extended to include an attack on Parliament. Milton responds: "That high treason may be committed against the kingdom as well as against the king can be denied by none of our jurists" (*CPW* 4:526). Milton relies pervasively on legal history in this chapter, and he cites the laws of Henry I and legal authorities like Bracton, the anonymous author of *Fleta*, and the twelfth-century ju-

12. Cowell, *Interpreter*, Vvv1v.

rist Ranulf de Glanville. However, Milton does not simply confine his argument to legal precedent:

> What would be the point, however easy it might be for me, of citing more of our laws when the truth is so plain? Especially when it would be so completely ridiculous and unreasonable that treason could be committed against the king but not against the people for whom, on his account, and so to speak by whose favor, the king is what he is. It is then vain for you to babble about all our statutes, vain for you to vex and torment yourself with old English lawbooks; for Parliament always had power of determining whether to confirm or repeal the laws, and it alone has the task of deciding what treason is, or lèse-majesté. (*CPW* 4:527)

Milton makes two arguments here. The first is an appeal to reason or Natural Law. Assuming that the good of the people, *salus populi*, is both the warrant and the ultimate goal of the king's reign, it is illogical to say that treason can be committed only against the king and not against the commonwealth that represents the people. Second, Milton argues that searching for legal precedents in English law has ultimately a limited value. Since Parliament has the right to make laws, Parliament can redefine treason. We see here another instance of Milton's support for statutory law.

Milton's claim that "treason could be committed . . . against the people" as much as against the king raises the question of what exactly counts as treason against the people. Increasingly in the late sixteenth and the seventeenth centuries, the answer was any tampering with the fundamental laws of the nation. In his speech to Parliament calling for the attainder of Strafford, John Pym declared, "The Law is the safeguard, the custody of all private interest: Your Honours, your Lives, your Liberties and estates are all in the keeping of the Law; without this, every man hath a like right to any thing." As a result, Pym argued, Strafford's attempt "to subvert the Fundamentall Lawes of England" qualified as treason. Similarly, the jurist Sir Matthew Hale, in his effort in *Pleas of the Crown* to address what he calls "some mixture of Introductions of new Treasons," counts as treason both traditional offenses like threatening the king's family and any action that interferes with the "Administration of Justice."[13] Milton echoes this idea of treason as a disruption of the law. In *Eikonoklastes* he claims that Charles I is a traitor because he has "denie[d] to govern us by that which ought to be our Law" and has instead intruded "his own privat reason, which to us is no Law" (*CPW* 3:360). Echoing Pym's language, he says that Strafford is a traitor because he has exerted all his efforts "to subvert Fundamental Lawes" (*CPW* 3:369). And in *Tenure of Kings and Magistrates*, Milton famously makes disregard for the law into the hallmark of tyranny, for a tyrant is defined as one who regards "neither Law nor the common good" (*CPW* 3:212).

Repeatedly in *Paradise Lost*, Milton shows that Satan's worst crime is to defy the law, and so Satan emerges as a traitor in the impersonal sense. For example, Satan's first overt defection is framed less as a rebellion against God per se than as a rebellion against the law. Whispering to Beelzebub in book 5, Satan says,

> New laws thou seest imposed;
> New laws from him who reigns, new minds may raise
> In us who serve, new counsels. (5.680–82)

In effect, Satan claims that he has the right to determine which of God's laws are binding and which are not, and in the process he attempts to enlarge his own jurisdictional authority at the expense of God's. Thus, well before Satan becomes a traitor in the 1351 sense of one who assaults the monarch, he becomes a traitor in the impersonal sense of one who defies not just a single law but the substance of the law itself. In *A Defense of the English People*, Milton argues that in the hierarchy of crimes, the one who "does away with the law to avoid the appearance of crime" is worse than the one who merely "sins against the law" (*CPW* 4:529). Satan does precisely this. In the process of refusing allegiance to God, Satan "does away with" the law of God and claims a lawmaking

13. Pym, *Declaration of John Pym*, 5, 3; Hale, *Pleas of the Crown*, 9.

authority for himself. Abdiel recognizes the jurisdictional nature of Satan's argument, for in their later confrontation he responds, "Shalt thou give law to God[?]" (5.822). In the seventeenth-century courts, a violation of the law's jurisdictional boundaries fell easily within the new scope of treason, since any "disruption of the ordinary course of justice at common law constituted the erection of a sovereign jurisdiction."[14] For example, one of the major charges against the Earl of Strafford was that he had enlarged the legal purview of the Council of the North (a prerogative court) and thereby reduced the scope of the common law. Archbishop Laud was similarly charged with a treasonous erosion of the common law's jurisdiction, since he had expanded the powers of the ecclesiastical courts in an attempt to enforce Stuart policies. The common lawyer Sir John Maynard said at Laud's treason trial, "Nothing can bee more fundamentall then that [which] bends Jurisdiction."[15] Milton agreed, and he argues in *Eikonoklastes* that Charles I was a traitor in part because he had sought to "abolish both Laws and Jurisdictions" (*CPW* 3:444).[16]

Satan commits a related act of treason when he questions the justice and thus the legality of God's laws. He tells his followers that they should not "submit [their] necks, and choose to bend/ The supple knee" (5.787–88). In Aristotelian rhetorical terms, Satan first subjects God's law to a forensic analysis ("Was God's action just?") in order then to make a deliberative appeal to his followers ("Should we then obey him?"). Abdiel recognizes the judicial elements in Satan's speech, for he offers the following rebuke: "Canst thou with impious obloquy condemn/The just decree

14. Orr, *Treason and the State*, 125.

15. Quoted in Orr, *Treason and the State*, 72. Maynard was speaking at Laud's trial three years later, although the legal principles were much the same. On the importance of jurisdictional questions to early modern law and literature, see Cormack, *Power to Do Justice*.

16. As Conrad Russell argues, one major impetus for the new interpretation of treason came from Parliament's desire to defend its own role as the sole legislative body in England. Charles I had undermined Parliament's legislative sovereignty by passing and enforcing acts of state as if they had the same legal standing as Acts of Parliament. Russell, "Theory of Treason," 39–40.

of God, pronounced and sworn[?]" (5.813–14). Abdiel identifies two reasons why God's decree is "just." The first is a substantive argument. God's laws are made by God himself, which means they meet Aquinas's definition: a law is "nothing else than an ordinance of reason for the common good, made by him who has care of the community."[17] Abdiel adds that God has made good laws (they are "indulgent" and provide for the angels' "good" and "dignity"), but their benignity is secondary to the fact that God made them (5.883, 827). The second, more surprising argument is a procedural one: God's new law is just because it has been duly "pronounced and sworn." Milton twice shows that God's practice is to formulate a rule or intention and then to swear it into law. In this passage from book 5, God first proclaims the law and then says that he has "sworn" "by [him]self," and in book 2 Beelzebub says that God's intention to create was first "pronounced" and then "by an oath,/That shook Heav'n's whole circumference, confirmed" (5.607, 2.352–54). Milton's emphasis on these divine oaths—binding the lawgiver as well as his subjects—echoes Milton's pervasive emphasis in his political prose on the English king's obligation to keep his coronation oath to uphold the laws. God's lawmaking echoes the process that produced human laws. Parliament's role was to write new laws, and as Milton emphasizes repeatedly in *Eikonoklastes*, the king's was to provide formal assent and enforcement. As the perfect lawgiver, God combines both of these functions, but Milton suggests that even God follows a kind of two-stage legislative procedure: the divine will must be first articulated and then attested by oath in order to achieve the full force of heavenly law.

Yet, despite what Milton shows as the overwhelming legality of God's law of obedience to the Son, Satan protests its injustice. In Abdiel's words, Satan feels that it is "flatly unjust, to bind with laws the free" (5.819). (Milton may be indulging in a pun here, since *lex*/*leges* shares a root with the Latin *ligare*, "to bind.) With

17. Aquinas, *Summa theologica*, vol. 2, pts. I–II, q. 90, art 4.

his claim, Satan tries to drive a wedge between God's laws and God's justice, claiming that since he and the other angels are "free," God's decision to bind them with laws is "flatly unjust." Animating this critique of a single law—the law of obedience to the Son—is an attack on God's basic legislative authority and thereby on the law itself. In early modern terms, this is unquestionably treason. In the 1619 case of *Rex v. Williams*, Henry Yelverton, acting as King's Attorney, argued that it was treasonous to hold that the government itself was "erroneous, heretical, and unjust" and thereby to "impeach[]" the authority and integrity of the laws.[18] We venture onto something of a legal tightrope here, because while it was treason to impugn the legitimacy of the law as a whole, it was not treason to criticize any given law or even subset of laws (had it been, a work like *Areopagitica* would have been dangerous indeed). Sometimes the dividing line between treasonous and nontreasonous protests against the law could be very thin. Coke argued that one sixteenth-century uprising was treason because it was "generally against the Kings Law"; that is, it was an attack on the law in general as opposed to a protest against a single law, an instance of questionable legal hairsplitting since the protest in question targeted one statute, the Henrician Statute of Laborers. Coke reasons, "The offenders took upon them [the] reformation thereof, which subjects by gathering of power ought not to do."[19] The Chief Justice would have had no trouble convicting Satan on similar legal grounds, for Satan likewise makes a general critique of God's laws and then instigates a "gathering of power" in the interests of remaking—or abolishing—those laws as he sees fit.

18. Quoted in Orr, *Treason and the State*, 26. In the 1649 *Act Declaring What Offenses Shall Be Declared Treason*, Parliament similarly made it treasonous to declare publicly that the government is "tyrannical, usurped, or unlawful" or to announce the equivalent "by any open deed." See Gardiner, *Constitutional Documents*, 389.

19. Coke, *Third Part of the Institutes*, 10. See also Bellamy, *Tudor Law of Treason*, 78–82, for discussion of other riots that were construed as treasonous.

In Death's address to Satan outside the gates of Hell, Milton similarly emphasizes that Satan's fundamental crime is to traduce the law. Death offers an accurate recap of Satan's crimes:

> Art thou that traitor angel, art thou he,
> Who first broke peace in Heav'n and faith, till then
> Unbroken, and in proud rebellious arms
> Drew after him the third part of Heav'ns sons
> Conjured against the highest[?] (2.689–93)

According to Death, Satan's first crime is against the entire polity of Heaven: he has broken "peace in Heav'n and faith." His second crime is to draw off "the third part of Heav'ns sons" and thus diminish the social order of Heaven. And his third is an offense against God: the rebel angels have "conjured against the highest." Significantly, Milton pushes the personal crime to the end, and even within the confines of this line, legal inflections make Satan's treason seem more impersonal than personal. Milton editors usually gloss "conjured" as "united in conspiracy" or "sworn together," but these explanations do not capture Milton's legal wordplay.[20] "Conjure" comes from the Latin stem *jus*, whence we get words like "jury" and "justice." Thus to "con + jure" literally means to come together to make laws or to oppose existing ones. In this line where Death seems to be talking about a personal, armed attack on God, Milton suggests that this conflict is, at heart, about law and jurisdiction, and the passage that begins by identifying Satan as a "traitor angel" ends by locating that treason in an act of legal conjuring.

In book 3 God foresees that Adam will commit a substantively similar kind of crime:

> Man disobeying,
> Disloyal breaks his fealty, and sins
> Against the high supremacy of Heav'n,
> Affecting Godhead, and so losing all,

20. Kerrigan, Rumrich, and Fallon, *Paradise Lost*, 346n; Roy Flannagan, *Paradise Lost*, 401n.

> To expiate his treason hath naught left,
> But to destruction sacred and devote,
> He with his whole posterity must die. (3.203–9)

Milton is careful here to indicate that Adam is not actually offending God himself. Rather, Adam commits a crime against the "high supremacy of Heav'n," and this phrasing echoes Satan's determination to "leave/Unworshipped, unobeyed the throne supreme" (5.669–71). At least within these poetic lines, Adam and Satan are offending something other than the person of the heavenly king: respectively "supremacy" and a "throne." While advocates for the divine right of kings held that sovereignty was inseparable from the person of the sovereign, republican political theorists called for "the necessary separation, by law, of power from the persons who hold it."[21] At a theological level, Milton would not see power or authority as in any way distinct from the person of God. At a syntactical level, he suggests this separation nonetheless. Law and supremacy emanate from God, and rebels like Adam and Satan sin primarily against these emanations and only secondarily against God himself. Adam's impersonal crime against the "high supremacy of Heav'n" recalls the interpretation of treason emerging in the early modern courts. For example, Cowell defined treason as crimes against the "amplitude and majestie" of the commonwealth, and in passing a bill of attainder against the Irish peer Shane O'Neil, Parliament accused him of treasonous offenses against the "Majestie" and "dignitie" of the Crown.[22]

By suggesting that Satan is punished more for traducing the law than for assaulting his king, Milton shows that God's justice does not respect persons. When he sentences Satan and Adam, God is protecting the legal order of Heaven and Earth more than responding to a personal affront, and so he is not what Milton elsewhere calls a "partial Judge" (*Tenure of Kings and Magistrates*, *CPW* 3:198–99). Repeatedly in *Eikonoklastes*, Milton criticizes

21. Bennett, *Reviving Liberty*, 51.

22. Quoted in Orr, *Treason and the State*, 48.

King Charles for doing the opposite. Discussing the king's professed reluctance to sign the bill for Strafford's execution, he says, "Had half [Strafford's] crimes bin committed against his own privat Interest or Person," the king would have gladly signed the execution order. In Milton's view, Charles had a corrupt definition of treason: the king "thought nothing Treason against the Common-wealth, but against himself only" (*CPW* 3:371). Milton returns to the same theme in his discussion of Sir John Hotham's treason, arguing that King Charles's "vengefull act of proclaiming him Traitor before due process of Law" resulted from the king's personal "anger for [Hotham's] affront" rather than from a desire to enforce impartial justice (*CPW* 3:426, 427). And in the context of Charles's attempted arrest of the five members of Parliament in January 1642, Milton writes, "Certainly for a King himself to charge his Subjects with high treason, and so vehemently to prosecute them in his own cause, as to doe the Office of Searcher," indicates that the king's motive is not impartial justice but rather "revenge" (*CPW* 3:440). Whereas Charles cared more for personal treasons than for impersonal ones, Milton's God does the opposite, and his justice is indifferent to what Milton calls the monarch's "Personal Rights" (CPW 3:417).

Adam is also a traitor because he has "affect[ed] Godhead," or pretended to godlike powers (9.936). He imagines in book 9 that eating from the Tree will result in "proportional ascent," by which he and Eve will literally transform into "gods, or angels, demigods," and his hope echoes Milton's earlier description of Eve at the moment of sin: "Nor was Godhead from her thought" (9.937, 790). We might ask, however, why imagining that one has or might attain divine powers falls within the scope of treason. After all, since the fruit does not impart heightened abilities, Adam and Eve's fantasy about becoming divine has an absurd quality, and unlike Satan's rebellion, it hardly seems a noteworthy affront to the "supremacy of Heav'n." Adam's aspiration to godhead, however, contains within it a more sobering offense, for, like Satan, in the process of aspiring he questions the justice and authority of the law itself. Adam reasons,

> Nor can I think that God, creator wise,
> Though threat'ning, will in earnest so destroy
> Us his prime creatures. (9.938–40)

By concluding that the law is not binding and will not really be enforced, Adam denies the very nature of the law. Milton argues strenuously against precisely this kind of travesty of justice when he says in *Eikonoklastes* that laws without real penalties are mere "cobweb laws" (*CPW* 3:524).

In assuming that the law will be set aside in his case, Adam misapplies the idea of the legal dispensation that he has earlier learned from the angel Raphael. Before he begins the story of Satan's fall in book 5, Raphael says that while it is "perhaps/Not lawful to reveal" the secrets of Heaven, this law has been "dispensed" for Adam's sake (5.569–71). Milton suggests that Adam and Eve have been the recipients of a dispensation, an arrangement that allowed for a law's penalties to be waived in certain circumstances or that absolved certain persons from the obligation to comply with the law. In the entry "Of Laws, Dispensations from Them, and Indulgences" in his *Commonplace Book*, Milton writes that "Dispensations from man-made laws are permitted because of the imperfection of the law-maker who has not provided satisfactorily for all things. Accordingly, they have no place in the laws of God, to whom nothing is hidden" (*CPW* 1:467).[23] Having said that dispensations are incommensurate with divine justice, however, Milton immediately makes room for them: "Being born of the most honorable motives [dispensations] are therefore themselves honorable. Otherwise, they are utterly unworthy of being granted by God" (*CPW* 1:467). God approves of and will grant dispensations that proceed from a desire to do true justice, as opposed to those that just encourage sin. This is the kind of dispensation that Raphael says God has granted to Adam and Eve. The hypothetical law against revealing the secrets of Heaven conflicts

23. Milton registers his scorn for the dispensations that had been traditionally granted by the Papacy when he includes "Indulgences, Dispenses, Pardons, Bulls" in the Paradise of Fools (3.492).

with Adam and Eve's need for knowledge, and so the solution is for the lesser law of heavenly secrecy to be dispensed in the interests of the greater one of Edenic obedience, an action that Milton says "fulfilled/All justice" (5.246–47).

In book 9 Adam misapplies this principle of divine dispensation to his actions in eating from the Tree. In claiming that God will not punish his "prime creatures," Adam effectively claims that his high rank should exempt him and Eve from punishment (9.940). Milton repeatedly attacks this kind of lawless thinking in his prose. In *Tenure* he argues that "the ways of justice are in exactest proportion" to the high status of the offender. Kings are punished more, not less, for even petty trespasses, and if a king commits "heinous crimes," then the law "requires of him twenty fold" (*CPW* 3:253). Similarly in *Eikonoklastes*, Milton writes that the "unsparing sword of Justice" is heaviest "by how much greater and in highest place the offender. Els Justice . . . were not Justice, but a fals counterfet of that impartial and Godlike virtue" (*CPW* 3:346). This insistence that justice must not respect persons was a common subject of judicial treatises and Assize sermons in the period. Discussing the overwhelming mandate for judges and juries to render impartial verdicts regardless of rank or status, the minister William Est writes, "Surely there is not one point in the Judges office whereunto the scripture speaketh more then to this."[24] When Adam assumes that the law does not apply to him because of his position at the top of creation's hierarchy, he reasons completely athwart the most basic early modern assumptions about justice, and he also sounds ominously like those early modern monarchs—such as Charles I—who claimed that they were above the penalties of the law.[25]

24. Est, *Judges and Juries Instruction*, 12.

25. Milton echoes widespread sentiments about the application of justice, such as that in the *Agreement of the People*, which required that "no person, by virtue of any tenure, grant, charter, patent, degree or birth, shall be privileged from subjection" to the laws "or from being bound thereby, as well as others." See the reprint in Gardiner, *Constitutional Documents*, 369.

The profoundly public nature of Adam's crime pushes it even further over the bar of treason. In early modern debates, the definition of what counted as treason often turned on the distinction between public and private acts. As Coke explains, if a group of men gather to attack an enclosure, they commit "riot, a Routh, or an unlawfull assembly, and no Treason" because the crime is a private one, affecting just one or two landowners. But if the same group goes from town to town casting down multiple enclosures, they commit treason, because the offense "is publick and general, and not private."[26] A similar legal reasoning can be applied to Adam's offense. If Adam commits a private crime in eating from the Tree, then he is guilty only of a felony like theft. However, Adam knows that there is no such thing as a private fall. Because he has been "set over all [God's] works," Adam understands that the Earth "in our fall,/For us created, needs with us must fail,/Dependent made" (9.941–43). Indeed, the fact that his fall would ripple outward through creation is the basis on which Adam erects his false confidence in receiving a dispensation. Adam returns again to the public nature of his crime a few lines later when he equates his own ruin with that of "mankind" (9.950). By corrupting everything and thus creating "distance and distaste" between God and his subjects, Adam effectively commits the crime of alienating a portion of the realm (9.9). This crime fell comfortably within the early modern scope of treason. In the bill of attainder of Shane O'Neil, Parliament based the treason charge on O'Neil's attempt to "deprive your Highnesse, your heirs and successors, from the reall and actuall possession of this your Majesties kingdome of Ireland."[27] Milton refers to this same crime in his *Observations upon the Articles of Peace* when he asks, "What greater [crime] . . . then . . . to disalliege a whole Feudary Kingdome from the ancient Dominion of *England*[?]" (*CPW* 3:307). Adam's ultimate treason is to sever

26. Coke, *Third Part of the Institutes*, 9. See also Manning, *Village Revolts*, 56.
27. Quoted in Orr, *Treason and the State*, 48.

Earth from Heaven, giving Satan, Sin, and Death apparent dominion over territories that once were God's.

By showing that God's judicial process runs along recognizable legal lines, Milton tacitly asserts the soundness and rationality of the more recent English interpretation of treason. In *Eikonoklastes* he writes, "I hold reason to be the best Arbitrator, and the Law of Law it self" (*CPW* 3:403), and in *Brief Notes* he says that the only binding law is that which is "grounded on the light of nature or right reason" (*CPW* 7.479). These are classic expressions of Natural Law, the idea that there is a higher moral order that authorizes all human laws and is accessible to the light of reason. In Natural Law theory, the best way to judge any individual law is to ask, "Would God himself act this way?" and "Is the reason of this particular law consonant so far as we can tell with the divine reason?" In *Paradise Lost* Milton suggests that if these questions were asked of the seventeenth-century law of impersonal treason, the answer would be a decisive "yes." God sees treason exactly same way that Parliament did when it condemned Strafford, Laud, and Charles I as traitors for having betrayed the laws of the land. As works like *Doctrine and Discipline of Divorce* and *Areopagitica* amply attest, Milton was often a vocal critic of laws that he saw as unjust, but his depiction of treason in *Paradise Lost* suggests that in this one area, the administration of justice by the English common law was reasonably well aligned with the will of Heaven.

The Legal Deity

In *Reviving Liberty*, Joan Bennett reminds us that Milton was translating the first eight Psalms around the time that he began writing *Paradise Lost*, and so the same celebrations of God's law and justice that characterize Milton's translations of Psalm 1 ("in the great Jehovah's law is ever his delight,/And in his law he studies day and night" [vv. 5–6]) and Psalm 7 ("Then will I Jehovah's praise/According to his justice raise" [vv. 61–62]) equally inform the epic poem. Milton does not regard God's laws as a source of oppressiveness or constraint. For Milton, "as for the ancient Jews, God's judgment is the cause of great joy, the revelation of his beneficent goodness." Bennett argues that Milton's God is obedient to the laws that he creates, and she cautions against the error of seeing "God's right as based on his omnipotence rather than on the justice which defines his divine nature."[28] In a general sense, I follow Bennett's lead in this section, for, like her, I suggest the profound importance of justice, judgment, and law to Milton's depiction of God. In a more specific sense, however, Bennett and I follow different paths. She thinks of law in a broadly abstract moral and theological sense, and she finds it primarily at those moments when God speaks in the poem, as with the elevation of the Son in book 5 and God's reference in book 3 to the divine decree ordaining free will. My goal is to show that the law is more pervasively present than even Bennett recognizes, for God's moral and theological laws interact dynamically in the poem with early modern ideas of temporal law. As a result, early modern legal debates and juridical practices provide a useful window through which readers are invited to look into the workings of Heaven and see and assess a perfect rule of law.

Chronologically speaking, God's very first sentence in *Paradise Lost* comes in book 5 when he says, "Hear my decree, which unrevoked shall stand" (5.602). From the beginning, Milton presents God as a lawgiver as he instructs the assembled angels that they are to love and obey the Son:

> Your Head I him appoint;
> And by myself have sworn to him shall bow
> All knees in Heav'n, and shall confess him Lord:
> Under his great vicegerent reign abide
> United as one individual soul
> Forever happy. (5.606–11)

God practices a form of perfect judicial transparency by publicly proclaiming the exact provisions of the law that now binds

28. Bennett, *Reviving Liberty*, 63, 130.

the angels. Although its enumeration of penal sanctions ("that day/Cast out from God and blessed vision, [the offender] falls/ Into utter darkness, deep engulfed" [5.612–14]) has not endeared this passage to the hearts of readers, Milton's depiction reflects contemporary juridical concerns. Locke, in his *Second Treatise of Government*, emphasizes that a legitimate government must rule by laws that are "promulgated and known to the people."[29] Locke was responding in part to events earlier in the century when law enforcement without clear legal backing had become an important civil rights issue. For example, a major tenet of the Petition of Right was that "no man ought to be adjudged to death; but by the laws established in this . . . realm," and Leveler pamphlets like the *Petition of January 1648* and the *Petition of 11 September 1648* held that no one should be molested or imprisoned for "such Matters as are not Crimes, according to Law" or "punished for doing of that against which no Law hath [been] provided."[30] Milton himself complains of this same offense in *Eikonoklastes*. Because King Charles could find no "temporal Law" against those who opposed him, the king alleged scandals and made those "the argument to inflict his unjust penalties both on thir bodies and Estates" (*CPW* 3.511). In *Paradise Lost*, Milton deflects any comparable critique of God's government, for those who offend are not just breaking tacit principles of obedience but also clear statutes. In addition to his call for laws to be clearly promulgated, Locke also adds that a legitimate government must rule by "established *standing laws* . . . not by extemporary decrees."[31] The question in book 5 of *Paradise Lost* is whether the elevation of the Son is an extemporary decree or merely a new aspect of God's standing laws. Certainly Satan, with his allegation of "new laws," feels that due process has been lacking and that God has acted capriciously. Milton was clearly sensitive to the critique of arbitrariness, since he has Abdiel argue to Satan that this appar-

29. Locke, *Second Treatise of Government*, 68.

30. Gardiner, *Constitutional Documents*, 68; Wolfe, *Leveller Manifestoes*, 266, 287.

31. Locke, *Second Treatise of Government*, 68 (emphasis in original).

ently extemporary decree is rather a manifestation or elaboration of an existing legal protocol: the laws of God and nature sanction the rule of one who is "worthiest" and "excels/Them who he governs" (4.177–78). As a result, God's laws are not simply positive impositions of the divine will but also expressions of "right reason" (12.84).

What critiques of God's legislative decree in book 5 typically miss is that this is by no means the only law of Heaven. God is imposing a new statute for the angels to obey, but he is not thereby ushering them from a nonlegal order into a legal one, from a cosmos bereft of statutes into one where the angels' behavior is suddenly hemmed in by law. For example, Abdiel uses the plural three times in referring to the legal code of Heaven. Speaking to Satan about the nature of the angels' lives, he says that God has provided "indulgent laws" and that God's "laws" are "our laws" (5.883, 844). Similarly, when Raphael muses that it is "perhaps/Not lawful to reveal" the secrets of Heaven to Adam and Eve, he reasons like one who lives under a general body of statutory law but who is unsure about whether a given action conflicts with one of the existing legal provisions. When God says in book 3 that he cannot justly revoke the "high decree" that ordains humanity's freedom, he indicates that there is a law on this subject as well and that it also applies to the angels: "Such I created all th' ethereal powers" (3.126, 100). Thus far, we have a law stipulating the necessity of free will, one requiring obedience to the Son, possibly one that restricts revealing the secrets of Heaven, and arguably some other unspecified statutes that all combine to make up what Abdiel thinks of as "indulgent laws." God's will for his creatures is expressed not only in the law written in their hearts but also in positive statutes that order the cosmos and angelic society. These laws are all certainly derivatives or reflections of God's perfect reason, but Milton's sheer insistence on their presence also indicates that they have some degree of independent ontological standing.

The striking thing is that these laws are not, strictly speaking, necessary. An omnipotent God does not need to rule through the medium of a corpus of laws. Since Raphael says that the angels are possessed of an "intuitive" reason, they would hardly seem to need laws to instruct them in how to act righteously (5.488). In his royalist tract *Patriarcha*, Robert Filmer argues that laws ventriloquize the king's desires, and so when the king is off at war or busy with affairs of state, every subject can find "his *Prince's Pleasures* deciphered unto him in the Tables of his Laws." If an omnipotent God does not need laws to help extend his will throughout his realm, neither does an omnipresent God need laws to make his "*Pleasures*" known to his angelic subjects. The fact that Milton insists that Heaven has laws despite their lack of any real utility indicates his desire to show that Heaven operates according to legal principles that resemble the human ideals of stable, objective, and impartial justice. Furthermore, as Bennett argues, God is obedient to his own laws.[32] In *Samson Agonistes*, the Chorus criticizes those who try to hold God to his own laws:

> As if they would confine th' interminable,
> And tie him to his own prescript,
> Who made our laws to bind us, not himself. (307–9)

However, in *Doctrine and Discipline of Divorce*, Milton argues the exact opposite: God "swears to keep [his own law], binds himself like a just lawgiver to his own prescriptions" (*CPW* 2:292). Given the legality that surrounds God in *Paradise Lost* and God's strict obedience to his own laws (as when he confesses himself bound by the "high decree/Unchangeable, eternal" that ordains human freedom [3.126–27]), the Chorus seems to misunderstand the fact that, for Milton, God is not only the source of the divine law but also that law's most obedient subject. Moreover, whereas the Chorus argues that it is pointless to try to fathom God's laws ("down Reason then" [322]), *Paradise Lost* presents an alternative view. While human reason cannot fully reconstruct or replicate the workings of divine justice on Earth, core ideas of temporal legal justice provide at least a partial entry point into the work-

32. Filmer, *Patriarcha*, 92; Bennett, *Reviving Liberty*, 67–71.

ings of God's laws, and so there is no need to beat reason back with a stick in the way that the Chorus claims.[33]

Comments by the fallen angels further reinforce the sense that Heaven is ruled by means of law. When Belial says, "To suffer, as to do,/Our strength is equal, nor the law unjust/That so ordains," he apparently alludes to a heavenly law that "ordains" that punishment be commensurate with the crime (2.199–201). What the fallen angels can "do" (i.e., the crime they commit) is "equal" to what they should "suffer," and, remarkably enough, Belial admits that the "law" establishing this equitable ratio is not "unjust." Satan has a different law in mind when he tells his fallen followers in book 2, "Me though just right, and the fixed laws of Heav'n/Did first create your leader" (2.18–19). Here, he alleges that his preeminence in Heaven was one part of the "fixed laws" that governed Heaven, and so we can infer that the legal code of Heaven ordained a hierarchy in which more excellent angels outranked less excellent ones. Satan's use of the plural "laws" also supports Abdiel's claim that there was a variety of laws in Heaven. Furthermore, when Satan complains to Beelzebub in book 5 that God has passed "new laws," his adjective "new" posits the existence of old laws, and so—again—we see a hint that Heaven is not simply a society where the angels more or less regulate themselves through the exercise of what Raphael calls their "intuitive" faculty and where larger systems of order result spontaneously from the choice to love God (5.680). Although Heaven is surely full of such forms of rational self-governance, Milton indicates that God has also provided clear laws that are themselves perfect expressions of his will for his creations. As a result of these many references to heavenly laws, we should not believe Satan when he says to his assembled, soon-to-be-fallen angels that God has no right to "introduce/Law and edict on us,

33. Indeed, as Karen L. Edwards argues, the Chorus fails to understand the reasons why God dispensed with the law against marrying Gentiles in Samson's case: see her *Milton and the Natural World*, 31–32.

who without law/Err not" (5.797–98). Satan implies that at the presentation of the Son to the hosts of Heaven, God introduces law into an otherwise prelegal society. To the contrary, Milton emphasizes that Heaven was from the beginning a legal order. Indeed, the presence of law makes Heaven what it is, for without law, Heaven would resemble nothing so much as Chaos.

Milton's vision of heaven as a legal order is particularly visible when he describes the War in Heaven. The great Dutch jurist and Natural Law theorist Hugo Grotius, in his masterwork *De jure belli ac pacis* (The rights of war and peace), rebuts the commonly held idea that war lies entirely outside the sphere of law and justice. He argues that "war is made against those who cannot be restrained in a judicial Way" and that for a war to be just, it must be "waged with no less Care, and Integrity, than judicial Proceedings." Grotius's influence on Milton was considerable, and Milton follows Grotius in *Tenure of Kings and Magistrates* when he writes that "lawfull warr is but the execution of justice against them who refuse Law" (*CPW* 3:254). We can also hear echoes of *De jure belli* at the beginning of book 6 when God tells the good angels that they will fight against foes "who reason for their law refuse,/Right reason for their law, and for their King/Messiah" (6.41–43). In Grotius's words, the fallen angels are "those who cannot be restrained in a judicial Way," and so war is the best means of enacting justice. By implication, the good angels are going to war primarily to protect the law of Heaven and the order it supports and only secondarily to defend the honor of their king. Julie Stone Peters, in her discussion of how both Milton and Grotius depict the emergence of sovereignty and a global world order, argues that the law appears in *Paradise Lost* only at the moment of creation in book 7, when the Son uses his golden compasses to bring order out of Chaos. As a result, the prior War in Heaven shows "the condition of a disordered cosmos not yet subject to territorial order or the rule of law." However, Milton is careful in *Paradise Lost* to show that law predates armed conflict, and so this war is not what Peters calls a "primal anarchy" that catalyzes the imposition of a later legal order.[34] To the contrary, for Milton as for Grotius, war is law by other means.

The Abdiel-Satan confrontation provides another instance of how Milton threads justice and legality through his depiction of war. Abdiel's challenge to Satan reprises both the biblical story of David and Goliath and moments from classical epics when heroes like Achilles and Hector engage in single combat. Milton, however, gives legal overtones to his encounter that are not present in his sources. Abdiel says to himself,

> His [Satan's] puissance, trusting in th' Almighty's aid,
> I mean to try, whose reason I have tried
> Unsound and false; nor is it aught but just,
> That he who in debate of truth hath won,
> Should win in arms, in both disputes alike
> Victor. (6.119–24)

We are witnessing here the entire war in miniature, for, as Grotius explains in *De jure belli*, wars and formal single combats have the "same Nature" and essentially the "same Name": "the Latin Word *Bellum* (War) comes from the old World *Duellum* (a Duel), as *Bonus* from *Duonus*, and *Bis* from *Duis*." When Abdiel uses the verb "to try" twice in a single line (having "tried" Satan's reason, Abdiel will now "try" his strength), Milton shows that this is not a test of strength but rather of the justice of each combatant's—and, by extension, each army's—claim. Michael Lieb argues that Milton returns often in his works to the ideology of holy war. I would add that in book 6 of *Paradise Lost*, Milton is careful also to make it a just war, by which I mean that in addition to being fought in the name of the Holiest of Holies, it is impelled by certain clear dictates of justice.[35]

34. Grotius, *Rights of War and Peace*, 1:101–2; Peters, "Bridge over Chaos," 276, 279.

35. Grotius, *The Rights of War and Peace*, 1:135; Lieb traces the ways in which the War in Heaven conforms to the holy war ideology, both in the scriptural tradition and in historical sources. See his *Poetics of the Holy*, 246–312. For other discussions of the War in Heaven, see Revard, *War in Heaven*; Freeman, *Milton and the Martial Muse*. On early modern ideas of the just war, see Tuck, *Rights of War and Peace*.

Milton's emphasis on justice and the holy war–just war distinction come more clearly into focus if we compare this passage from book 5 to Milton's primary biblical source, the story of David and Goliath. In 1 Samuel 17, David wins because he is the Lord's anointed. God has empowered him to slay lions and bears while guarding sheep, and so David has faith that he will similarly prevail against Goliath: "The Lord that delivered me out of the paw of the lion, and out of the paw of the bear, he will deliver me out of the hand of this Philistine" (I Samuel 17:37). When Abdiel says he goes "trusting in th' Almighty's aid," Milton shows him with a David-like faith that God will guide his sword arm. But Milton puts a stress on justice that is not present in his biblical source, in that Abdiel is thinking specifically about the way divine justice works. As a result, there is an impersonal quality to the Abdiel-Satan encounter that is missing from the biblical story: the outcome results from the impartial processes of justice as well as from the nature of the persons involved. It is instructive to compare Abdiel's confrontation with Satan to Michael's later in book 6, for Milton does not cast the same judicial light across the Michael-Satan encounter. Instead, the image seems to come straight out of classical epics: the two angels end "parle" and, "both addressed for fight," wield their "fiery swords" and wear shields like "two broad suns" (6.296, 304, 305). Milton is free to render the Michael-Satan encounter in heroic terms precisely because Abdiel's earlier confrontation with Satan gives the entire war a judicial framing.

Abdiel's challenge to Satan has a close analogue in early modern legal practices, obliquely reinforcing Raphael's point that things in Heaven and on Earth are "each to other like, more than on Earth is thought" (5.576). When he reasons that in justice he should be able to defeat Satan, Abdiel speaks the logic of trial by combat. While from a modern viewpoint, trial by combat is likely to seem a highly primitive alternative to the legal system, it was actually the last stage in the formal legal proceeding known as the appeal of felony. A panel of jurors or magistrates heard the aggrieved party's appeal, and if it appeared to have substance, the matter was referred either to trial by combat or trial by ordeal, depending on the gender and fitness of the parties involved. The appeal of felony remained a viable (albeit uncommon) legal option under English law throughout the seventeenth century, as when Cowell refers to those who prefer to "trie the truth [of an appeal] by combat rather then by Jurie."[36] Details at the beginning of book 6 suggest the affinities between Abdiel's actions and the appeal of felony. Having witnessed Satan in the commission of a crime, Abdiel has presented his accusation before God, who commends him for having supported the "cause/Of truth" and having given the "testimony of truth" (6.31–33). Although the fallen angels have "judged" Abdiel wrongly, he stands "approved" in the sight of God ("approve" is cognate with words like "prove" and "proof") (6.37, 36). The next stage in this legal process is for Abdiel "to subdue/By force" his opponent, thus further demonstrating the truth of what he has alleged (6.40–41). Abdiel cannot ultimately defeat Satan (only the Son can do that), but when he sends Satan reeling, Abdiel demonstrates the justice of his own position. The Abdiel-Satan confrontation begins in book 5 with a disagreement over the authority of God's laws, and it ends with Abdiel proving the binding force of the very laws that Satan rejects.

At the end of book 4, when Ithuriel and Zephon arrest Satan and bring him before Gabriel, Milton shows the judicial process of the war being modulated into another key. Grotius writes that "judicial Proceedings are of Force against those who are sensible of their Inability to oppose them; but against those who are or think themselves of equal Strength, Wars are undertaken."[37] A just war and a just lawsuit have the same motive and the same ultimate end, and the choice of one over the other simply depends upon the opponent's idea of his strength. Since, in books 5 and 6, Satan and his followers "think themselves of equal Strength" to God, justice can be achieved only by means of war.

36. Cowell, *Interpreter*, F4v.
37. Grotius, *Rights of War and Peace*, 101–2.

By the time of his arrest in book 4, however, Satan has grudgingly learned, in Grotius's terms, his "inability to oppose" God, and so a different implementation of justice comes to the fore. Twice in this section of the poem, Milton shows battlefield justice being replaced by courtroom justice. Encountering Satan's defiance, Zephon thinks along the same lines that Abdiel does during the war. He wonders about making "trial" of Satan who is "wicked, and thence weak," precisely the logic of trial by combat (4.855–56). However, having brought events up to the edge of another eruption of armed justice, Milton shows trial by combat being replaced by judicial examination. The angelic swords stay sheathed, and Satan, the accused, is led before Gabriel, the magistrate, for questioning.

This same pattern repeats itself when the forensic debate between Satan and Gabriel escalates toward violence. Satan threatens Gabriel with his "prevailing arm," and in response,

> th' angelic squadron bright
> Turned fiery red, sharp'ning in moonèd hornes
> Their phalanx. (4.973, 977–79)

Right at the moment when "dreadful deeds/Might have ensued," a different kind of judgment intervenes (4.990–91), another indication that orderly systems of legal justice are usually preferable to the clash of battle. Gabriel says, "Satan, I know thy strength, and thou know'st mine," and he adds, "for proof look up" (4.1006, 1010). God has "hung forth in Heav'n his golden scales, yet seen/Betwixt Astrea and the Scorpion sign," and seeing these scales, Satan knows that he has been weighed and found wanting (4.997–98, 1011). Milton further ratchets up the judicial overtones when he says that Satan fled "murmuring," for, in addition to its general meaning to grumble, "to murmur" meant to cast aspersions on a judge or on a legal ruling (4.1015).[38] While this scene revisits moments from the *Iliad* and the *Aeneid* when Zeus/Jove weighs the outcome of battle in a set of scales, Milton gives the

38. "Murmur," v., def. 1b, *OED Online*.

act of weighing more specifically legal overtones than it has in his classical sources, for the scales of Libra were associated with the Roman goddess Justitia. The scales appear again in book 10, for before he sends the Son down as judge, God refers to the "even scale" that has determined Adam's guilt. Drawing attention to the impartiality of his verdict, God says that the scale's balance arm has been free from any "touch with lightest moment of impulse" (10.47, 45).

The scales in books 4 and 10 serve as a metaphor for the law, and they allow Milton to make two interrelated points. First, the image of the scales demonstrates that the source of all justice, God, is also the source of all law. Satan had tried to pry apart law and justice with his book 5 argument that God's laws were "flatly unjust." Milton, however, rebuts this claim by putting the scales of law unambiguously into the hand of divine justice. Stephen Dobranski associates the scales of justice in book 4 with the Son's agency, but I see Milton arranging the emphases differently.[39] Later Milton shows the Son wielding the tools of destruction and creation: in his "right hand," the Son grasps "ten thousand thunders" by which he ends the war, and then he uses his "golden compasses" to form the world (6.835, 836; 7.225). The Son even seems to hold the prayers of Adam and Eve in book 11, for Milton says that their prayers are "clad/With incense" by the Son who then "present[s]" them "before the Father's throne" (11.17–20). The scales of law, however, are the only implement that God himself unquestionably wields in the poem. That said, I am not trying to draw a firm distinction between what God does and what the Son does. As I have argued in this section, the War in Heaven is itself a form of judicial process, and by ending it, the Son acts as both the agent and the fulfillment of God's justice. And, as I argue in chapter 7, the Son's judgment of Adam and Eve similarly shows him as the effectual means by which divine justice works in the created world. My point is that while war, creation, and intercession all happen via the Son, justice can be

39. Dobranski, *Milton's Visual Imagination*, 43.

enacted differently. Sometimes it is the result of the Son's agency, as in the War in Heaven, but sometimes God applies it directly himself, as in the scales of book 4. Milton seems intent on reminding readers of the way justice is central to the divine nature.

Second, like the law, the scales make the workings of justice legible from the outside, for the precise tilt of the scale's beam helps us see why God does what he does. The image of the scales hung there for all to see thus reinforces Milton's often-repeated point that God's laws are knowable. In *Doctrine and Discipline of Divorce*, he writes the following:

> God indeed in some wayes of his providence, is high and secret past finding out: but in the delivery and execution of his Law, especially in the managing of a duty so daily and so familiar as this is wherof we reason, hath plain anough reveal'd himself, and requires the observance thereof not otherwise then to the law of nature and of equity imprinted in us seems correspondent. And hee hath taught us to love and to extoll his Lawes, not onely as they are his, but as they are just and good to every wise and sober understanding. (*CPW* 2:297–98)

While large parts of God's providence are an impenetrable mystery ("high and secret past finding out"), his laws are accessible to human reason. They are "plain anough reveal'd" to "every wise and sober understanding." In book 4 God can see the slope of the scale's armature, and so too can Satan, Gabriel, and all the other assembled angels. As a result, the scales of law take something as potentially inscrutable and unfathomable as divine justice and open up its operations to public view.

4

The Arch-Felon

Like the scales of justice explored in the previous chapter, the criminal language that increasingly attaches to Satan in book 4 helps readers make sense of how divine justice is applied in the poem. Milton often uses the word "crime" to characterize Satan (e.g., "next in crime" [1.79]; "The fellows of his crime" [1.606]; "crime and punishment" [5.882]; "the crime/Of [his] rebellion" [6.268–9]; etc.). While "crime" had the general meaning of sinfulness or wrongdoing in the early modern period, it also carried the specific meaning of an offense against the law. As I argue throughout this book, Milton consistently uses words with an eye to both their theological and their legal meanings, and "crime" is a prime example of how he wraps legal implications around religious actions and religious implications around legal ones. In book 4 Milton shows that as Satan moves through Paradise, he commits actions that are readily recognizable in early modern terms as legal crimes, and Milton thereby invites readers to view Satan through the lens of the laws he is violating. Moreover, the trajectory Milton plots is a careful one: Satan begins with relatively minor offenses such as trespass and contempt, moves through more serious crimes such as burglary, and ends with what Milton calls an "attempt" on Eve.

This criminal trajectory has specific jurisprudential and theological stakes, and Milton announces these stakes at the opening of the book when he calls Satan "the Tempter ere th'Accuser of mankind" (4.10). Noting this moment in *Paradise Lost* and a similar one in the book of Job, Neil Forsyth calls Satan a "kind of prosecutor or attorney general."[1] Forsyth offers this comment half-playfully, since in the modern judicial system, only a massive corruption of justice could result in someone such as an attorney general prosecuting a crime that he or she had abetted. But the early modern judicial system operated differently, and Milton is not being ironical in the same way that Forsyth is. We give the work of prosecuting to legal professionals, and so plaintiffs and defendants alike sit on the bench as spectators while the machinery of law enforcement does its job. In the seventeenth century, despite the increasing role of constables and justices of the peace, the work of criminal investigation and prosecution still fell largely on the shoulders of private individuals. While the volume of private prosecutions made the judicial system more efficient, it also made the system more partial, since these prosecutors were hardly detached, objective voices. The early modern world understood quite clearly that sometimes men and women accused others for a variety of reasons that had little to do with the crime in question. Sometimes the motive was spite; sometimes it was revenge; sometimes it was a strategic decision to eliminate a rival; sometimes it was an attempt to earn an informer's fee.[2] In an attempt to discern which prosecutions had merit and which ones resulted from malice, judges and juries looked to the characters of those involved. In our modern system, the defendant's good or bad character is less important than what the evidence says. In the early modern system, in contrast,

1. Forsyth, *Satanic Epic*, 37. My argument complements that of John Leonard, "Satan as Con Man."

2. Shuger provides a compelling description of the way private prosecutions under common law could lead to unjust outcomes: Shuger, "Prison Diaries of Archbishop Laud." Kneidel discusses the role of early modern informers in the judicial system in *Donne and Legal Culture*, 115–23.

the good or bad character of those involved in a lawsuit was arguably the single most important piece of evidence.[3] Even if presented with clear indications of a defendant's guilt, juries and judges often acquitted or mitigated the sentence if the plaintiff had been shown to be a man or woman of ill repute.[4]

Thus, as his "audience" of juror-readers crosses the threshold into book 4, Milton tells them that the plaintiff in question, Satan, also aided and abetted the crime in question: the accuser was previously a tempter. He thus signals that a just verdict will involve a careful consideration of character—of who the plaintiff was as opposed to simply what the defendants did—in precisely the same way that the character of the accusers stiffened or softened the outcome for defendants in so many early modern courtrooms. Attempting to assess the character of plaintiffs and defendants, magistrates and jurors applied the criterion of malice: did the accused or accuser act with mens rea (literally, an evil mind or intent)? Milton answers this question in *Paradise Lost* by repeatedly applying the word "malice" to Satan: despite "all his malice," Satan's actions serve God's greater good; he has "so deep a malice"; he is full of "malice"; he conceives "deep malice" (1.217; 2.382; 3.158; 5.666). In contrast, Milton stresses that Adam and Eve had a different intent. Adam sinned "not of his own malice," and he and Eve were "fall'n" through the "malice" of others (3.arg.; 3.400). Because they do not meet the important legal and theological bar of mens rea, Adam and Eve are not sentenced in the same way as Satan and his followers. As God declares in book 3,

3. Early modern judges and juries "tended to take a hard line with certain prosecutors, especially those they suspected of acting out of malice or of being suspicious themselves." Beattie, *Crime and the Courts*, 346. See also Jones, *Elizabethan Court of Chancery*, 315; Brooks, *Lawyers, Litigation and English Society*, 18.

4. Beattie gives as an example a shrimp seller who brought charges against two men whom she claimed had robbed her—and since one man was later hanged for a different robbery, her accusation probably had factual merit. But the two men were acquitted when neighbors testified that the shrimp seller herself was a woman of "very ill character." Beattie, *Crime and the Courts*, 442. Stretton provides other examples in which an assessment of the accuser's bad character was crucial to the case's outcome. See Stretton, *Women Waging Law*, 132–35.

"man falls deceived/By the other first: man therefore shall find grace" (3.130–31). Adam and Eve can be the beneficiaries of God and the Son's redemptive plan precisely because they have been the victims of an unscrupulous seducer. Like those in the early modern courtroom charged with determining just sentences for the accused facing the penalty of law, readers of book 4 are being shown the character and malice of the Satanic accuser and then tacitly asked on that basis to evaluate God's judgment toward that accuser's victims/accessories.

Misdemeanors

Satan's first offense in Eden is trespass, an offense that had "multiplied at an unprecedented rate" in early modern England, "in keeping with the heightened emphasis on private ownership in the period."[5] Near the beginning of book 4, Milton describes Satan as momentarily deterred by the "thick entwined" and "tangling bushes" surrounding the Garden (4.174, 176). Satan's solution to this impasse is typical of his impulse to transgress boundaries:

> Due entrance he disdained, and in contempt,
> At one slight bound high over leaped all bound
> Of hill or highest wall, and sheer within
> Lights on his feet. (4.180–83)

This passage is dense with legal language, as when Milton uses the verb "bound" to put extra emphasis on the noun "bound." A "bound" was "the boundary line of a territory or estate," so with his bound over the bound, Satan trespasses onto land that belongs

5. Greenberg, "Paradise Enclosed," 165. The writ of trespass on the case first began to be widely used in the fourteenth century to cover wrongs done accidentally or consequentially instead of directly. It was a means whereby plaintiffs could have actions heard at common law that had previously fallen outside of the common law's cognizance (for instance, it allowed questions of debt, negligence, and trade to be heard in common law venues that had traditionally been more focused on land and crime). Because this writ was so adaptable, trespass became one of the dominant forms of legal action in the late medieval and early modern periods.

to God and over which Adam has been given dominion.[6] The phrase "due entrance" also has a strongly legal ring. "Due" came from the Latin *debitum*, indicating that which is legally owed, and "entrance" was a term in property law derived from the verb "to enter," which meant "to make entry (into lands) as a formal assertion of ownership; to take possession."[7] By scorning "due entrance" into Paradise and jumping its "bound," Satan illegally intrudes onto the lands of another, and it seems likely that he first tempts Eve to commit "petty trespass" in book 9 because his own criminal career in Eden starts with this minor property crime (9.693). Although trespass to land did not require any intent to be demonstrated (even accidental trespass was actionable), Milton stresses that Satan knows precisely what he is doing: he leaps the wall "in contempt." In this context, "contempt" refers not only to a general attitude of scorn but also to the crime of scoffing at judges or actively disobeying the orders of a court. (It may be relevant in this context that Milton's father was subject in 1637 to an action for contempt from the Court of Requests, which issued a writ of attachment against him [*LR* 1:313–14].) Milton's legal use of the word at this point in *Paradise Lost* echoes other places in his writings where "contempt" has a distinctly judicial ring. For example, in *Areopagitica*, he compliments those with the nerve to publish unlicensed books "in contempt of an *Imprimatur*," and in *Tenure of Kings and Magistrates*, he criticizes King Charles for acting "in contempt of all Laws" (*CPW* 2.568; 3.214). Judicial contempt was a more serious offense when the offender was a stranger, and Satan is precisely this kind of nonresident alien who flagrantly disobeys the rules governing who may enter Paradise and how.[8]

The sense of Satan as a trespasser becomes more pronounced when he answers Gabriel's examination at the end of book 4. Unlike trespass to land, trespass to persons required that the plaintiff

6. "Bound," n. 1, def. 2a, *OED Online*.
7. "Enter," v., def. 2, *OED Online*.
8. Fox, *History of Contempt of Court*.

prove intent; while unintentional harm done to another was actionable in a few select circumstances, it could not be prosecuted as trespass to persons. Satan seems to understand how the early modern common law works. In response to Gabriel's questions, he first defends his decision to escape from Hell ("Lives there who loves his pain?/Who would not, finding way, break loose from Hell" [4.888–89]) and then addresses his presence in the Garden: "The rest is true, they found me where they say;/But that implies not violence or harm" (4.900–901). Here, Satan openly admits that he has committed trespass to land. Ithuriel and Zephon "found [him] where they say," and so Satan is thereby guilty of "bold entrance" (4.882). But Gabriel has also charged him with trespass to persons, for he claims that Satan was "employed it seems to violate sleep, and those/Whose dwelling God hath planted here in bliss" (4.883–84). Satan answers law with legalism by pointing out that Gabriel cannot prove evil intent, since his mere presence in the Bower "implies not violence or harm." In effect, while Gabriel can allege a charge of trespass to persons, he cannot substantiate it. At this moment, Milton invites readers to apply not only an ethical but also a judicial measuring stick to Satan and Gabriel's debate and to weigh this exchange in light of what they know of legal processes and standards of proof.

In entering the Garden, Satan is trying to do more than simply trespass on another's property; he is actively plotting to seize control of it. To appreciate Satan's land grab, we have to move chronologically back to a moment in book 6 when Milton stresses Satan's newly landless identity. Musing to himself before confronting Satan in battle, Abdiel characterizes Satan as one whose "faith and realty/Remain not" (6.115–16). "Realty" registers in two ways at once. It is most commonly glossed as meaning "reality" or "sincerity," but in its widespread legal meaning, it referred to real property, or land. In this latter context, the idea that Satan has no "realty" means quite literally that he has no real estate. In what seems to be a loosely feudal arrangement, God gives "mighty regencies" in Heaven to the higher angels, and Lucifer held those regions in "the limits of the north" (5.748, 755). In the history of early modern English common law, betraying one's lord typically resulted in the forfeiture of one's land holdings, and Milton suggests that Satan's treachery has similarly resulted in his loss of "realty." Abdiel's use of the verb "remain" also suggests a legal, land-ownership context, since "remain" could denote legal ownership, as in the Geneva version of Ezekiel 46:17: "His inheritance shal remain to his sonnes."[9] Abdiel concludes that since Satan's "faith" or loyalty to his lord has lapsed, he has been rightfully stripped of his "realty" in all senses of the term (no assets "remain" to him), a testament to the profound early modern attachment to land as an indicator of status and identity. Satan has effectively become a vagrant, a category of persons that stirred deep anxieties in the early modern consciousness.[10] It is not surprising in this context that "Lucifer" also becomes the more generic "Satan" ("Satan, so call him now, his former name/ Is heard no more in Heav'n" [5.658–59]), since under English law traitors lost their titular, landed names. At the moment he was attainted by an act of Parliament, the Earl of Strafford, a peer, became merely Thomas Wentworth. In a legal register, it is also fitting that Satan's children have the generic names Sin and Death. Sir Edward Coke writes that the traitor "shall lose his children," by which he means that the children lose any titled identity or inheritance rights and "become base and ignoble."[11] Having been stripped of his name and his land, Satan the heavenly traitor can only father legal nonentities, those whose identity is reduced to the lowest common denominators of sinfulness and mortality.

Since Satan has no "realty," he can only have possession, as when he says in apostrophe to the landscape of Hell, "Receive thy

9. *Bible and Holy Scriptures.*

10. Satan's restlessness makes him Milton's literary equivalent of the vagrant, a figure that loomed in the early modern imagination as a fertile seedbed of crimes. On anxieties about vagrancy, see Fumerton, "London's Vagrant Economy"; Beier, *Masterless Men*; Woodbridge, *Vagrancy, Homelessness.*

11. Coke, *Third Part of the Institutes*, 211.

new possessor" (1.252). To modern ears, phrases like "my property" and "my possession" register as synonyms, but in the early modern legal world, "possession" had a different set of inflections. In his *Epitome of All the Common and Statute Laws of This Nation Now in Force*, the lawyer William Sheppard divides property into three kinds. First, there is absolute property; a man "hath such a Right" in the property in question "that therein he hath no dependence on any other." Then there is "qualified or limited" property, such as the property a husband might have in the real estate his wife brings into the marriage, as opposed to her chattels, where his property rights are absolute. Third, Sheppard refers to "possessory Property of Lands, Goods and Chattels," and he clarifies that sometimes "a man may have a Possession" of lands and goods "to which he hath no Right at all." Since possession was not the same as full legal ownership, when Satan calls himself the "possessor" of Hell, he obliquely acknowledges his contingent relationship to this property. The same overtones apply when Milton describes Satan as "possessing" the snake (9.189). Animals were the most common early modern form of possessory property; in fact, almost all of Sheppard's examples concern animals. For instance, he writes, "Such a [possessory] Property only a man hath in things which are *fera natura*, *(i.)* of a wild nature, as Fish in a Pond or River; wild Beasts, as Deer, Conies and Hares, and the like in a Field or Park."[12] Unlike a fish or a wild deer, which was a possession only as long as it resided on one's land, a sheepdog or a dairy cow could be claimed as absolute property. The fact that Satan "possess[es]" the snake speaks to his desire to acquire what Sheppard calls things "to which he hath no Right at all." As I argue in chapter 6, Satan shortly passes this possessory impulse on to Eve, for the fall happens in part because Eve seeks a form of illegitimate private ownership of the garden and its material things.

12. Sheppard, *Epitome*, 813.

Larceny and Burglary

In a January 1679 pamphlet on the most recent spate of executions at Tyburn, one anonymous writer observes laconically that "the nature of Malefactors is so amply known, I need not much inlarge upon the subject." He contents himself with a brief recap of the stereotypical criminal career. Beginning with "crimes of a smaller note," these bad men and women become "by degrees emboldened in the cursed Trade" until they "trample upon fear and stifle all remorse" and so arrive at the gallows.[13] This author was reiterating the commonplace view that small crimes led insensibly but inexorably to more heinous ones, a view echoed a half century later by the author of *Lives of the Most Remarkable Criminals*, who notes the "old saying" that "nobody becomes superlatively wicked at once."[14] In book 4 Milton shows that this "old saying" holds true even for Satan, for Satan the trespasser next becomes Satan the "arch-felon" (4.179). As the lawyer John Rastell explains in his *An Exposition of Certaine Difficult and Obscure Words, and Termes of the Lawes of This Realme*, felony is "a generall terme, which comprehendeth diverse heinous offences, for which the offendour out [ought] to suffer death, and loose their lands."[15] When he calls Satan a "felon," Milton draws on a contemporary social inflection, one that comes more clearly into view if we contrast this epithet with one that Death gives Satan in book 2: "traitor angel" (2.689). Although treason was more heinous than felony in that it struck at the heart of the social order, it was also considered an elite crime, one hardly surprising in those lordly men who, in Satan's words, thought that "one step higher" could put them in power (4.50).[16] In contrast, felony was

13. *Execution of the 11 Prisoners*, 4–5.

14. Hayward, *Lives of Remarkable Criminals*, 451.

15. Rastell, *Difficult and Obscure Words*, 96r–96v.

16. Donald Veall points out that while peers could be punished as traitors, they were not typically punished as felons. The Earl of Castlehaven provides a notable seventeenth-century exception. The sensationalism of this trial may have been further amplified by

associated with the lower orders of society, and felons "were spoken of with contempt or with rough, unsympathetic humour."[17] We see this scorn for felons in Milton's *Defense of Himself* when he criticizes the rhetorical thinness of Alexander More's peroration: "What odious felon, with beard unkempt, foul and squalid, ever entreated his judges in so wretched a preface?" (*CPW* 4:775–76). Given this very typical attitude of derisiveness toward the convicted felon, Satan's move from being a "traitor angel" in book 2 to an "arch-felon" in book 4 is a key example of the dwindling that forms so consistent a part of his characterization.

In the extended simile that follows Satan's decision to leap the hedge, Milton pinpoints his first felony:

> As when a prowling wolf,
> Whom hunger drives to seek new haunt for prey,
> Watching where shepherds pen their flocks at eve
> In hurdled cotes amid the field secure,
> Leaps o'er the fence with ease into the fold:
> Or as a thief bent to unhoard the cash
> Of some rich burgher, whose substantial doors,
> Cross-barred and bolted fast, fear no assault,
> In at the window climbs, or o'er the tiles;
> So clomb this first grand thief into God's fold:
> So since into his Church lewd Hirelings climb. (4.183–93)

The image of Satan as "the first grand thief" draws intensity from rising early modern fears about theft, robbery, and burglary. Although by Milton's day the nation's crime rate was tapering from a record high in the 1620s, London defied the nationwide trend and experienced a steady, century-long increase in crime.[18] The government responded to this urban threat with acts like *A Proclamation for the Better Discovery and Prevention of Burglaries, Rob-*

the fact that a peer was being tried for a lower-class crime. See Veall, *Popular Movement for Law Reform*, 4.

17. Pendry, *Elizabethan Prisons and Prison Scenes*, 265.

18. On early modern crime rates, see J. A. Sharpe's two books *Crime in Early Modern England* and *Crime in Seventeenth-Century England.*

beries, and Other Frauds and Abuses in 1630 and *A Proclamation for Discovery of Robberies and Burglaries, and for a Reward to the Discoverers* in 1661. The opening sentence of this second act succinctly states the perceived problem: "Robberies upon the Highways, and Burglaries have been more frequently committed of late, then heretofore, and more audaciously in the open Streets, and other ways, and places, in, and about the Cities of London and Westminster."[19] London's crime problem was such that "one of the prevalent anxieties of the Londoner was fear of criminal assault."[20] Milton himself was not immune to such concerns. In *Eikonoklastes* he laments the "robberies, and rapines" characteristic of society under Charles I (*CPW* 3:435), and under the entry "Of Theft, and Highway Robbery" in his *Commonplace Book*, he explores past periods in England's history when roads and cities were safer. He particularly singles out the efforts of monarchs such as Edwin, Alfred, Edgar, and William the Conqueror to control crime, noting, for instance, that "Edwin, King of Northumbria, so checked thefts and highway robberies that it was possible for anyone to make a journey in safety wherever he wished throughout the realm" and that King Alfred proverbially "hung chains of gold" on highway crossroads in the confidence that no thief would dare touch them (*CPW* 1:386). Similar observations appear in his *History of Britain*, as when Milton praises King Harald as one who charged "all his Officers to punish Theeves, Robbers, and all disturbers of the peace" (*CPW* 5:394).

Satan isn't just a regular thief; he is a "grand thief," and the adjective signifies in two ways. First, in the early modern period as today, "grand" meant "great or important above all others of the kind," so that Satan is the "grand Thief" in the same way that he is the "arch-felon": the chief example of the crime.[21] But the word

19. Charles II, *Proclamation for Discovery*. Similarly, Bacon, in his charge to Assize judges, asked them to investigate "how there is a rising of robberies more now than in former times was wont." Bacon, *Letters and the Life*, 6:306.

20. Faller, *Turned to Account*, x. For London's rising crime rate, see Beattie, *Crime and the Courts*, 14–15.

21. "Grand," adj., def. 5a, *OED Online*.

"grand" also had a specific legal meaning. Larceny was the general criminal category that encompassed all thefts that did not involve physical assault or burglary. In Coke's words, "Larceny, by the Common Law, is the felonious and fraudulent taking and carrying away by any man or woman of the meer personal goods of another, neither from the person nor by night in the house of the owner."[22] Larceny, in turn, was divided into petty larceny and grand larceny. The latter was defined as theft of goods valued more than 12*d* and was a capital offense. Milton carefully spells out the division between petty and grand larceny in his *Commonplace Book*, where he dates it to the reign of Athelstan, grandson of Alfred, referring to "Athelstanes law to attach such as stole above the valew of 12d. at above the age of 12 yeers" (*CPW* 1:387). By calling Satan a "grand thief" in book 4, Milton dryly notes that he is not the kind of petty criminal who nicks handkerchiefs or loaves of bread. By coupling the label "grand thief" to the image of Satan as one who climbs into "hurdled cotes," he also raises the specter of sheep stealing, the most prevalent kind of grand larceny in England's rural areas and the crime that was the particular focus of Parliamentary statues in the late sixteenth and early seventeenth centuries.[23] In one direction Milton's image castigates the "lewd hirelings" that prey upon the metaphorical flock of God's church, and in another it indicts those criminals who would prey more literally on the livestock and livelihoods of others.

Perhaps because centuries of inflation had made even grand larceny seem a tolerably minor crime, Milton is careful to specify that Satan also commits burglary, seen as a much more serious offense in the period.[24] Milton likens him to one "bent to unhoard the cash/Of some rich burgher, whose substantial doors,/Cross-barred and bolted fast, fear no assault." Finding the doors blocked, the burglar "in at the window climbs, or o'er the tiles."

22. Coke, *Third Part of the Institutes*, 107.

23. Dean, *Law-Making and Society*, 188–90.

24. On the particular anxiety surrounding burglary, see Herrup, *Common Peace*, 171–73.

Patrick Hume, in his 1695 commentary on *Paradise Lost*, clarifies in a note that these thieves usually "get up by help of a Ladder."[25] Milton's image of the mechanics of burglary—testing doors and then opting for the high, dangerous route over slippery roof tiles—recalls the proliferating pamphlet literature of the seventeenth century, for many of these works describe the criminal's ruses and ploys. Milton had at least a rudimentary familiarity with these works, for in *Animadversions* he likens judges in the ecclesiastical courts of the Arches to "bow men of the Arches" (*CPW* 1:675). As one early modern canting dictionary explains, a "bowman" was a slang term for "an eminent Thief or Villain; a dexterous Cheat, or House-breaker."[26] The logistics of burglary was a common topic in canting dictionaries and works about contemporary crime. The convicted robber John Hall, writing from Newgate, details the various duties of burglars, including the "hoister" who boosts another to the eaves and the "stealer" who slinks across the roof.[27] Thomas Dekker, in his *Belman of London*, similarly anatomizes the subspecialties of house breaking, including the "Kinchin Coes," whose practice "is to creep in at windows or Celler doors."[28] By book 9, Satan acts even more like one of Dekker's kinchin coes. Under cover of darkness and on the side of Paradise "averse/From entrance or Cherubic watch," Satan "by stealth/Found unsuspected way," entering the Garden through the subterranean passages "at the foot of Paradise" (9.67–69, 71).

Although Satan is like one who hopes to "unhoard the cash," Milton tacitly reminds the readers that this crime is about more than money. Burglars tapped into society's worst fears about violent invasion of the home, increasingly regarded as a place of security and safety. Samuel Pepys provides a vivid example in his diary entry for July 11–12, 1664. He awoke during the night in a

25. Hume, *Annotations on Milton's "Paradise Lost,"* 136.

26. *New Canting Dictionary*, C1v.

27. Hall, *Memoirs of John Hall*, 5. On the general rise of early modern crime literature, see Salgado, *Elizabethan Underworld*.

28. Dekker, *Belman of London*, D4v.

"mighty sweat," and then, "knowing what money I have in the house and hearing a noise, I began to sweat worse and worse, till I melted almost to water. I rung, and could not in half an hour make either of wenches hear me, and this made me fear the more, lest they might be gag'd [bound and gagged]."[29] The sixteenth and seventeenth centuries witnessed a dramatic increase in house building, and new concerns about privacy and security resulted in new forms of architecture: "Renaissance great houses were lockable; and they had courtyards within courtyards and private spaces deep within the house." The houses of the well-to-do were "circummured because the world beyond them was seen as dangerous, full of criminals."[30] The palpable fear associated with burglary appears in Coke's definition of the crime: "A Burglar . . . is . . . a felon, that in the night breaketh and entreth into a mansion-house of another, of intent to kill some reasonable creature, or to commit some other felony within the same." While the modern world generally associates burglary with the mere theft of goods (and indeed, cat burglars can have a certain roguish charm, like Cary Grant in *To Catch a Thief*), Coke ties burglary first to the "intent to kill." God has given Paradise to Adam as his "mansion" (8.296), and so Satan's illicit entry into what Coke calls the "mansion-house of another" makes him into the most feared kind of criminal, the one who threatened the home and family, that fundamental early modern unit of fixity and stability. This image of him as a burglar also anticipates the later moment when he actually steals into Adam and Eve's Bower as they sleep. Commenting on intrusions that occur when the owners are in the house, Coke writes that "when the owner or dweller, etc. is put in fear, etc. or when the owner or dweller, etc is sleeping or waking within any place within the precinct of the same house, these circumstances do aggravate the Burglary."[31]

29. Pepys, *Diary of Samuel Pepys*, 5:201. The noise turned out to have been made by the dog.

30. Woodbridge, *Vagrancy, Homelessness*, 169, 171.

31. Coke, *Third Part of the Institutes*, 63, 65.

Satan's burglary results in precisely this outcome in which the dweller is "put in fear." As a result of his intrusion, Eve awakes full of "offense and trouble" and with her first experience of "damp horror."[32]

Milton's simile puts the reader into a bind. Since the burglar is stealing from a "rich burgher" and not from a poor cottager, we might well wonder who the real villain is. Clearly, Milton intends us to decry Satan's actions, but does that mean that he approves of the sleek, well-fed burgher? Katherine Bootle Attie, although she does not frame the issue in these terms, seems to recognize the interpretive difficulty here. Examining this simile, she concludes that Milton is not "inviting us to sympathize with the victims of invasion" but is rather encouraging us "to recognize the ease, even the naturalness, with which boundaries are transgressed and the enclosed are victimized." She continues, "Compared to 'this first grand thief,' the burgher is petty and insignificant: imagining him hoarding his case, smugly self-satisfied behind locked doors, we almost feel he deserves it."[33] Attie's claim does not, to my mind, take seriously the real terror that accompanied the idea of home invasion or the fact that gangs of burglars often bound or killed the homeowners. I would argue that Milton *does* intend his readers to sympathize with the victims of invasion and that the victim's relative wealth or poverty is beside the point. Moreover Milton displays a persistent concern to protect private property. In his *Second Defense*, he argues that "to be free is precisely the same as to be pious, wise, just, and temperate, careful of one's property, aloof from another's" (*CPW* 4:684). In *On Christian Doctrine*, he makes "respect for Property" a central part of commutative justice (*CPW* 6.674). And in the second edition of *A Readie and Easie Way*, Milton argues against Harrington's proposed Agrarian Law on the grounds

32. I tend to agree with Balachandra Rajan, who argues that the seventeenth-century reader's primary reaction to Satan's grandeur, power, and rhetorical cunning would not have been admiration but rather fear. Rajan, *"Paradise Lost" and the Reader.*

33. See Attie, "Enclosure Polemics and the Garden," 150.

that it would require an "injurious alteration or circumscription of mens lands and proprieties" (*CPW* 7:445). He displays similar sentiments in his *Commonplace Book* entry "Of Navigation and Shipwrecks," where he notes "the evill custom in England, of seiseing all shipwracks as forfeit to the Lord of the Mannor, or the inhabitants of that shoar where the ship was wrackt" (*CPW* 1:507). The local practice in most coastal areas was to regard timbers and goods salvaged from shipwrecks as the rightful property of the coastal dwellers. Milton, however, sides with the law and the merchants: the rights to the cargo and the ship's carcass should stay with the owners.[34] While Milton supported politically radical ideas like regicide and theologically radical ones like antitrinitarianism, he did not support the upending of systems of wealth and exchange. Assuming that the rich burgher in Milton's simile gave to the poor and had amassed his estate through honest business practices (much as Milton's father implicitly had), I think Milton would have defended his right to sleep in peace and safety.

Hunting in Purlieu

Almost no one in early modern England disputed the wrongness of crimes like burglary or larceny, but other kinds of actions looked illicit or allowable depending on one's viewpoint. Historians call these "social crimes," actions that only some sectors of society considered criminal. Examples included smuggling and "wrecking," the practice described just above of pilfering shipwrecks.[35] Milton's disapproval of the practice of wrecking is consistent with his treatment of a different social crime in book 4, for he gives Satan all the trappings of the early modern poacher. Milton's grandfather, Richard Milton, was the ranger or forest keeper at Shotover, so Milton's own awareness of forest laws and

34. By the middle of the eighteenth century, wrecking was a capital offense. Hay, "Property, Authority," 20.

35. Briggs, *Crime and Punishment in England*, 87–92.

his intolerance for poaching may reflect a certain familial bias.[36] Milton's implicit statement on the evils of poaching is a carefully poised one. Forest rights were increasingly contentious in the period because they were associated with the privileges of the upper classes. Although the poaching vocabulary he applies to Satan offers a tacit comment on the need to protect forest animals and plants from unlawful conversion, in criticizing Satan's poaching, Milton is not thereby suggesting that forests should be preserved for the elite. John Manwood, in his 1598 *Treatise of the Lawes of the Forest*, writes that a forest "is, for the delight and pleasure of the King onely, and his nobles, and for no other end nor purpose, nor for no other person or persons." Manwood justifies the policing of forests and game on the grounds that the beasts and birds "do most properly belong unto the king onely."[37] However, by Milton's day, Manwood's serene vision of the forest as exclusive royal property had come under enormous pressure. The Stuarts both expanded the forests and passed a raft of game laws restricting hunting rights, and these laws caused a sharp uptick in poaching offenses.[38] Contrary to the popular stereotype, poaching was rarely about putting a haunch of venison in front of a hungry family. Instead, it was a highly political act, and men preyed on the animals of other men as means to express social resentments and rivalries. For many, poaching was also profitable. The growing restrictions on forest use had led to a robust black market in game, and poachers formed organized and well-armed gangs that often killed gamekeepers and threatened local villagers.[39]

Satan embodies all the worst qualities of the violent, political poacher. He enters this forest not because he is interested in the prey animals themselves but because he wants to express his fury at the owner:

36. Shawcross, *Arms of the Family*, 7.

37. Manwood, *Treatise and Discourse*, A3, B4v.

38. Theis, *Writing the Forest*, 48–49. See also Munsche, *Gentlemen and Poachers*, 8.

39. Two key studies of early modern poaching are Manning, *Hunters and Poachers*; and Beaver, *Hunting and Violence*.

> Then from his lofty stand on that high tree
> Down he alights among the sportful herd
> Of those four-footed kinds, himself now one,
> Now other, as their shape served best his end
> Nearer to view his prey, and unespied
> To mark what of their state he more might learn
> By word or action marked: about them round
> A lion now he stalks with fiery glare,
> Then as a tiger, who by chance hath spied
> In some purlieu two gentle fawns at play,
> Strait couches close, then rising changes oft
> His couchant watch, as one who chose his ground
> Whence rushing he might surest seize them both
> Gripped in each paw. (4.395–408)

The poaching overtones implicit in this act of covert stalking are heightened by the fact that he comes in disguise. Central to the proliferating early modern game laws were specific bans on wearing disguises.[40] Coke offers this comment: "It is enacted and stablished, that if any person or persons hereafter be convict of any such huntings with painted faces, vizors, or otherwise disguised, to the intent they should not be known, or of unlawfull hunting in time of night," then that person should be treated as if convicted of the felony.[41] By the end of the seventeenth century, simply being caught wearing a disguise in a game preserve was a capital crime. In this respect, Satan outdoes all human poachers. Whereas they blacked their faces and threw animal skins over their shoulders for camouflage, Satan takes the shape of whatever animal he pleases ("himself now one,/Now other, as their shape served best his end") so that he can approach his prey "unespied."

By likening Satan to a lion or a tiger that has seen animals in a "purlieu," Milton pushes even deeper into his poaching anal-

40. Men blacked their faces before poaching raids; hence the names of poaching gangs like Windsor Blacks and Waltham Blacks. For a landmark study of the class tensions that led to the Waltham Black Act and the general rise of property crime in the period, see Thompson, *Whigs and Hunters*.

41. Coke, *Third Part of the Institutes*, 76.

ogy. A "purlieu" was an area on the margins or fringes of a forest, and Hume, in his 1695 commentary, notes that Milton is using one of "our Law Terms."[42] The *OED* specifies that a purlieu is an area "formerly included within the forest boundaries and still partly subject to the forest laws, esp. those relating to the hunting or killing of game."[43] As Jeffrey Theis points out, the expansion of and restrictions on forest lands under the Stuarts had made "purlieu" into "a particularly contentious and politically resonant word" in the seventeenth century.[44] Satan is venturing onto land clearly governed by the restrictions of forest law, and when Milton adds that Satan is like one who menaces "two gentle fawns at play," he makes the poaching associations almost inescapable. Deer, by definition, were considered "royal beasts," and Manwood stresses that hunters must carefully observe all bans on "any unseasonable Deare in the Purlieus." Indeed, such was the concern about the health and safety of young deer that any man who simply set foot "into the Forest in Fawning time . . . and is not Sworne to be true to the Kings game" would be prosecuted as a poacher.[45] The image of Satan, tigerlike, adjusting his "couchant watch" and planning how he can "seize" both young deer makes him the embodiment of the most lawless form of early modern predation. Just as the burglar simile at the beginning of book 4 prefigures Satan slinking into the Bower at the end of the book, the image of Satan the poacher has a similar forward tilt. The phrase "hunting in purlieu" could be used metaphorically to mean poaching on someone's wife, so over the course of book 4 Satan moves from the purlieus of the Garden to the purlieus of Adam's Bower, becoming a sexual poacher who whispers in Eve's ear.

42. Hume, *Annotations on Milton's "Paradise Lost,"* 85. Hume is glossing 2.333, where Satan refers to Earth as in "the purlieus of Heaven." When Hume says that purlieus are "pure and free from the Laws of the Forest," he gets his jurisdictional details wrong.

43. "Purlieu," n., def. 1a, *OED Online*.

44. Theis identifies all of creation as a purlieu, and thus "Satan's entrance is framed within a legal discourse that explicates the spatial and ontological relationship between heaven and creation." Theis, *Writing the Forest*, 270, 271.

45. Manwood, *Brefe Collection*, Aa1v, P2r.

But Milton's image of Satan as a poacher does not imply his sympathy for early modern forest owners and their social ilk. To the contrary, Milton's whole depiction of the Garden seems aimed at creating a different understanding of how a forest might be used. Legally speaking, a forest did not mean simply a body of woods, in the modern sense of the term. Rather, a forest could include fields, moors, even villages.[46] In this sense, the varied landscape of Paradise, with its dells, grottoes, and open fields, qualifies it as God's forest, one that he has in turn given to Adam and Eve. Manwood specifies that the forest is meant to provide "pleasure and delight" for the lord, and the Garden does just that. It supplies "all delight of human sense" and "to the heart inspires/Vernal delight and joy" (4.206, 154–55). But despite these similarities, God's forest preserve differs from England's forests in several crucial ways. Whereas James I wrote in a 1609 proclamation that his forests existed solely for his aristocratic "recreation," God's forest is primarily a place of creation (recreation for its own sake enters Paradise after the fall when Adam says to Eve, "now let us play" [9.1027]). Whereas the forests of England were increasingly closed to all but the aristocracy, the Garden will be open to all of Adam's descendants. And whereas James describes his "affection and delight in that exercise" of hunting, Adam and Eve's affections and delight are directed toward sustaining one another and the natural world around them.[47]

Violent Crime

Soon after he leaps the perimeter fence around Paradise, Satan sits atop the Tree of Life "devising death/To them who lived" (4.197–98). Milton here indulges in a pun. "Devise" had both a general meaning of creating or concocting and also a legal meaning of bequeathing or disposing of property by will.[48] In "devis-

46. Theis, "'Ill Kill'd' Deer," 46–47.
47. James I, *We Had Hoped*, 1.
48. "Devise," v., def. 4, *OED Online*.

ing Death," Satan is both planning destruction and imagining how he can make death part of humanity's permanent inheritance, handed inexorably from father to son. Whereas God bequeaths life and righteousness, Satan hopes to erase this legacy and instead bequeath mortality. Milton thus dramatizes the pithy description of Satan offered in John 8:44: "He was a murderer from the beginning." He continues this characterization when he calls Satan's plot a "dire attempt," for legally speaking, an "attempt" was an assault upon a woman's chastity or upon a person's life (4.15).[49] Just as Satan's stalking of the Garden's fawns in purlieu will later be realized in human predators like Nimrod, his "attempt" on Adam and Eve will result in a history of human homicide, and it is not surprising that in his first vision of humanity's future in book 11, Adam watches Cain murdering Abel. This primal crime was seen as the quintessential expression of Satan's legacy on Earth, for Cain was "of that wicked one," the devil (1 John 3:12). The early modern period was quick to attribute all murders to the promptings of Satan. One Jacobean Assize judge told a jury that no other crime "makes a man soe like the Devill as Murder . . . ffor hee was a Murderer from the beginning."[50] Lincoln Faller argues that by the middle of the seventeenth century, murder was beginning to rival treason as the paradigmatic expression of criminal behavior.[51] In showing Satan "devising death" to all the Garden's inhabitants, Milton reminds readers of the tragic course of human history that links Satan's first crime in Paradise to all the forms of human homicide they saw around them.

Satan's general "attempt" on Adam and Eve takes a specific form when he enters the Bower and whispers to the sleeping Eve. While the sexual threat Satan presents has been widely remarked upon, the homicidal implications of a toad at the ear have not.[52]

49. "Attempt," n., def. 3b, *OED Online*.

50. Quoted in Gaskill, *Crime and Mentalities*, 211.

51. Faller, *Turned to Account*, 22.

52. Lehnhof, "'Impregn'd with Reason.'" On the overtones of witchcraft, see Benet, "Milton's Toad, or Satan's Dream."

The details of Satan's entry into Adam and Eve's Bower invite us to read his actions in the context of the most feared and loathed of all forms of homicide: poison. Addressing a jury in 1614, Sir John Croke, justice of the King's Bench, explained that "of all murders poisoning is the worst and more horrible 1 Because it is secret 2 Because it is not to be prevented 3 Because it is most against nature and therefore most heinous 4 It is also a Cowardly thing."[53] It was also quintessentially a work of Satan. Milton draws on the Satan-poison link when Comus presents a "baneful cup" full of "pleasing poison" (525, 526), and in the first entry of his *Commonplace Book*, Milton notes that just as no one "combines poison with gall, and with hellebore, but with savory sauces and delicacies," so too "the devil steeps whatever deadly dish he prepares" in seeming virtue (*CPW* 1:362). Moderns might object that we should not take Milton's poison references here too literally, since he merely uses the image of "natural" poison as a metaphor for Satan's supernatural influence. While at one level this is true, the seventeenth-century mind did not categorically separate physical poisoning from spiritual poisoning in the way that the modern one does. Chemical poisons were themselves regarded as sources of supernatural force and contamination.[54] We see this mingling in a 1603 murder pamphlet about the "strange invasion of Sathan, lately on the persons" of two poisoners, Elizabeth Caldwell and her lover Jefferie Bownd. When Caldwell repents of yielding to the devil's "hellish instruments," she refers simultaneously to the ratsbane that she put in her husband's oatcakes and to the devilish wiles of "wicked people" who tempted her.[55]

In describing Satan as "squat like Toad" at Eve's ear, Milton draws on widespread associations between toads and venom.[56] William Ramesey, in his 1663 *De venenis, or, A Discourse of Poysons*, describes the toad as a "creature extreamly poisonous, and

53. Quoted in Gaskill, *Crime and Mentalities*, 207.

54. Mollenauer makes this case in her fascinating *Strange Revelations*.

55. Dugdale, *True Discourse*, A3, C1v.

56. Edwards notes that Milton draws on the toad-poison association. See her "Milton's Reformed Animals."

no less pernicious" than any serpent or spider, "offending by the emission of their venom." In book 1 of *The Faerie Queene*, Spenser shows Envy chewing on "a venemous tode," and in book 3, Malbecco eats "toades and frogs, his pasture poisonous."[57] Milton himself echoes such beliefs about toads in *Colasterion* when he speaks of the antipathy that a man might bear to "a Toad or Poyson" (*CPW* 2:739). Unlike most other forms of venom, toad poison was believed to be readily diffused through the skin. In Ramesey's words, the "venomous quality of their poyson" is conveyed "through all and ever part of the Body, by the pores."[58] Satan the toad nestled in close to the sleeping Eve is thus an image full of threat. Bartolomeo Eustachio's discovery in 1564 of a tube connecting the ear and the throat (the eponymous Eustachian tube) had given the ear even greater significance as a gateway into the body's interior and had heightened "early modern concerns about the vulnerability of the ear." *Hamlet* provides the most famous example of ear poisoning, but the early modern period furnished other examples. In 1538 the Duke of Urbino was alleged to have been poisoned by a lotion that his barber poured into his ears, and the French medical pioneer Ambroise Paré was at one time accused of blowing poison into the ear of Francis II.[59] When Satan crouches "inspiring venom" into Eve, literally trying to breathe or blow toxin into her ear canal, early modern readers might have recalled Marlowe's stage assassin Lightborn (whose name is a dark pun on "Lucifer"), who boasts that he knows how to "take a quill/And blowe a little powder in [the victim's] ears."[60] Milton reminds us that when Satan pours his

57. Ramesey, *De Venenis*, 226; Spenser, *Faerie Queene*, 1.14.30, 3.10.59.

58. Ramesey, *De Venenis*, 227. The threat of the poisonous toad was spectacularly realized in the Affair of the Poisons in France, when sorceresses were discovered to have been selling "inheritance powers"—powders made of toads steeped in arsenic—to highly placed court women to use in ridding themselves of their husbands. See Mollenauer, *Strange Revelations*.

59. Pollard, *Drugs and Theater*, 128. Pollard discusses the cases of Urbino and Paré on the same page.

60. Marlowe, *Edward II*, 21.34–35.

metaphorical venom into Eve's ear, he is attempting to cause her death.

Criminal Biography

Milton's depiction of Satan as trespasser, thief, burglar, poacher, and would-be murderer resonates with contemporary trends. The late seventeenth and eighteenth centuries were marked by a growing national fascination with lawbreakers. For example, when the street robber Jack Sheppard was hanged in 1724, more than two hundred thousand people attended his execution—roughly one-third of the city's population—and a century after his death, Sheppard's name was more widely known in some places than the queen's.[61] As crime became one of the reigning preoccupations of the late seventeenth and eighteenth centuries, it also became a dominant theme in the popular press. Earlier in the period, writings about criminal behavior had typically focused either on specific events (e.g., late-sixteenth-century pamphlets retailing stories of horrific murders and dramatic scaffold conversions) or on the operations of an imagined criminal underclass (e.g., coney-catching works and canting dictionaries). However, beginning around the middle of the seventeenth century, the genre known as criminal biography, in which an author narrated the life and actions of a single individual, began to emerge.[62] *The English Rogue Described in the Life of Meriton Latroon* (published in four parts between 1665 and 1671), *The Life and Death of Major Clancie, the Grandest Cheat of This Age* (1680), and *The Complete Memoirs of the Life of That Notorious Imposter, Will. Morrell* (1694) are just three examples of a flourishing genre. By the beginning of the eighteenth century, multivolume collections of criminal lives were being published, and contrary to the stereotype of crime as a "low" interest, these often cost as much as ten shillings. Also contrary to ideas of crime as a nonelite in-

61. Linebaugh, *London Hanged*, 8.
62. See Stymeist, "Criminal Biography."

terest, criminal biography had a wide-ranging literary impact. It fueled plays such as Gay's *Beggar's Opera* and novels such as Fielding's *Amelia*. Lincoln Faller argues that four of Daniel Defoe's novels—*Captain Singleton*, *Captain Jack*, *Moll Flanders*, and *Roxanna*—were direct responses to the criminal biography tradition, which was familiar enough by the early eighteenth century that Defoe could manipulate its generic conventions.[63]

Milton and contemporary writers of criminal biographies were all reacting in their different ways to the same pervasive cultural concerns. The late-seventeenth-century anxiety about crime was the symbolic expression of a general sense of social instability, which had been created by cultural, religious, and political upheavals in the middle of the century. As Faller observes, it is no coincidence that criminal biography emerged as a recognizable genre during the Commonwealth period, when the whole world seemed to have been turned upside down.[64] After the initial access of national joy at the Restoration, the autocratic and pro-Catholic tendencies of Charles II only increased this uneasy feeling of tenuousness. There was a widespread sense that, far from being firmly reestablished by the return of the Stuarts, England's social and political structures could change again in an instant—as indeed they did in 1688. The criminal, the shadowy, opportunistic, sometimes violent figure who menaced other people's safety and property, became the walking epitome of this vague sense of threat and instability. Milton concentrates this sense of threat and unease onto the figure of Satan, who becomes the archetypal criminal, one who stalks the Garden instead of the streets of London. Milton's Satan has often been associated with political figures such as Charles I or Cromwell. While these allusions are at work in politically minded portions of *Paradise Lost*, such as the epic council in Hell and Satan's temptation of his angelic host, Satan is a more domestic figure in book 4. Not surprisingly, he also becomes a more domestic

63. Faller, *Crime and Defoe*, 4.
64. Ibid.

kind of adversary, one more likely to be seen in the shadowy alleys of London than in the towered halls of Westminster.

The link Milton forged in *Paradise Lost* between Satan and crime was not lost on two of the early eighteenth century's foremost writers. Defoe, in his 1726 *Political History of the Devil*, finds Milton's depiction of Satan as a criminal even more objectionable than his Arianism. To clarify, Defoe is not bothered that Milton actually likens Satan to a felon. This he takes more or less for granted: "[Satan's] crime, whatever particular aggravations it might have, 'tis certain, amounted to High-treason against his Lord and Governor."[65] Rather, Defoe objects to the *kind* of criminal Milton makes Satan into, complaining that Milton brings "little Devils and great Devils together" by making Satan seem too much "like our *Newgate* thieves." For example, when Satan escapes from Hell with the help of Sin and Death, Milton shows "the *Devil* able to break Gaol, knock off his Fetters and come abroad," an outcome that makes a laughing-stock of God: "The comparison must suggest, that the power which has cast him down could be deluded, and the under-keepers or jaylors, under whose charge he was in custody, could wink at his excursions, and the Lord of the place know nothing of the matter."[66] Unhappy with Milton's version of Satan-the-criminal, Defoe proposes his own alternative: rather than a thief who has escaped from a prison like Newgate, we should instead think of Satan as "in this World like a transported Felon."[67]

Henry Fielding noticed this same Satan-criminal link, but instead of quibbling with it, he put it to parodic use in his 1754 anti-epic *The Life of Mr. Jonathan Wild the Great*. By the time Fielding was writing, Wild had taken Sheppard's place as the most sensational criminal of his day, and his exploits had captured the imaginations of both John Gay and Defoe, who wrote his own life of Wild. Early in Fielding's fictionalized version of Wild's life, the

65. Defoe, *Political History of the Devil*, 26.
66. Ibid., 80, 31.
67. Ibid., 26.

young Wild meets Count LaRuse, who is being held in semi-custody at the inn where Wild lives. Taken with Wild's native abilities as a cardsharp and pickpocket and hoping to introduce the young con man to more lucrative poaching among London's elites, the count offers to kit Wild up like a gentleman. Wild initially resists on the grounds that he would "rather stand on the Summit of a Dunghil, than at the bottom of a Hill in Paradise."[68] The Miltonic allusion becomes clearer on the next page when the Count responds, "I have often heard that the Devil used to say, where, or to whom, I know not, *That it was better to reign in Hell, than be a* Valet de Chambre *in Heaven*." The count continues: "Perhaps [Satan] was in the right; but sure if he had had the Choice of both, he would have chosen better."[69] While the adolescent Wild says he would prefer to reign in Hell (i.e., be the dominant thief in a small province) than to serve in Heaven (i.e., be a minor thief in London), the count reasons that a man of Wild's talents can "reign" in both. The count bases his logic on the fact that there is "a nearer Connection between high and low Life than is generally imagined," a seeming allusion to Raphael's claim that things in Heaven and on Earth are "each to other like, more then on Earth is thought" (5.576).[70] Taking to heart the count's adaptation of *Paradise Lost*, Wild embarks upon a new career as a cheat and thief and ultimately is apotheosized as London's criminal mastermind.

Milton has often been seen as a poet who looked backward toward the values of the Good Old Cause even as his Restoration world moved resolutely onward. The Presbyterian Sir John Hobart said upon reading *Paradise Lost* that the author was a "criminall and obsolete person."[71] Milton's decision to write an epic (definitely an old-fashioned genre by 1667) and to scorn the "modern bondage" of rhyming contributes to this sense of the poem as temporally out of step with its milieu. Commenting on

68. Fielding, *Life of Mr. Jonathan Wild*, 16.

69. Ibid., 17.

70. Ibid., 19.

71. Quoted in von Maltzahn, "First Reception of *Paradise Lost*," 491.

Milton's eschewal of heroic couplets, Fielding observes in *The True Patriot* that Milton's poem almost vanished into obscurity because Milton failed to do what authors should and conform to "the reigning taste."[72] But while Milton's verse form was unfashionable, other aspects of *Paradise Lost* were not, as Fielding's own borrowing from book 1 amply attests. During the same period when Milton was composing his poem, crime was steadily becoming a salient preoccupation of contemporary culture and a dominant theme in the press. In this context, *Paradise Lost* participates in one of the most robust strands of eighteenth-century literature, and by dressing Satan in the language of the early modern criminal law, Milton points us forward toward characters like Fielding's Jonathan Wild, Gay's Captain Macheath, and Defoe's Moll Flanders.

72. Fielding, *True Patriot*, 8.

5

The Sole Propriety of Adam and Eve

The allure of the gallows has resulted in a deeply lopsided idea of the early modern law. Those interested in the way the early moderns punished criminals can lay hands on scores of studies of the variety of penal offenses and sanctions, and there are multiple books just on the subject of capital punishment. In contrast, those interested in the substance and implementation of the civil law have far fewer options. This lopsidedness is at odds with early modern realities. First, England's corpus of criminal law was cursory and primitive compared to the extensive, intricate, and sophisticated corpus of civil law. Second, most of the period's legal transformations happened on the law's civil side, such as the rapidly evolving jurisprudence related to contracts, trusts, and commerce. Finally, while England's crime rate declined over the course of the seventeenth century, the rate of civil litigation exploded at a rate significantly in excess of population growth. In its civil aspects, English common law was overwhelmingly about property, about who could own, use, inherit, or bequeath what, under a vast array of varying circumstances. This almost obsessive concern with ownership is epitomized by the fact that Coke's commentary on Littleton's *Tenures*—an encyclopedic disquisition into all the modulations of what we could call real estate law—was arguably the single most important legal text of the period. Coke succinctly sums up the main preoccupation of English common law when he calls it an exploration of "those two great pronouns *Meum* and *Tuum*."[1]

This chapter traces the way Milton uses terms and ideas drawn from English property law to depict Adam and Eve's relationship. Before the fall, these legal terms and ideas paradoxically provide him with a flexible tool for representing his ideal marriage, a set of relations that he pointedly calls "just" (4.755). The law can serve as this tool precisely because, for Milton and the early modern period, law could still be regarded as one expression of God's will for humanity. Counterbalancing this erected form of property, Milton shows the emergence of more corrupted proprietary relationships after the fall. When Adam refers to Eve as "mine" in book 9, he is not applying to her a concept of property ownership that has sprung suddenly into existence (9.957). Rather, he is distorting the unfallen model of sole propriety by moving its center of balance. Milton suggests that a major consequence of the fall is that Adam's legal rights in Eve increase and Eve's legal rights in Adam dwindle, and the two lose their mirrored legal rights in each other.

"All Things Common Else"

During the early modern period, there were two general strands of thinking about the origins of private property and of the laws that enabled and regulated it. The dominant strand saw private property as a necessary evil in a fallen world, a means to prevent the strong from preying on the weak. Seventeenth-century radicals such as Diggers and Ranters amplified this view and claimed that, rather than being merely a response to sin, property was itself sinful. For example, in his *Fiery Flying Roll*, the Ranter Abiezer Coppe writes that "propriety," among other sins, has been

1. Coke, *Third Part of the Institutes*, B1.

"the cause of all the blood that ever hath been shed," from Abel to the "last Levellers that were shot to death." However, others resisted the contemporary tendency to associate property with humanity's fallen condition. In support of his argument that kings are the ultimate owners and dispensers of property, Robert Filmer claims that Adam was given outright ownership of Eden.[2] Others of a less absolutist bent also made room for private property in Paradise. John Selden, in his *Of Dominion, or Ownership of the Sea*, the 1652 English translation of his *Mare clausum* and a pioneering work in maritime law, counters the traditional view that Noah was the first man who had ownership of the Earth (a view based on Genesis 10:5, "By these [i.e., to Noah's sons] were the isles of the Gentiles divided in their lands"). He suggests instead that "Private Donations or Possessions" originally date to "the daies of *Adam*," concluding, "Neither the Law Natural nor Divine . . . hath expresly commanded or forbidden, but permitted both." The early-seventeenth-century writer George Saltern generally agreed with Selden: "I take it the distinction of properties was enacted by Almightie God in the beginning, and by him imprinted with other Lawes, in nature, by virtue of the wordes, Beare rule over the earth: which gave to man, both dominion and propertie of all thinges."[3]

In a comment that seems representative of the critical orthodoxy about *Paradise Lost*, J. Martin Evans writes that "the concept of private property is as alien to [Adam and Eve] as it was believed to be to the native Americans."[4] For Evans, Milton belongs

2. Coppe, *Fiery Flying Roll*, 4; Filmer, *Patriarcha*, 13.

3. Selden, *Of the Dominion*, 19, 20; Saltern, *Of The Antient Lawes*, F3. Saltern's name appears as "Salteren" in the Short Title Catalog and Early English Books Online. Sommerville references both Selden's and Saltern's opinions in his useful *Politics and Ideology*, 146–47.

4. Evans, *Milton's Imperial Vision*, 96. Greenberg also discusses property ownership in Eden in her "Paradise Enclosed." While my argument has been stimulated in part by hers and I acknowledge subsequent debts below, our basic orientations differ. In a claim that resonates with Filmer's, Greenberg sees Adam as the owner of everything in Paradise, and she explores to what degree Eve participates in this ownership. My argument (which I develop in greater detail in chapter 6) is that this kind of ownership

squarely in the first group, among those who saw private property as a purely postlapsarian phenomenon. Milton would have agreed that the unchecked desire for ownership and the competition to control resources were results of the fall. Writing in *Tetrachordon*, he says that "prime Nature made us all equall, made us equall coheirs by common right and dominion over all creatures." As a result, the use of "propriety to divide all things" and the inequitable division of resources through laws ("some to bee undeservedly rich, others to be undeservingly poore") are both symptoms of humanity's corrupt condition (*CPW* 2:661). However, he accepted the fallenness of private property only up to a point. As I argue in this section and the next, *Paradise Lost* does not represent private property as originally and intrinsically a fallen set of relations; to the contrary, Milton grants property a privileged role in the unfallen world. Filmer, Selden, and Saltern all implicitly think of property as something that Adam has in the world around him. In Selden's words, Adam and Eve had "a common enjoiment, as well as a private dominion or possession of the Things of this life."[5] Milton, however, situates private property exclusively within the domain of marriage, and he repeatedly uses images of legal ownership to describe marriage, a pattern epitomized when he calls Adam and Eve's lovemaking the "sole propriety" of Paradise (4.751). Rather than being predictive of the fall, this propertied language attests to what is exceptional about Edenic marriage.

Milton's image of Edenic property appears during the hymn to wedded love in book 4, right after Adam and Eve amorously turn toward one another in their Bower. Milton writes:

> Hail wedded love, mysterious law, true source
> Of human offspring, sole propriety
> In Paradise of all things common else.
> By thee adulterous lust was driv'n from men

---

of physical things is a result of the fall. Before the advent of sin, ownership is strictly vested in one another.

5. Selden, *Of the Dominion*, 19, 20.

Among the bestial herds to range, by thee
Founded in reason, loyal, just, and pure,
Relations dear, and all the charities
Of father, son and brother first were known. (4.750–57)

Editors of *Paradise Lost* typically pause over the phrase "sole propriety" long enough to clarify that "propriety" was a common seventeenth-century word for property. James Holly Hanford adds in a note, "Their love for each other is the one thing in Paradise which Adam and Eve have as their exclusive possession," and Stephen Orgel and Jonathan Goldberg explain, "Marriage was the only property exclusively ordained for Adam and Eve in paradise—the relation of husband to wife is conceived as a property relation." Alastair Fowler seems more conflicted about the idea of unfallen property: "The exclusive and mutual rights of Adam and Eve were the only *propriety* (proprietorship, ownership) in Paradise. The institution of marriage was prelapsarian, but not that of property rights."[6] Fowler puts property in unfallen Eden in the first sentence and then takes it away in the second, a testament to the tensions and contradictions that critics implicitly see in the idea of Edenic property.

Despite such routine, albeit uneasy, editorial references, and even though this passage has been widely quoted by scholars interested in Milton's representation of marriage, it has to my knowledge only once been examined for what it might say about ownership in Eden. In "Milton's Natural Law: Divorce and Individual Property," Michael Komorowski convincingly argues that an idea of marriage as a form of private property is central to the divorce tracts. Because Milton sees marriage as instituting "a form of property ownership and not an unbreakable bond," marriage "could be dissolved" in much the same way that private ownership could be relinquished in the event that it proves damaging to the owner. Komorowski extends this idea to *Paradise Lost*, noting the presence of "sole propriety" in book 4, and

6. Hanford, *Poems of John Milton*, 303n; Orgel and Goldberg, *John Milton*, 882n; Fowler, *Paradise Lost*, 658n.

he claims that "Milton takes great care that his Eden should accurately embody a natural law in which respect for property, including the special case of marriage, is at the center of Adam and Eve's relationship with each other and with God."[7] However, Komorowski primarily discusses the "propertied" nature of Edenic marriage in relationship to events of book 9 such as the separation colloquy, Satan's temptation of Eve, and Adam's choice to join Eve in sin. As a result, in Komorowski's reading, the sole propriety model of marriage becomes most visible when Adam and Eve's marriage is most problematic, and his acute analysis tilts toward the idea that property relations are more characteristic of a fallen world than of an unfallen one. But Milton's idea of marriage as a set of property relations is neither as wary nor as pessimistic as Komorowski implies, for sole propriety also points to what is best and most unique about Adam and Eve's relationship.

When he characterizes the human relations of Eden as a form of propriety, Milton engages with a vigorous contemporary debate about the meaning of private property. Surprisingly enough, property was not given an actual legal definition until the beginning of the seventeenth century.[8] While lawyers from earlier centuries had often used the words "property" and "propriety" in legal argumentation, the first actual definition of "property" appeared in Cowell's controversial 1607 law dictionary *The Interpreter*. Cowell writes: "*Property* (*proprietas*) signifieth the highest right that a man hath or can have to any thing, which is no way depending upon any other mens courtesie. And this none in our kingdome can be said to have in any lands, or tenements, but onely the King in the right of his Crowne. Because all the lands through the realme, are in the nature of fee, and doe hould either mediately or immediately of the Crowne. See *Fee*." Although only the king can truly be said to own property, Cowell allows that the word is often "used for that right in lands and tenements, that

7. Komorowski, "Milton's Natural Law," 70, 81.
8. Aylmer, "Meaning and Definition of 'Property.'"

common persons have" because it "importeth" their use rights in these things ("*utile dominium*") without indicating actual ownership ("*directum*"). Faced with a contest between a Roman law idea of property that allowed absolute ownership to individuals and a common law idea that vested all property in the king, Cowell opts for the common law model, even though he was a Civil lawyer. Over the course of the seventeenth century, however, the Roman law definition made deep inroads on Cowell's feudal one. For example, Oliver Cromwell's law reformer, William Sheppard, defined property in 1656 as "the Right that a man hath to anything which no way dependeth upon another mans courtesie: And he that hath this, is called a Proprietary."[9] Sheppard borrows from Cowell's definition in areas of lesser import (his reference to property as free from "another mans courtesie" is a clear echo of Cowell's "any other mens courtesie"), but in fundamentals, he pointedly excludes the feudal language that in Cowell's view confines all property to the Crown. Although royalist jurists after the Restoration often asserted a version of Cowell's definition, eventually the political theories of Locke migrated into English legal terminology, and property became almost inseparable from an idea of absolute individual ownership.

This changing seventeenth-century definition of property provides a useful coordinate field against which we can plot Milton's idea of "sole propriety." As Mary C. Fenton argues, Milton supported the changing land laws of the seventeenth century, and he wanted to extend land ownership rights to ordinary men of age and of sound mind.[10] We see a version of this stance in book 4, for he actually gives Adam and Eve their own form of property. Significantly, however, they do not have property in Eden itself. In fact, Milton is interestingly cagey about what kind of proto-legal relationship Adam has to the world around him. In book 8 the Son says to him, "This Paradise I give thee, count it thine/To till and keep" (8.319–20). To modern eyes, "thine" connotes ownership

9. Cowell, *Interpreter*, Ffff4–Ffff4v; Sheppard, *Epitome*, 813.
10. Fenton, *Milton's Places of Hope*, 39–64.

as does a phrase like "I give thee." But in early modern law, I could be "given" a variety of rights in land, tenements, or even chattels—and could call these things "mine"—without actually having full proprietary rights in them. Although it is possible that Milton imagines Adam as having something like the prelapsarian version of absolute ownership of Eden, on balance he seems inclined toward the idea of communal use rights, for in the words of Psalm 24:1, "the earth is the Lord's, and the fullness thereof."

But while Milton does not spell out the exact nature of the first couple's proprietary relationship to the land and material resources of Eden, he is explicit that they are joint owners of their marriage. Indeed, this passage is the only time in *Paradise Lost* when the word "propriety" or its variant "property" appears. Milton further emphasizes that marriage is a realm of mutual ownership when he says that outside this sphere of sole propriety, all things are "common else" (4.752). Marriage is the one exception to the Garden's no-property economy, and Adam and Eve relate to one another in a fundamentally different way than they relate to anything else. As a result, marriage is more than simply what John Halkett calls a "parallel ideal of nature" and a "reflection of the sensuousness and order of the Garden itself."[11] Adam and Eve do not appear to own the flowers, animals, and fertile earth of the Garden, but they do have shared ownership rights in the marital relationship. Indeed, Edenic marriage is constituted and defined by the exclusive system of mutual ownership that obtains only inside it and nowhere else.

When Milton describes wedded love as "loyal, just, and pure" (4.755), he further reinforces the distinction between the marital exchange and all other forms of Edenic relations. The first and third terms in this sequence need little comment, since it is not difficult to understand what it means for a marriage to be both loyal and pure. The idea of a marriage as "just," however, raises more questions. For Aristotle, domestic justice is founded in respect (as opposed to political justice, which is founded in law),

11. Halkett, *Milton and Matrimony*, 109.

so in this sense, Adam and Eve's marriage is "just" because it is based on an appreciation of each other's dignity and integrity. But Milton's adjective also points to the idea that Adam and Eve inhabit their own miniature judicial system. Justice was considered a uniquely human trait, and so by calling the Edenic marriage "just," Milton reminds readers that it is the fulfillment of a "mysterious law" not available to the rest of the created order.[12] He also draws on a foundational definition of justice as rendering up to each person that which is his own.[13] For Milton, marriage can be described as "just" because it is a system in which Eve gives to Adam rights in herself, and Adam gives to Eve rights in himself. This idea of justice as a uniquely human trait subtends Milton's depiction of the Bower as an exclusive and protected space. Describing Eve's labor to adorn the Bower, Milton says that Eve "decked first *her* nuptial bed" (4.710, emphasis added). The possessive adjective does not mean that she and Adam actually own this bed. Instead, they have use rights in it, use rights that approach a form of de facto ownership.[14] I think it is not accidental that Milton edges closest to an idea of private ownership of material things when he describes the one place that most represents the "mysterious law" conferring sole propriety on Adam and Eve (4.750). It is as if the mysterious model of reciprocal ownership that exists solely within their marriage and that has its highest expression in the act of lovemaking

12. For example, Grotius draws on a long-standing vein of classical thought when he writes that there is no crime in animals killing one another, since "justice doth not take place amongst them," and "the Law of Justice, which is the most excellent Thing in the World," has been prescribed only to human beings. Grotius, *Rights of War and Peace*, 1:157.

13. Seipp, "Concept of Property," 32. See also Aquinas, *Summa theologica*, vol. 3, pts. I–II, q. 58, art. 11.

14. This idea of use right was articulated by Grotius as an unfallen precursor to legal property rights. In turn, Locke relies on Grotius's ideas in his influential discussion of property in the *Second Treatise on Government*. As Seipp points out, historians tend to assume that the history of private property begins with Locke. Seipp, "Concept of Property," 30. Whereas Seipp traces the genesis of thinking about private property back through the legal rolls, my argument is that Milton uses *Paradise Lost* to provide an imaginative account of its origins.

filters out onto the bed that is the primary setting for wedded love. Even Paradise's fauna instinctively respect the exclusive rights that Adam and Eve have in the Bower. Milton writes, "Other creature here/Beast, bird, insect, or worm durst enter none" (4.703–4).

Before pushing further into some of the implications of Milton's sole propriety conception of marriage, I want to pause and address the counterintuitive aspect of my argument. When I characterize "sole propriety" as part of what is best and most unique about Adam and Eve's relationship, it may sound as if I am attempting to redeem ideas of competitive ownership—what the great eighteenth-century jurist Sir William Blackstone called that "sole and despotic dominion" that one person has "in total exclusion of the right of any other individual in the universe"[15]—by finding them on the other side of the innocence-sinfulness divide. This is not my intent, nor is it an accurate understanding of Milton's poem. The problem for modern readers is that property has become almost inextricably entangled with objects and commodities. As a result, any discussion of marriage as a property relation sounds like one party to the marriage is being owned by the other, in the way that one might own a refrigerator, a pet, a car, or—more troublingly—a slave. Thus "mutual Edenic propriety" can ring in the ear as "mutual Edenic commodification," hardly an apt image for Milton's prelapsarian marriage, however unequal one might think its gender relations.

However, the word "property" or "propriety" had a different set of inflections in earlier periods. As legal historian David Seipp explains, "property" and its cognates were not originally used to refer to material possessions: "One did not say 'this is my property,' as we use the term now. Rather, one said 'I have property in it' or 'the property of it is to (or with) me.' Property was thus a characteristic or attribute . . . of a cow or a jewel or a sum of money, not a shorthand referent to the thing itself."[16] Further-

15. Blackstone, *Commentaries*, 2:2.
16. Seipp, "Concept of Property," 33.

more, one used "property" to designate rights in those things not currently in one's possession. A hand tool or a necklace jealously locked away was not "property." These items became "property" only when they were loaned into circulation. Thus property was outward-looking and inherently communal in a way that has been lost in modern usage. Milton seems intent on recovering this earlier idea of property as a set of rights and attributes, an idea that was still dimly visible in his own day. When he suggests that Adam has sole propriety in Eve, he does not mean that Eve is herself a piece of property. Instead, he means that one of the attributes (or "properties") of Eve is Adam's marital rights in her—and vice versa. As both Arnold Stein and Christopher Ricks observed decades ago, Milton often uses a word with later, pejorative associations to describe unfallen Eden in order to "re-create something of the pre-lapsarian state of language." Particularly with his Latinisms (of which "propriety" is a prime example), Milton attempts to recover "an earlier purity."[17] Like the "mazy error" of the Garden's rivers or Eve's "wanton ringlets" (4.239, 306), the word "propriety" as applied to Adam and Eve in their Bower asks readers to peer around property's later associations with greed and purely material accumulation and to imagine what unfallen ownership might have looked like.

Milton's depiction of marriage as a space of sole propriety can modulate how we think about Eve, since it casts her as an independent legal agent. This does not mean that she and Adam have a fifty-fifty share in their joint marital property, for Milton applies more of the language of proprietorship to Adam than he does to Eve. Upon first seeing Eve, Adam says, "Part of my soul I seek thee, and thee claim/My other half" (4.487–88). To "claim" meant to "affirm one's possession of." Similarly, the verb "to seize"—appearing when Eve says "thy gentle hand/Seized mine"—was primarily a legal term meaning to come into ownership of, as evident in the tenure known as seisin, one of the most

17. Ricks, *Milton's Grand Style*, 110, 111. See also Stein, *Answerable Style*, 66–67; Picciotto, *Labors of Innocence*, 464–65.

complete forms of land ownership available under feudal law (4.489).[18] In the sole propriety model of Eden, for Adam to "seize" Eve's hand does not mean that Eve is being reduced to a thing that he owns. Rather, she becomes one of the attributes or characteristics of him, and he also becomes one of the attributes or characteristics of her. While their marriage is built around a reciprocal exchange of proprietary rights, this exchange is not a fully equal one: Milton provides no corresponding moment when Eve seizes Adam. Despite the legal imbalance here, Milton gives Eve enormously more legal agency than was available to early modern women. While scholars sometimes oversimplify the disabilities that early modern women suffered under English common law (for example, a feme covert could, under certain circumstances, inherit property and execute wills), married women definitely did not have unfettered rights of property ownership. For example, while Sheppard extends property ownership rights to all men regardless of rank, he follows English legal tradition in denying them to married women: "A Feme Covert alone can do nothing during the Coverture [i.e., during her marriage], with any her lands, goods or chattels . . . for that she is *Sub potestate viri.*" Therefore "all Feoffments, Deeds, Gifts, and Grants, by her alone, are void" and "a Devise by her of her Land by Will is void." Indeed, even a legal document transferring land to her can be annulled by "a bare *Verball* agreement of the Husband."[19] Thus, unlike Eve, who has sole propriety, early modern married women had no propriety. The way Edenic property comes into being reinforces the sense that Eve is an enfranchised part owner. Milton writes,

> Strait side by side were laid, nor turned I ween
> Adam from his fair spouse, nor Eve the rites
> Mysterious of connubial Love refused. (4.741–43)[20]

18. "Claim," v., def. 2a; "seize," v., defs. 1, 2, *OED Online.*

19. Sheppard, *Epitome*, 734.

20. Turner gives extended consideration of this passage in his *One Flesh*, although he does not discuss it in the context of property and law.

When Adam and Eve unite in the act of sex, the boundary between their bodies becomes most blurred. Insofar as Milton calls this a moment of property exchange, it is one that completely overturns the logic of Coke's *meum* and *tuum*. Indeed, in place of these exclusionary pronouns, Milton uses the adjective "sole," which confounds any attempt to sort out who owns what.

Perhaps even more surprising than its legal enfranchisement of Eve is what sole propriety suggests about Adam and Eve's relationship to God. In the modern world, debates about private property are conducted between ordinary individuals, and so they operate along what we might think of as a horizontal social axis. Typical examples include disputes between neighbors about land boundaries, legal scuffles between business partners about who owns company assets, and fights between ex-spouses about who gets the house and furniture. If we apply this horizontal thinking to Eden's sole propriety model of marriage, then the issue is whether Adam and Eve have to share one other with other human beings. In this register, sole propriety means that Eden is not an incipient free love society. Milton relegates the indiscriminate sharing of bodies to the "bestial herds," whose sex is literally improper, that is, indifferent to proprietary relations. However, the seventeenth-century legal debate about private property was not primarily conducted along this horizontal social axis. Rather—as we see in the legal writings of Cowell, on the one hand, and Sheppard, on the other—it addressed the "vertical" question of the respective rights of subjects vis-à-vis their monarch.

While Milton's sole propriety model makes a proto-republican statement about equal rights of ownership, it also makes a theological point about Adam and Eve's freedom in relationship to God. In an Assize sermon preached at Worcester in 1654, the Puritan minister Richard Baxter argues that "no man hath any absolute Propriety, but only the use of the Talents that God doth entrust him with."[21] Milton's ascription of sole propriety

21. Baxter, *Three Treatises*, 18.

to Adam and Eve suggests that however much he might have agreed with Baxter that talents are loaned rather than given outright, marriage remains one place where ownership can be called absolute, where Adam and Eve are proprietors and God is not. Marriage is both enabled and ennobled by God, but once bestowed on Adam and Eve, it becomes theirs to own and manage. This position echoes early modern English thinking about the fundamental links between property and liberty, a particularly sensitive issue during what looked like the Stuart erosion of property rights. The English equivalent to slavery was villeinage, and the crucial dividing line between villeins and nonvilleins was property ownership. As the early modern lawyer Thomas Headley writes, "the king may by commission at his pleasure seize the lands or goods of his villeins, but so can he not of his free subjects."[22] Almost by definition, free men were propertied men, and to strip someone of property rights—or to deny him ownership rights in the first place—was the first step to enslaving him or making him a villein. Milton imports an unfallen version of this property-liberty connection into *Paradise Lost.* As long as Adam and Eve have sole propriety, they also have perfect liberty. Whereas seventeenth-century political thinkers made material property into the cornerstone of individual male freedom, Milton makes property a central part of the "mysterious law" of male and female marital freedom.

Dowries, Coins, and Collateral

While Milton's hymn to wedded love in book 4 contains his clearest description of how property works in Eden, this same idea also appears at other points in the prelapsarian books. For example, when he describes Adam and Eve gardening in book 5, Milton likens the loving reciprocity of marriage to a dowry exchange:

22. Quoted and discussed in Sommerville, *Politics and Ideology*, 148. See also Dickinson, *Liberty and Property.*

They led the vine
To wed her elm; she spoused about him twines
Her marriageable arms, and with her brings
Her dow'r th' adopted clusters, to adorn
His barren leaves. (5.215–19)

Like the sole propriety of book 4, this lovely description of marriage is not a repudiation of ownership but rather a sanctification of it. Milton puts a transaction—the vine's "dow'r" being given to the "barren elm"—at the very heart of marriage, and he thereby indicates how much the later ideas of ownership and exchange are corruptions of this perfect ideal. In the early modern dowry system familiar to Milton and his contemporaries, the wife was a conduit through which property passed into the ownership of the husband. Milton, however, suggests a model of co-ownership that was impossible under English common law without elaborate prenuptial contracts and tenuous even then. In the logic of his image, the dowry (the grapes) remains a distinct property of the vine, since we cannot think of grapes being grafted onto the elm in the way that money and goods could be transferred to the husband. By calling the clusters of grapes "adopted," Milton calls attention to the fact that the husband/elm does not own them in any categorical way. As a result, his image of marital joining not only includes an exchange of property; it presents this exchange as one in which the female member retains both a distinct identity and some independent rights of proprietorship. These are not severable from the husband, but neither are they fully subsumed into him.

The idea of marriage as a sphere of sanctified ownership also marks Adam's conversation with the Son in book 8, for Adam several times uses the language of property to describe Eve. Arguing for his need for companionship, Adam says to the Son:

But man by number is to manifest
His single imperfection, and beget
Like of his like, his image multiplied,
In unity defective. (8.422–25)

Since words like "by number" and "multiplied" also ring in a financial register, Adam's language simultaneously glances at another means of replication: charging interest on loans, a topic that preoccupied Milton in many of his prose writings.[23] Like marriage, interest allows "Like" to be "multiplied" into "like," and so Milton suggests that interest is the sterile, spiritually empty alternative to marriage. In the process, he nods toward the common Christian argument that by making money breed unnaturally, interest—especially excessive or usurious interest—violated the Genesis mandate linking procreation to sexual intercourse.[24] Adam's image summons up the very idea that it repudiates, for Eve is a living alternative to coins, the figurative investment capital that will be the source of Adam's ongoing generativity.[25] As in the "dow'r" image, Milton embeds a reference to property exchange at the heart of a description of how a marriage should work. He does this not to commodify anything about wedded love but rather to show that the loving transaction of marriage is the unfallen ideal—the mysterious law that transcends any calculus of who benefits and how—and that subsequent, fallen forms of exchange are corruptions of this pure original. Adam's use of the word "amends" later in the debate works in the same way. When he first sees Eve, Adam exclaims to the Son, "This turn hath made amends" (8.491). The word "amends" comes from an Old French word meaning a pecuniary fine, and although it later broadened to mean any kind of recompense, it still had pro-

23. As one who made his living largely from loans, Milton displays considerable interest in and uneasiness about usury, which figures prominently in his *Commonplace Book* and in the section on commutative justice in *On Christian Doctrine* (*CPW* 6:776–77). For Milton's repeated comments on usury, see Shawcross, *Development of Milton's Thought*; Hawkes, *John Milton*; Hawkes, "Milton and Usury"; von Maltzahn, "Making Use of the Jews."

24. Dante provides a paradigmatic example of this argument in chapter 11 of *The Inferno*. On the widespread contrast between usury (which became symbolically affiliated with sodomy) and male-female marriage, see Hawkes, "Milton and Usury."

25. Hoxby has explored Milton's ambivalent relationship to markets and economics in his *Mammon's Music*, although his discussion of *Paradise Lost* focuses primarily on questions of international trade and empire.

nounced financial associations in Milton's day.[26] Coexisting with the general sense that the Son has made metaphorical "amends" for Adam's experience of lack and loneliness is the specific sense that Eve is herself the recompense. The Son has coined Eve, in a sense, and rendered her to Adam as payment, an idea furthered by the fact that Eve, like the face of a coin, bears the image of her lord. Eve herself seems to understand the nature of the exchange, for she says to Adam in book 4 that, when his hand seized hers, she "yielded" (4.489). To "yield" meant not only to submit but also literally to remunerate or repay.[27] By yielding to Adam, Eve is recompensing him with the coin of herself, participating with the Son in making Adam amends for the experience of yearning.

When Adam follows up this rejection of usurious "Like of his like" with a request for "collateral love," Milton makes a similar poetic move (8.426). He offers an allusion to the legal, contractual, and financial meanings of "collateral," only to invite readers to consider how much their fallen ideas of collateral serve as the palest derivatives of what Eden had to offer. Although our modern usage of "collateral" as a stand-alone noun meaning moneys or goods used to secure a loan did not appear until the early nineteenth century, it was already under construction in Milton's day. "Collateral" as an adjective appears widely in early modern legal phrases such as "collateral assurance," "collateral bond," and "collateral contract." In these contexts, it denotes something over and above, that which is extra. When Adam asks for "collateral love," he does not just mean that he wants the love of another created being who is equal to or coordinate with himself, the broad adjectival definition of "collateral." He is also making a specific kind of legal request, asking for something—here, a form of love—that is over and above what bare nature can provide. For example, the seventeenth-century term "collateral security" meant "any property or right of action, given as additional to the obligation of a contract or the like"; by extension, Adam's "collateral love" would

26. "Amends," n., etymology and def. 1a, *OED Online*.
27. "Yield," v., def. I.1, *OED Online*.

be love that is "given as additional to" his mere existence.[28] God has put Adam in a well-stocked Garden where he can live, work, and enjoy the homage of the creatures around him: these are the basic terms of Adam's tenure in Paradise. In asking for "collateral love," Adam argues that God should put up something extra to ensure Adam's happiness, and the almost cheeky quality of Adam's request is a prime instance of the playfulness that Rosenblatt finds in the prelapsarian books.[29]

Ultimately, Milton's use of early modern legal ideas of property allows readers to look into the unfallen world of Eden and see something that they can dimly recognize. Joanna Picciotto, in her *Labors of Innocence*, argues that the seventeenth-century language of experimentalism operates in *Paradise Lost* as "an instrument of magnification, to help us see further into the world Genesis describes."[30] "Rather than representing paradise as a permanently lost and foreign world, Milton's Baconian epic identifies it with an alien experience of the world we already know."[31] Images of law and property in books 4 and 8 work much the same way, for they make the unfallen relations of Paradise both familiar and yet distant. Milton's readers lived in a world full of property, dowry, coins, and collateral, and Adam and Eve's marriage shows them these same things, albeit arranged in a different way and attached to a different set of meanings. The upshot is that law and legal ideas serve as a means to link, however tenuously, the unfallen Paradise and the grubby, venal world of sin.

The Bond of Nature

While before the fall, the private ownership found only within a marriage has a holy aspect, afterward it becomes marriage's curse. In *Tetrachordon* Milton writes that after human beings be-

28. "Collateral," adj. and n., def. 5, *OED Online*.

29. Rosenblatt, *Torah and Law*, 78.

30. Picciotto, *Labors of Innocence*, 404.

31. Picciotto, "Reforming the Garden," 40. This essay is an earlier version of the chapter on Milton in *Labors of Innocence*.

gan mistreating one another, "then law more justly did permit the alienating of that evil which mistake made proper, then it did the appropriating of that good which Nature at first made common" (*CPW* 2:665). Once sin makes evil "proper"—that is, a form of property—within a marriage, then the best function of law is to allow for that property to be "alienat[ed]." As Komorowski puts it, "the marriage contract had allowed spouses to 'appropriate' each other but that form of ownership only held as long as their exclusive proprietary claim to each other facilitated their mutual help and sociability." When Eve comes to Adam bearing the fruit and thus threatening his relationship to God, he had the option to alienate his marital property rights.[32] Instead, Milton shows him making a different kind of property decision: rather than relinquishing his property, he clings more tightly to it, and in the process he reframes it entirely. Milton shows that the perfect model of sole propriety can go wrong in two ways. First (and this is the subject of chapter 6), proprietary relations can be relocated outside the realm of marriage and applied to the things of Eden. Satan is the primary agent of this relocation, for he encourages Eve to look at the world through the lens of ownership. Second, the system of mutual propriety can lose its former equilibrium as one spouse acquires disproportionately more rights than the other.

The sole propriety model of marriage first begins to wobble in Adam's conversation with Raphael in book 8. Adam tells Raphael that Eve seems "so absolute" and "so well to know/Her own" (8.547–49). "Absolute" had a range of meanings inferring completeness and sovereignty (as when Milton says that Adam is created for "absolute rule" [4.301]), but in a legal register, it denoted outright ownership. Thus an absolute title was one unencumbered by restrictions of any kind.[33] The overtones of ownership inherent in "absolute" are amplified by Adam's reference to "her own." By saying that Eve has, in effect, a clear title to herself, Adam is forgetting that he and Eve participate in a system that

32. Komorowski, "Milton's Natural Law," 70 (quote), 94.

33. "Absolute," adj. (and adv.) and n., def.5a, *OED Online*.

gives them joint proprietorship of their marriage and of one another. In book 9 Adam's language veers to the other extreme, for as he makes the decision to sin, he addresses Eve as "my own,/ My own in thee, for what thou art is mine" (9.956–57). Adam's language at this point has commonly been read in a spiritual and moral register as pointing to his growing narcissism, idolatry, and lust. I would add that it also indicates the emergence of a profoundly inequitable legal and property relationship in which Adam now takes even greater proprietorship of Eve and Eve loses both her rights over herself and the shared ownership she once had in Adam and in their marriage. Whereas in book 8 Eve had "her own," here she becomes "his own." In early modern political terms, by stripping Eve of her proprietary rights, Adam reduces Eve to the level of a villein or—as I suggest in the next section—a feme covert. The idea of mutual joyful ownership inherent in Adam and Eve's lovemaking also disappears, and a different, more ominous mutuality takes its place. When Adam and Eve have sex in the wake of the fall, Milton describes the act as the "seal" of their "mutual guilt" (9.1043). A seal was the impression of a signet ring used to indicate a claim to possession and was used figuratively for any mark of ownership. The only kind of "mutual" property left to Adam and Eve after the fall is their co-ownership of "guilt," an image reminiscent of Milton's claims in *Tetrachordon* that sin makes evil "proper" to marriage.

On the threshold of his fall, we see Adam using the same language of finance and ownership that earlier characterized his conversation with the Son. However, both the tone and the context are different, suggesting that he has begun to think about Eve in a different, more acquisitive way. Explaining to Eve why he has chosen to sin with her, Adam says:

> If death
> Consort with thee, death is to me as life;
> So forcible within my heart I feel
> The bond of nature draw me to my own,
> My own in thee. (9.953–57)

In his preceding interior monologue, Adam refers to his sense of connectedness as the "link of nature" (9.914), but here, in his more formal declaration of intent, he uses the phrase "bond of nature." The word "bond" has conventionally been read in the sense of a tie or ligature that connects him to Eve. In this sense, Adam reasons that his primary "bond" is the one wrought by Nature and not by God, and he privileges fleshly desires over spiritual duty. But a "bond" had a legal meaning in the period that is equally applicable and that provides us with a different perspective on Adam's fallen thinking. A bond was a legal instrument whereby one party "confessed himself to be bound and obliged" to another party, and it was "the most significant single legal ligament in early modern society, a fact which is no less true because it has received so little attention from scholars."[34] Milton knew plenty about bonds, since many of his Chancery dealings arose in the wake of bond agreements. For example, in *Ashworth v. Milton*, Milton argued that he had a claim on Richard Powell's Wheatley property because Powell had "come bound unto this [defendant] in the Some of five hundred pounds of lawfull English money" (*LR* 3:358). Similarly, in his long and complex suit against the Cope family, Milton declared that Sir John Cope "became jointly and severally bound to [Milton] in the penal sume of 300[L] of lawfull English money Condiconed for the paym[en]t of 150[L] principall money lent and 3[L] Interest for the same" (*LR* 1:358).

In referring to the "bond of nature," Adam implies not only that he has a natural tie to Eve but that he and Nature have entered into a legal "bond." This image strategically erases the Son's agency. Whereas earlier Adam asked the Son to grant him "collateral love," now he imagines that his receipt of Eve was a purely private transaction between himself and Nature. Unlike the earlier vine-elm image in which the vine herself brought a dowry to the elm, Adam's "bond of nature" also excludes Eve as an active participant in the exchange, demoting her instead to the role of

34. Simpson, *Legal Theory and Legal History*, 112; Brooks, *Pettyfoggers and Vipers*, 68. See also Muldrew, *Economy of Obligation*.

mere currency. We might contrast Adam's talk of bonds to his book 4 address to Eve persuading her to be his wife:

> Whom thou fli'st, of him thou art,
> His flesh, his bone; to give thee being I lent
> Out of my side to thee, nearest my heart
> Substantial life. (4.482–85)

Eve is both the direct object and the indirect object of his verb "lent." That is, he has loaned (i.e., produced or generated) her out of his side, and he has loaned *to her* out of his side. In this latter sense, Eve is the recipient of his loan, a phrasing that figures them as joint parties to the marital agreement and that echoes their "sole propriety" in one another. While he has "lent" his own substance to her, he wants Eve to join him not because she owes him and his loan must be repaid but rather because doing so will be the source of love and joy for both of them.

The language of bonds in book 9 reframes the terms of this loan. In a typical sealed bond, A loaned B money or goods, and B promised to pay a penalty—often double the amount of the original loan—in the event of default. When Adam considers the "bond of nature," in a legal sense he construes his rib as a loan he made to Nature. Now that the deal has gone wrong, he claims the forfeiture (the ownership of Eve) owed to him under the terms of the bond, and his logic transforms Eve from the recipient of his loan to its transactional substance. This refusal to forfeit a "bond" is strongly reminiscent of Shylock's insistent claim in *The Merchant of Venice*: "I would have my bond."[35] Whether or not Milton modeled this moment in *Paradise Lost* on Shakespeare's play, the significant point is that both Milton's Adam and Shakespeare's Shylock speak a common early modern language of debt bondage. As Amanda Bailey argues, since penal bonds allowed the body of the debtor to be used as financial security, debt bondage functioned as a precursor to slavery.[36] In

35. Shakespeare, *Merchant of Venice*, 4.1.86.
36. Bailey, *Of Bondage*, 24–25.

their different ways, both Shylock and Adam are exerting proprietary rights over the person of another, and so Milton, like Shakespeare, suggests the kinds of spiritual disfigurement that results when one human concentrates on what he thinks is owed to him, even to the extent of commodifying or exploiting another. We might think of Adam in book 9 as exchanging one kind of property for another: instead of the unfallen mutuality inherent in the sole propriety model of marriage, he opts instead for a more individualistic and materialistic conception of material property, one in which he can think of Eve and use the word "mine." Thus the fall does not suddenly introduce Adam into a world of property. Instead it changes and darkens the property relations that were already there.

The Feme Covert

Adam's shift away from thinking of Eve as a full participant in sole propriety and toward thinking of her instead as a piece of property indicates that fallen Eve has taken on a legal status similar to that offered women under early modern coverture. Before the fall, she is clearly not a feme covert, for she has proprietary rights within the sphere of marriage. Although she disclaims a direct relationship to the law when she says to Adam, "God is thy Law, thou mine," she later qualifies this statement of legal handicap (4.637). She tells the serpent that except for the prohibition on the tree, she and Adam "live/Law to ourselves, our reason is our law," describing herself as possessed of the capacity both to legislate for herself and to be accountable to the law of reason and the Law of God (9.653–54). In the aftermath of the fall, however, Eve's legal status changes, and Milton shows her becoming a feme covert in the full early modern sense of the term. In support of the legal principle of coverture, the early modern law took the Genesis "one flesh" model to mean that married women forfeited most of their legal rights. Blackstone, in his definition of the feme covert, writes that "the very being or legal existence of the woman is suspended during marriage," and the author of *The Lawes Resolution of Womens Rights* notes drily, "A married woman perhaps may either doubt whether shee bee either none or not more then halfe a person."[37] Under coverture, a man could not co-own property with his wife any more than he could co-own with himself.[38] As Sheppard puts it, "if one enter into a Covenant to make his Wife a Feoffment, it is impossible, and therefore void."[39] The sense of fallen Eve as a feme covert appears in Adam's book 10 soliloquy when he thinks about the "fair patrimony" that he will leave his "sons" (10.818–19). In the prelapsarian books, Adam generally refers to his future children in nongendered terms, such as his reference to "more hands than ours" and to "younger hands" (4.629, 9.246). But after the fall, Adam considers the lethal inheritance that will come specifically to his "sons," and he reinforces the patriarchal tilt with the term "patrimony," a term that carried the sense of property inherited from a male forebear. Although Adam is talking about the burden of original sin, which is transmitted equally from mothers and fathers to both sons and daughters, he uses the vocabulary of male legal inheritance. Milton thereby suggests that Adam imagines himself as part of new legal system in which fathers bequeath property to sons, a system that excludes mothers and daughters or that uses them as carriers of exchange value.

The sense that postlapsarian Eve is now, legally speaking, a feme covert is further reinforced in book 11. Hearing that she and Adam must leave the Garden, Eve laments, "Must I thus leave thee Paradise? thus leave/Thee native soil, these happy walks and shades[?]" (11.269–70). Her complaint rests on the idea that she has a relationship to the land not mediated through Adam. Earlier,

37. Blackstone, *Commentaries*, 1:430; Edgar, *Lawes Resolutions*, 4. My discussion of the legal status of married women in early modern England is generally indebted to the introductions in Greenberg, *Legal Treatises*. See also Sokol and Sokol, *Shakespeare, Law, and Marriage*, 117–38.

38. As Stretton notes, other jurisdictions that did not recognize coverture (e.g., equity courts and ecclesiastical courts) granted women a wider scope of legal rights. See his *Women Waging Law*.

39. Sheppard, *Epitome*, 723.

in book 8 when Eve goes to tend a place Milton calls "her nursery," Greenberg sees a similar instance of Eve's connection to the landscape, and while I think this relationship stops shy of the outright ownership Greenberg wants to ascribe to it, she is right to call attention to this moment as indicating Eve's direct link to and thereby use-rights in the natural resources of Eden.[40] However, the angel Michael soon clarifies Eve's new legal status in the wake of the fall:

> With thee goes
> Thy husband, him to follow thou art bound;
> Where he abides, think there thy native soil. (11.290–92)

Under English common law, when a woman married and exchanged her status as a feme sole for that of a feme covert, among other legal disabilities, she also lost the right to determine where she would live.[41] In a fallen world, Eve can have no independent relationship to real property. The "native soil" of Paradise where she has tended and bred flowers is replaced by the "native soil" beneath her husband's wandering feet.

Milton's account of the origins of coverture differs in a subtle but crucial way from that current in his contemporary legal world. Early modern jurists who defended coverture saw it as instituted by God in his judgment of Eve. Writing in the 1659 *Manby v. Scott* case about a fugitive wife, Judge Hyde says that God's judgment upon Eve—"Thy desire shall be to thy Husband, for thy Will shall be subject to thy Husband, and he shall Rule over thee,"—sanctions not only the domestic but also the legal subordination of married women. As a result of the punishment imposed on Eve, a married woman "is disabled to make any Grant, Contract, or Bargain, without the allowance of her Husband."[42] Milton, however, suggests that the rise of coverture takes place even before the Son comes down to the Garden in

40. Greenberg, "Paradise Enclosed," 171.
41. Stretton, *Women Waging Law*, 22.
42. *Lady's Law*, 179.

book 10. The Son ratifies Eve's subordinate status, but this legal subordination has already begun, initiated by Adam's desire for what he calls "mine" and, as I argue in chapter 6, by Eve's own acquisitive gaze at the world around her. This change is epitomized in Milton's changing use of the word "partner." Etymologically, "partner" is cognate with "parcener" (both springing from the Anglo-Norman *parcener*), and in its widespread legal meaning, a parcener was "a person who shares equally with another or others in the inheritance of an estate from a common ancestor; a coheir."[43] When in book 4 Adam refers to Eve as his "sole partner," he characterizes her as his coheir, one who joins with him in the shared ownership of marital property (4.411). "Partner" appears in a different context in book 9, however. After she eats the fruit, Eve contemplates whether or not to share with Adam, and she toys with the idea of having knowledge "without copartner" (9.821). She does not want a parcener or coheir to split the profits on her new "odds of knowledge" (9.820), and so the "mysterious law" of sole propriety that was such a distinguishing characteristic of Adam and Eve's unfallen marriage gives way to a fallen and thus all-too-familiar kind of legal thinking in which one person wants to acquire sole proprietorship at the expense of another.

43. "Parcener," n., def. 2, *OED Online*. On the legal implications of "partner" as it appears in Edmund Spenser's poetry, see Zurcher, *Spenser's Legal Language*, 262.

6

Acts of Possession

Jason Rosenblatt, in his *Torah and Law in "Paradise Lost,"* observes how easy it is for readers of Milton's poem to look through Pauline lenses—that is, to think about statements such as "The strength of sin is the law" (1 Cor. 15:56) and "The law worketh wrath" (Rom. 4:15)—and assume that every reference to Mosaic Law is also a reference to sinful behavior.[1] However, as Rosenblatt demonstrates, *Paradise Lost* is full of instances in which Mosaic Law does not point to sinfulness and instead characterizes prelapsarian righteousness. In previous chapters, I provided a complementary argument about the temporal law, for Milton shows that erected forms of law structure Edenic life just as law structures Heaven. I turn now to the wealth of legal language that characterizes Adam and Eve's fallen thinking in books 9 and 10. Following Rosenblatt's cue, I offer a reminder that if we adopt a Pauline angle of vision, we will likely emerge with a very partial understanding of how law works in these two books. For example, when Adam complains in his book 10 soliloquy about God's "terms" being "too hard," Milton alludes to the world of contract

1. Rosenblatt, *Torah and Law.*

law and specifically to developing ideas of legal liability (10.750–51). If we are thinking in Paul's terms, we are apt to conclude dismissively, "These legal allusions are hardly surprising. After all, Adam is now sinful, and we know that sin brings law into the world." This line of reasoning, however, oversimplifies the more nuanced and more surprising way that law functions in books 9 and 10. It is not simply the case that sin introduces the rigors of law into a legally pristine Edenic ecosystem. Rather, Adam and Eve misuse the forms of law that are already latent around them, just as they misuse other divine gifts such as reason and will.

In this chapter, I consider three different ways that Milton uses prevalent early modern legal and judicial ideas in books 9 and 10, and in each case my claim is that characters like Satan and Eve distort legal principles and sound forms of legal thinking in the interests of pride, greed, and aggression. The early modern period regarded law—in theory if not always in practice—as embedded within the larger framework of divine justice, so a just order like Eden is also a prototypically legal order. As part of betraying that justice, humans and angels also betray the law, putting its principles to the worst uses. In the first section, I survey several places in books 9 and 10 where Milton shows common jurisprudential ideas being misapplied or misrepresented, as when Satan skews early modern principles of statutory interpretation and when Adam imagines transferring his case to another jurisdiction to receive a more lenient verdict. In the second section, I look at the way Satan, Eve, and Adam all variously use the language of contract law to rationalize sin. Milton did not think the ban on the tree was part of a contract between humanity and God; it was instead part of God's direct positive law. When Satan and Eve apply common contractual assumptions and forms of reasoning to the ban on the tree, Milton shows them making a legal category error. The third section offers a complementary perspective to chapter 5's discussion of property rights. In early modern England, contracts were an important means of regulating the possession of things, and Satan uses the language of contract to usher Eve into a world of imagined ownership. Instead of resting content with the sole propriety of marriage, Eve learns to covet proprietorship of the material things around her. Throughout this chapter, I suggest that instead of simply producing law, sin warps it, and so books 9 and 10 tell a story about both the uses and the abuses of the law.

Legal Reasoning Gone Wrong

At several points in books 9 and 10, Milton shows characters misusing basic principles of law to persuade themselves or others to sin. The first of these occurs when Satan relies on a skewed form of statutory interpretation to tempt Eve. When, in the guise of the serpent, Satan asks Eve, "Indeed? Hath God then said . . . ?," he invites her to join with him in probing the real meaning of God's edict against eating from the Tree of the Knowledge of Good and Evil (9.656). As readers of *Paradise Lost* have long recognized, Satan's query is reminiscent of scriptural hermeneutics, and so Milton makes him into a grim parody of a figure like St. Augustine or Clement of Alexandria, attempting to distinguish between the letter and the spirit of biblical pronouncements. Satan simultaneously engages in an act of legal interpretation. Aristotle writes that because "a law is always a general statement," it might, when applied to a specific case, be "defective because of its generality."[2] As a result, the gap between the abstract formulation of the law and the messy, contradictory, and varied reality of individual human action had to be bridged by an act of interpretation in which the judge determined whether or to what degree a given law applied to a given set of circumstances. Legal interpretation and particularly the interpretation of statutes had become a subject of widespread discussion and concern by the time Milton was writing *Paradise Lost*. The volume of statutes had increased dramatically over the centuries, and that rise accelerated in the middle of the seventeenth century with the growing power and independence of Parliament. Because the increase

2. Aristotle, *Nicomachean Ethics*, 5.10.4, 6.

often created conflicts with long-standing customs and case law rulings, it had become vitally important to understand how statutes should be interpreted. Works like Coke's report on *Heydon's Case* and Sir Thomas Egerton's *Discourse on the Exposition and Understanding of Statutes* show their jurist-authors trying to pin down how readings of the law could be fairly extended or restricted under varying conditions.[3] For example, Egerton writes, "Sommetymes statutes are taken by equytye more then the wordes, sommetyme contrary to the wordes, sommetyme it is taken strayctelye accordinge to the wordes, and sommetyme, where there are no wordes in the statute and yet a case happenethe upon an statute, the commen lawe shall make a construcion."[4] In a deliberative line of reasoning, Satan suggests that Eve needs to make the same kinds of discriminations that Egerton maps out so that she can properly decide how to act. Should God's law be taken "strayctelye according to the wordes"? Or is it rather the kind of law that needs a "construcion"?

In adopting this quasi-lawyerly stance, Satan deflects Eve's attention away from the fact that the prime law of Eden is not the kind that calls for interpretation at all. To be clear, Milton's message is not that God's laws must never be questioned or interpreted. Works like *Doctrine and Discipline of Divorce* and *Tetrachordon* provide ample evidence that Milton thought God's laws had to be interpreted properly so that they could be obeyed properly. Milton defends precisely this work of legal evaluation and interpretation when he argues in *Doctrine* that God "hath taught us to love and to extoll his Lawes, not onely as they are his, but as they are just and good to every wise and sober understanding," and he devotes the majority of his treatise to interpreting the Mosaic Law of divorce in light of what seems "just and

3. Jordan, "Interpreting Statute." Coke's vision of interpretation gave the judge a more radical degree of interpretive authority, while Egerton offers a more moderate view. In general, while statutes were assumed to have some elasticity, Coke was willing to flex them more than most early modern jurists were comfortable with, and so his views should not be taken as typical.

4. Egerton, *Discourse*, 140–41.

good" (*CPW* 2:297–98). We are to obey God's laws not only because God made them but also because they match our own sense of what is right. God's ban on the Tree of the Knowledge of Good and Evil needs no judicial interpretation not because God is its author and what God says is final. Rather, it simply does not have the kind of defective generality that, in Aristotle's view, makes interpretation a necessity. God created this law specifically for Adam and Eve to regulate their relationship in one particular place to one particular tree, and so—unlike the biblical laws on divorce that had been stretched across space and time to regulate early modern English marriages—there is no gap between the law as articulated and the circumstances to which it is applied.

Simply by moving the discussion into the realm of legal interpretation, Satan gains a significant advantage, since seventeenth-century assumptions about the law as a whole encouraged what might strike modern readers as a cavalier attitude toward the binding authority of any one law. Modern readers live in the wake of positivists like Bentham, who argued that laws were binding because they were duly enacted by a sovereign power. For Bentham and later thinkers such as Austin and Hart, laws were not to be measured against a priori ideas of justice and equity.[5] Although not all jurists today agree with positivism, these ideas have been influential enough that it can be difficult for us to see past them to the assumptions of an earlier world. For Milton and those like him committed to the supremacy of Natural Law, law was regarded as an expression of reason and not as itself a set of categorical mandates. Judges, in particular, were tasked with reconciling the law as written with larger ideas of justice and equity. In the words of legal historian Samuel E. Thorne, "If the application of a broadly phrased statute to a particular complex of facts led to injustice, a judge was under no constraint to follow its words but could disregard them. Contrary to modern practice under similar

5. For discussion of Hobbes's intervention into Natural Law debates, see White, *Natural Law*, 12–16.

circumstances, he need make no apology for this, nor was it necessary that he in some way attempt to reconcile his action with the statutory provision, though such justification was upon occasion made."[6] Even statutes were understood at least in part as "affirmations of a body of preexisting, unwritten, customary, fundamental law."[7] According to the principles of fundamental law, when Parliament drafted a statute, it was not so much creating a law where there had been no law before as it was giving new articulation to preexisting ideas of justice and equity. This idea should not be overstated, since as J. W. Tubbs points out, medieval and early modern jurists fully appreciated the degree to which statutes truly made new laws, even if they tried rhetorically to minimize this newness in the name of continuity and tradition. All the same, it is difficult to imagine a modern judge agreeing with Judge Hyde in the 1659 *Manby v. Scott* case that a judge "may alter the Law because an Inconvenience may follow thereon."[8]

Having implied that the ban on the tree is in need of interpretation, Satan invites Eve to consider God's intention in establishing it. When he asks, "Indeed? Hath God then said that of the fruit/Of all these garden trees ye shall not eat[?]," Satan not only asks her to rehearse the terms of the law under which she and Adam live; he also tacitly asks, "Yes, but what did God really mean? What was his intention in establishing this law?" (9.656–57). An important component of early modern legal interpretation was a consideration of the intention of the lawgivers. This principle was given its most influential articulation in Christopher St. German's *Doctor and Student*. Discussing the Elizabethan law against giving alms to able-bodied beggars, St. German's Student

6. Thorne, introduction to Egerton's *Discourse*, 106–7.

7. Orr, *Treason and the State*, 16.

8. Tubbs, *Common Law Mind*. In context, while Hyde agrees that laws can be adjusted, he warns against too quick a modification of the law and urges that the first course of action be to "provide against such Inconveniences as may arise." See the reprint of Hyde's finding in *Lady's Law*, 182. For a similar expression of the judge's authority over the law, see the discussion of Justice Hobart's views in Tubbs, *Common Law Mind*, 125–26.

of the Law raises the question of what to do if "a man meete with a valiant beggar in so cold weather and so light apparel, that if he hade no clothes he shall not be able to come to any towne to have succor, but is likely rather to dye by the way." The Doctor of Divinity says that while almsgiving would make a man guilty under the laws of England, such a man would be praised by God for his actions. After some thought, the Student concludes that the charitable man would also be legally clear, "because it shall be taken that it was the intent of the makers of the statute to except such cases. And the Judges may many times judge after the mind of the makers as farre as the letter may suffer."[9] While this idea was gradually shouldered aside in common law courtrooms as statutory interpretation grew stricter over the course of the early modern period, it remained the dominant interpretive approach in equity decisions.[10] Milton himself makes similar claims for intention in *Tetrachordon*: "Him wee count an ill Expounder who urges Law against the intention therof," and "For this is a confest oracle in law, that he who lookes not at the intention of a precept, the more superstitious he is of the letter, the more he misinterprets" (*CPW* 2:623, 667). In view of these opinions about the need for interpretation, Satan's tacit question to Eve—"What did God really mean?"—seems entirely aboveboard. After all, he is only doing what Milton himself recommends.

However, Satan's invitation to interpret the law detours strategically around the fact that this law does not need to have its true intention reconstructed. Aristotle writes that legal interpretation consists of "deciding as the lawgiver would himself decide if he were present on the occasion."[11] As if preempting Aristotle's dictum, Milton has shown that the law of Eden was delivered to Adam by a lawgiver, the Son, who was personally present on the occasion to make his meaning crystal clear. So while Satan

9. St. German, *Dialogue in English*, D4v.

10. See the discussion of common law views of interpretation in Tubbs, *Common Law Mind*, 116–28.

11. Aristotle, *Nicomachean Ethics*, 5.10.5–6.

presents himself as a good judge or lawyer trying to draw out the true sense of a law, he actually becomes Milton's "ill Expounder," for he presses on Eve an idea of the law that is directly "against the intention thereof." From his standpoint, this legal legerdemain about God's intention is a crucial part of convincing Eve that the law's penalties would not apply in her case. Satan asks,

> Or will God incense his ire
> For such a petty trespass, and not praise
> Rather your dauntless virtue, whom the pain
> Of death denounced, whatever thing death be[?] (9.692–95)

Satan pushes Eve to evaluate the ban on eating in light of what she takes to be, in St. German's words, "the mind of the makers" and to conclude that it was "the intent of the makers of the statute to except" such a case as hers. By eating, Eve would be acting like St. German's charitable traveler, one who displays what Satan calls a "dauntless virtue" in the teeth of the law.

Even when he concedes that eating from the tree would be an offense, Satan downgrades it to a "petty trespass." The lack of comment on this line implies that editors and critics have presumably read "trespass" in its spiritual sense as meaning a sin. However, this word was also dense with legal significance in the seventeenth century. Trespass cases had skyrocketed by Milton's day, because changes in common law practice had allowed a variety of legal matters to be litigated for the first time under the writ of trespass on the case. Satan's legal terminology brings a strategic advantage, for by labeling Eve's action a "trespass," Satan keeps it out of the realm of criminal offenses. To be clear, the early modern period did not draw the same fixed line between civil and criminal offenses that we do, and how and where a case was litigated often had more to do with the plaintiff's desired outcome than with a consistently applied judicial taxonomy. That said, while certain offenses fell into that murky middle category of common law cases that could be shunted either to a court like the King's Bench (criminal) or to Common Pleas (civil) depending on the circumstances, trespass was not one of them. It was consistently what the modern world would call a tort, and so those convicted of it were typically sentenced to make amends, often by financial compensation. God has been very clear about the criminal penalties for touching and eating the fruit: "He with his whole posterity must die" (3.209). By calling the sin a trespass, Satan demotes it from a capital crime to one for which the damages awarded rarely exceeded the actual harm sustained by the plaintiff. His use of the modifier "petty" adds to his argument, since this word was commonly used to indicate the lesser of two parallel offenses, as in petty treason/high treason and petty larceny/grand larceny.

Having suggested that eating from the fruit would be equivalent to a mere civil wrong, Satan makes this the basis for his claim that "God therefore cannot hurt ye, and be just" (9.700). When he asks, "What can your knowledge hurt him," Satan suggests that since Eve's knowledge will not "hurt" God, God cannot in justice "hurt" her in return (9.727). Satan's claim that God will surely not impose a penalty of death for a minor civil infraction like trespass echoes the Aristotelian idea that punishment should be calibrated to the amount of harm inflicted, an idea that was a staple in juristic texts. Milton himself takes up the issue of balancing crimes and punishment in *Tenure of Kings and Magistrates*, when he compares the kind of sentence pronounced upon a traitor to that pronounced upon a tyrant and concludes that the "ways of justice are exactest proportion" (*CPW* 3.253). Ultimately, Satan uses the assumption that God will not give an unjust punishment to reframe entirely the consequences of eating:

> So ye shall die perhaps, by putting off
> Human, to put on gods, death to be wished,
> Though threatened, which no worse than this can bring. (9.713–15)

Since a just lawgiver cannot possibly punish a petty trespass with real death, however much such a penalty is "threatened," some other punishment must have been intended. Thus, Satan argues, the only death that can result from eating the fruit is a "wished" transformation from a human state to a godlike one, and God can sentence them with "no worse than this."

Eve echoes Satan's brand of skewed legal reasoning when, on the threshold of sin, she calls the ban on the tree one of God's "prohibitions" (9.760). Like "trespass," "prohibition" had both a generic meaning and a specifically legal one. A "prohibition" could mean any kind of ban, but in the highly charged jurisdictional conflicts of early modern England, it referred also to an order issued by a superior court (e.g., the King's Bench) forbidding an inferior court (e.g., the Court of Requests or the Marshalsea) from proceeding in a given case or matter. Because our modern, unified idea of law has produced a judicial system with a relatively coordinated system of appeal, we can have trouble appreciating the depth and complexity of the period's jurisdictional struggles and the centrality of the prohibition as the main weapon some courts used in order to control others.[12] Although the central common law courts issued prohibitions against many other jurisdictions (for example, from 1590 until the accession of Charles I, the Court of Requests was virtually unable to hear cases, owing to the number of prohibitions issued against it), the majority of these prohibitions targeted the church courts.[13] When she thinks of God as having issued "prohibitions," Eve at one level makes a jurisdictional argument. She is not simply saying that God has banned an action; she is simultaneously suggesting that he has improperly tried to exert his authority in another jurisdiction. By rights, the action of eating the fruit should be decided not in some distant, centralized court of Heaven but rather in the local "court" of her own conscience. Eve sounds like one of England's canon lawyers complaining about the repeated intrusion of the common law onto their own jurisdictional turf. This impression is strengthened when Milton describes Satan as one "to some great cause addressed" (9.672), for *causa* was the legal term for a lawsuit in the ecclesiastical courts. Milton makes Satan the

12. Cormack, *Power to Do Justice*, 2. See also Gray, *Writ of Prohibition*.

13. Helmholz, *Roman Canon Law*, 158–95.

voice of the canon law, a characterization that recalls the moment in *A Masque Performed at Ludlow Castle* when Comus scolds the Lady for violating "the canon laws of [his] foundation" (808). Albeit with some reluctance, England's canon law courts consistently obeyed prohibitions issued by common law courts. In contrast, Eve concludes, "Such prohibitions bind not" (9.760), and she thereby claims the right to set limits on God's legal authority.

A similar kind of jurisdictional reasoning characterizes Adam's book 10 soliloquy. Having committed a crime against the law, Adam and Eve must be judged according to the terms of that law, but Adam imagines his case being transferred to a different jurisdiction:

Did I solicit thee
From darkness to promote me, or here place
In this delicious garden? As my will
Concurred not to my being, it were but right
And equal to reduce me to my dust. (10.744–48)

As Mark Fortier points out, when Adam thinks about what would be "right" and "equal," he uses the early modern language of equity.[14] Equity was important because laws, when applied to the extraordinary diversity of human circumstances, occasionally resulted in unfairness, and a verdict could be both legally correct and unjust. As St. German put it, "If thou take all that the words of the Law giveth thee, thou shalt sometime do against the law." Therefore, "in some cases it is necessary to leave the words of the law, and to follow that reason and justice requireth, and to that intent equity is ordained."[15] The question that vexed the early modern period was where equity was to be found. While St. German, a common lawyer, saw equity as a principle working within

14. Fortier, *Culture of Equity*, 147. See also Majeske, *Equity in English Renaissance Literature.*

15. St. German, *Dialogue in English*, D3, D3v. See also Maclean, *Interpretation and Meaning*, 181–85.

the law itself, equity in early modern England had also evolved into an autonomous arm of the judicial system, with Chancery as its primary court. Adam implicitly wants the kind of justice that Chancery provided; that is, he wants to escape from the law into another jurisdiction. He sounds exactly like those litigants that Milton complains of in his *Proposalls of Certaine Expedients*, one of the cluster of political works that he wrote right on the edge of the Restoration. In this work, Milton imagines a reformed, localized judicial system that will prevent suitors dissatisfied with a judgment from searching "for more equall Justice in another place" (*CPW* 7:338).[16] He responds here to the widespread jurisdiction hopping that had so grievously bogged down England's judicial system as litigants strategically transferred cases back and forth between courts in order to bankrupt opponents or secure a more favorable verdict. In his book 10 soliloquy, Adam acts just like one of these self-serving litigants, for, faced with a severe judgment, he turns his thoughts to whether a different judicial network might provide a "more equall" outcome.

Adam's use of the verb "solicit" also suggests that he hopes equity will rescue him from the clutches of law. In the early modern period, "soliciting" referred to certain kinds of actions that an attorney carried out on behalf of his client. For example, if an attorney of the Court of Common Pleas argued for his client in Chancery or in the conciliar courts, he was said to be a solicitor for them. As a result of such usages, solicitors as an independent branch of the legal profession appeared in the seventeenth century, and in keeping with the origins of the term, these men practiced in equity and in conciliar courts such as the Admiralty.[17] The important point is that one did not "solicit" in a common law setting. Adam's reference to soliciting has another strategic advantage: it subtly decriminalizes his actions in much the same way that Sa-

16. For a fuller discussion of this passage and Milton's other recommendations for judicial reform in his 1659–60 political pamphlets, see Chapman, "Milton and Legal Reform."

17. I am particularly indebted to Ben Darlow for clarification on this point.

tan demoted Eve's sin to a "petty trespass." By the middle of the seventeenth century, when the common law had a virtual monopoly on criminal cases, equity handled primarily civil cases. Cases where one "solicit[ed]" were not capital, and so when Adam uses a term pointedly associated with a venue like Chancery, he insinuates that his is a merely civil matter.[18]

Despite Adam's accusation that God only administers law, however, Milton has already shown that God combines all forms of just dealing. In book 3 God proclaims that he will not dispense with the basic law governing Adam and Eve's nature or "revoke the high decree/Unchangeable, eternal, which ordained/Their freedom" (3.126–28). At this moment when the rule of law seems most punishingly inescapable, Milton makes room for equity, for as Elliott Visconsi argues, the conversation between the Father and the Son in book 3 is, in effect, a conversation between law and equity. God spells out the strict provisions of the divine law, and then he and the Son together work out an equitable solution for humanity's salvation.[19] Where Adam in book 10 sees equity as a means to escape from law, Milton shows that God's justice incorporates all forms of justice. For example, when God says that he has issued a "high injunction" (10.13), Milton looks to a non–common law judicial system, since injunctions were Chancery's equivalent to the common law writ of prohibition and were a subject of pronounced interest, given seventeenth-century jurisdictional tensions.[20] Only the chancellor could issue an injunction, and so God's "high injunction" makes him the source of equity as well as law. Milton makes a similar poetic move when he refers to the tree as "interdicted" by God (7.46). Given the absence of editorial commentary on this line, scholars have

18. Louis A. Knafla, in his study of Lord Ellesmere's tracts, writes that equity "was used in the Chancery to supplement the rules of law in *civil* matters." Knafla, *Law and Politics*, 162, emphasis added.

19. Visconsi, *Lines of Equity*, 100–103. For a discussion of how Milton imagines equity as central to religious tolerance, see Silver, "'Taken Scandal Not a Given.'"

20. On Lord Ellesmere's writings about injunctions, see Knafla, *Law and Politics*, 155.

presumably read "interdict" in its general sense of an "authoritative prohibition."[21] However, an interdict was also a decree in Roman law typically used to ban private persons from taking actions related to possession.[22] Adam and Eve do indeed aspire to possession, and Milton invites us to understand the "interdict" in both its narrowly legal and its broadly generic senses. In the process he makes it clear that God's law incorporates Roman law ideas as well as common law and equitable ones, and he thereby prevents God's justice from being pinned to any one human legal system. Since God combines all possible forms of justice, Adam has no need to go jurisdiction shopping, and to do so misrepresents the nature of God's love.

The Contracts of Eden

Over the course of the early modern period, contracts increasingly structured early modern mercantile and financial dealings. As legal contracts became a ubiquitous feature of commercial life, contracts also became a defining paradigm for other forms of social organization. Ideas of the social contract transformed political thinking, and they also configured households across the nation, as the master-servant relationship—traditionally based in ideas of duty and allegiance—was reframed along contractual lines. The model of two individuals freely entering into a mutually beneficial bargain also became a means to understand marriage. Greenberg writes that "the contract emerged in seventeenth-century law as the predominant archetype for articulating the perimeters of individuals' associations with each other," and she shows how contract theory informs Milton's depiction of Adam and Eve's marriage.[23] While Greenberg's argument is a persuasive

21. "Interdict," n., def. 1, *OED Online*.

22. Ibid., def. 2a.

23. Greenberg, "Preliminary Study," 99. The body of scholarship on early modern contract theory is sizable. However, the most influential—and provocatively original—account in recent years of how and why the language of contract became important

one as applied to Edenic marriage in *Paradise Lost*, it weakens when she broadens the applicability of contract theory. As I argue in this section, contract was not, in fact, also "the principal frame for interpreting Adam's relationship to God."[24] Milton was deeply committed to ideas of contract, but he also knew that in order to use a thing properly, you also have to know where and when not to use it. In books 9 and 10, Milton shows that the fall happens in part because, under Satan's coaching, Adam and Eve apply contractual thinking to a prohibition that was instead the nonnegotiable cornerstone of God's positive law.

Milton is explicit about the fact that unfallen Adam and Eve were not parties to a covenant or contract with God. In Genesis, God places Adam in the Garden and says, "Of every tree of the garden thou mayest freely eat: But of the tree of the knowledge of good and evil, thou shalt not eat of it: for in that day that thou eatest thereof thou shalt surely die" (Gen. 2:16–17). While many theologians understood these provisions as establishing a covenant between God and human beings (whether it was a covenant of grace or a covenant of works remained a contested issue), Milton disagreed. In *On Christian Doctrine*, he considers and then rejects the idea: "A command, whether it comes from God or from a magistrate, should not be called a covenant just because rewards and punishments are attached: it is rather a declaration of power" (*CPW* 6:352). Furthermore, there was no covenant or contract because "Adam was not required to perform any works; he was merely forbidden to do one thing" (*CPW* 6:351). Discussing this passage, Shawcross writes, "The prohibition has *not* involved a contractual arrangement, although there is a reward or a punishment attached to the observance of that prohibition." Michael Lieb agrees, for he argues that instead of representing a

---

to seventeenth-century political culture is Kahn, *Wayward Contracts*. Craig Muldrew discusses rising ideas of contractual obligation in Muldrew, *Economy of Obligation*. For the use of contracts to define marriage, see Witte, *From Sacrament to Contract*.

24. Greenberg, "Preliminary Study," 107.

covenant between Adam and God, the ban on the tree was more like a primal taboo.[25]

Significantly, book 9 of *Paradise Lost* is not the first time that Milton shows a tempter resorting to the language of contract law, for Comus adopts the same strategy in *A Masque Performed at Ludlow Castle*. Confronting the captive Lady inside his castle, Comus argues that by spurning his offered cup in the name of abstinence, she misinterprets the humanity-Nature contract:

> But you invert the cov'nants of her trust,
> And harshly deal like an ill borrower
> With that which you received on other terms,
> Scorning the unexempt condition
> By which all mortal frailty must subsist,
> Refreshment after toil, ease after pain. (682–87)

While at one level this is a warped version of the parable of the talents, at another, it alludes to contemporary ideas of contractual obligation. Comus suggests that Nature has established a contractual "trust," which, in early modern law, was "the confidence reposed in a person in whom the legal ownership of property [was] vested to hold or use for the benefit of another."[26] As the metaphorical trustee of her own person, the Lady's job is to tend and safeguard herself for her future husband. Sounding like a litigant in the early modern Court of Wards, Comus argues that she misunderstands the "cov'nants" of the arrangement, for Nature never intended that a trustee should waste her physical resources in the execution of her duty. To the contrary, Comus argues, the "unexempt condition" of all trust arrangements is that the trustee is entitled to "refreshment after toil, ease after pain." This may be a sly reference to early modern wardship arrangements, for trustees notoriously used their positions and the wards' estates for their own gain. Unlike Eve in *Paradise Lost*, the Lady sees that her tempter has started with the wrong premise.

25. Shawcross, *John Milton*, 134; Lieb, "*Paradise Lost*."
26. "Trust," n., def. 6, *OED Online*.

Rejecting Comus's claim that she is one party to a contract with Nature (in which case the terms would be open to examination and renegotiation), the Lady says instead that Nature has provided "sober laws" and the "holy dictate of spare Temperance" (766, 767). Nature is a lawgiver, not a contracting equal.

As if taking his cue from Comus, Satan in book 9 uses the language of contract to push Eve to reevaluate the basic taboo of Eden. In his temptation of her, Satan assiduously promotes the very position that Milton rejects. He suggests that Adam and Eve's life in the Garden is a reciprocal arrangement between themselves and God, one that should be rooted in a sense of mutual benefit. Specifically, Satan draws the ban on the tree into the realm of contracts and contract law. In a now classic work, Sir Henry Sumner Maine argued that the early modern period witnessed a move from a status society to a contract society, and although the thoroughness and the suddenness of the shift Maine traces are open to question, it seems undeniable that, in Luke Wilson's words, "the meaning of contractual relations was a matter of particular concern" in the sixteenth and seventeenth centuries. Generally endorsing Maine's thesis, Wilson argues that "where social relations had once been understood as depending on who you were (your status), they were increasingly determined by what you did, that is, by the (legal) relationships you voluntarily entered into."[27] Milton shows Satan turning Eve's attention away from the fact that she lives in a status relationship to God, where obedience is an intrinsic part of her existence as a human being. Satan promotes instead the idea that obedience is one provision of a contract between human beings and God, and his argument frequently crosses into the rapidly evolving world of contract law.[28]

When he reminds Eve of the contradiction between the ban on the tree and the fact that Adam and Eve are "lords declared

27. Wilson, *Theaters of Intention*, 70. See also Maine, *Ancient Law*, 139–41, 252–302.

28. On Milton's use of the political and social dimensions of early modern ideas of contract in *Paradise Lost* and his prose works, see Kahn, *Wayward Contracts*, 120–33, 196–222.

of all in earth or air" (9.658), Satan tacitly raises a version of the legal doctrine of consideration. In the early modern law of contract, consideration was the legal value or the benefit to the contracting parties. Under English law, contracts without some kind of mutual exchange of value or benefit were not considered binding. For example, if Party A pledged to give Party B his annual crop of rye and Party B offered nothing in return, under the English common law this contract would not be binding, since there was no mutual exchange of consideration. Party B would have to offer reciprocal consideration—a monetary sum, goods or services, even a pledge to refrain from some specified action—for the contract to hold. As Milton writes in *Tetrachordon*, consideration (which he here refers to as "equity") "is understood in every Covnant, . . . though the terms bee not exprest" (*CPW* 2:624). Satan is suggesting that the considerations offered by the two sides in this contract are vastly unequal. Adam and Eve have agreed to refrain from eating of the tree, but this consideration is not matched by an equal one on God's part, since they are already "lords declared of all in earth or air." As a result, their quid does not have a corresponding quo. In his discussion of contracts, Hobbes says they must be grounded in a "mutuall transferring of Right," for a man enters into a contract only "in consideration of some Right reciprocally transferred to himself; or for some other good he hopeth for thereby."[29] According to Satan's logic, the "transferring of Right" in the Garden of Eden has not been "mutuall" because, under the pretense of giving freely to Adam and Eve, God continues to monopolize available rights and resources. Hobbes's vision of contracts is particularly apt for Satan's purposes, since it moves the discussion away from Aristotelian ideas of justice and toward the pragmatic question of who benefits.[30] And in both Hobbes's and Satan's legal calcu-

29. Hobbes, *Leviathan*, 94, 93. For a fuller discussion of the origins of consideration, see Baker, "Origins of 'Doctrine' of Consideration."

30. Sacks, "Promise and the Contract," 43. Much of my discussion of consideration is based on Sacks's essay. See also Simpson, *History of the Common Law*.

lus, benefit is gauged according to the contracting parties' assessment of where the greatest good to self lies.

The obvious response to Satan's suggestion that Adam and Eve's quid lacks a quo would be that the consideration God offers is life in Paradise, so that Party A, the married couple Adam and Eve, "contracts" not to eat from the tree, and in return Party B, God, pledges them the otherwise unlimited enjoyment of the Garden. But Satan preempts this line of reasoning by suggesting that God is not the true creator/owner of the Garden, and so its use or ownership is not legally his to endow. He argues,

> The gods are first, and that advantage use
> On our belief, that all from them proceeds;
> I question it. (9.718–20)

Satan is suggesting that God (rendered as "gods") uses his status as "first" to create the fiction that everything "proceeds" or derives from him, thus giving him the right to grant or withhold ownership and access. To this, Satan poses a lawyer's demur: "I question it," drawing on the specific meaning of "to question" as to challenge or interrogate in a judicial context.[31] He explains,

> For this fair Earth I see,
> Warmed by the sun, producing every kind,
> Them nothing. (9.720–22)

In effect, the "gods" have not produced the Earth or the things on it, and yet they claim ownership and the right to dispose of it at will. He asks Eve, "What can your knowledge hurt him, or this Tree/Impart against his will," and then he adds a crucial disclaimer: "if all be his?" (9.727–28). Satan is here implicitly accusing God of contractual fraud, of pretending to have a legal right—in this case, the right to convey property to another and to stipulate the terms of that property's use—and of trying to benefit by that imposture.

31. "Question," v., defs. 2a, 2c, *OED Online*.

Satan promotes the same idea of breachable legal contracts that the royalist Robert Filmer does in his *Patriarcha* to debunk the idea of the social contract: "Now if a private person makes a Contract, either with Oath or without Oath, he is no further bound than the Equity and Justice of the Contract ties him: for a man may have Relief against an unreasonable and unjust promise, if either Deceit, or Errour, or Force, or Fear induced him thereto. Or if it be hurtful or grievous in the performance."[32] Filmer is correct that "Deceit," "Force," and "Fear" were legitimate grounds for challenging a contract. However, as I explore below, by the middle of the seventeenth century, the doctrine of strict liability was newly being applied to contracts in a way that made the contractee's "Errour" or the fact that the contract was "hurtful or grievous in the performance" legally irrelevant. Satan is trying to convince Eve that she, like Filmer's rueful contractee, has simply made "an unreasonable and unjust promise," and he suggests too that God has practiced the kinds of fraud that would invalidate the arrangement anyway. Accordingly, she is free to walk away from this bad bargain.

Eve clearly internalizes this logic, because she shortly begins using basic principles of contract law to convince herself that God's ban on the tree is not a binding one. In early modern practice, a contract could be successfully challenged if it violated public policy.[33] For example, one banning an individual from having children would be declared void because procreation was essential to the good maintenance of the commonwealth. Eve reasons along comparable lines when she says that God "forbids us good, forbids us to be wise" (9.759). In an English court of common law, a contract in which A stipulated that B could not learn and thereby become good and wise would have been declared illegal, a rule that made contract law consonant with the Natural

32. Filmer, *Patriarcha*, 97.

33. While a strict doctrine of public policy was not established until 1711, the idea of an equitable public policy had existed for centuries, an idea that was generally tied to principles of illegality and the common good.

Law principle *Lex iniusta non est lex.* Contracts also had to be internally consistent. William Sheppard, in his legal textbook *Actions on the Case for Deeds*, stipulates that in addition to being "lawful," a valid contract must also be "clear and certain," and "it must be co-hering, and agreeing in itself."[34] Eve plays upon this idea when, reflecting on the penalty of death God has pronounced, she asks, "How dies the serpent? He hath eat'n and lives" (9.764). The penalty is not clear (what is this thing called Death?), nor is it certain (why does the penalty not apply to the serpent?).

Milton shows a similar instance of mistaken contractual thinking when Adam in his book 10 soliloquy claims that he was "unable to perform/Thy terms too hard" (10.750–51). According to Adam, God has initiated an unjust contractual relationship whose "terms" were impossible to fulfill.[35] As Milton makes clear in *On Christian Doctrine*, however, he did not think the ban on the tree established a contract or covenant; that is a line of reasoning that tempters such as Comus and Satan adopt and one that leads Eve into sin. Even if it were a covenant or contract, common sense tells us that a contract in which one party's primary stipulation is that the other party refrains from touching a single tree is clearly not "too hard." Adam's logic also fails to hold up for more technical legal reasons. By roughly the middle of the seventeenth century, contracts under common law could no longer be invalidated owing to the difficulty of performing them, a change that reflects the general Puritan emphasis on the binding nature of promises. The doctrine of strict liability in contracts acquired one of its most classic formulations in the 1647 *Paradine v. Jane* case, in which a

34. Sheppard, *Actions*, 84. For a fuller discussion of Sheppard's rules, see Simpson, *History of the Common Law*, 506–38; on the need for contracts to be "clear and certain," see Teeven, *History*, 83.

35. Observing the "unremittingly legalistic" language of Adam's lament, Rosenblatt focuses on the Pauline sense of the Law evident in this soliloquy. Milton's thinking about law is even more pervasive than Rosenblatt allows, for as the Law comes flooding into Adam's consciousness, we also see evidences of law. Rosenblatt, "Law in Adam's Soliloquy," 186.

defendant argued that he could not pay his rents because Prince Rupert's army had kept him from cultivating the land and selling his crops. The King's Bench ruled in favor of the plaintiff, arguing that "when the party by his contract creates a duty or charge upon himself, he is bound to make it good . . . notwithstanding any accident by inevitable necessity, because he might have provided against it by his contract."[36] In *Leviathan*, Hobbes arrives at a similar conclusion: "To promise that which is known to be Impossible, is no Covenant. But if that prove impossible afterwards, which before was thought possible, the Covenant is valid, and bindeth."[37] Adam sounds like Hobbes or one of the King's Bench judges when, having complained about the impossibility of meeting God's terms, he then catches the flaw in his own logic. He concedes,

> Too late
> I thus contest; then should have been refused
> Those terms whatever, when they were proposed. (10.755–57)

He admits to himself, "Thou didst accept [the terms]; wilt thou enjoy the good,/Then cavil the conditions?" (10.758–59). Adam here offers an accurate summary of the new legal rules of strict liability: the terms of the contract "should have been refused" by the defendant when "they were proposed"; once the contract is accepted, the defendant cannot argue in retrospect that the terms were impossible to fulfill because they were unreasonable or unjust. Although Adam and God are not parties to a reciprocal contract, even if they were, Adam would be liable for breach.

36. Quoted and discussed in Berman, *Law and Revolution: II*, 281. See also Stoljar, *History of Contract*, 189–90. Strict liability emerged unevenly over centuries. Ideas of strict civil liability in relationship to keeping fires contained had appeared as early as the fourteenth century, while strict criminal liability did not appear solidly until the nineteenth century. The seventeenth century applied ideas of strict liability to commercial matters such as contracts and the obligation of carriers to keep goods safe.

37. Hobbes, *Leviathan*, 97. For a modern view, see Epstein, "Unconscionability," 288.

In *How Milton Works*, Fish contrasts the world of Milton with the world of the "modern moment." In the modern world, "choices are complex and persons are always pulled this way and that by equally compelling values, and reason, as a technical faculty, becomes one of the tools you have recourse to in the face of moral ambiguity." In Milton's world, in contrast, there is no complex clash of equally compelling values: "There is only one value—the value of obedience." In one sense, the opposition Milton creates between contracts and law supports Fish's point about the importance of obedience. Laws are not negotiable in the way that contracts are. Had Adam and Eve understood that their relationship to the tree was governed by law and not by contract, and had they simply obeyed that law, the fall would never have happened. But the fact that Milton uses legal and contractual terms at all in his account of the fall complicates the opposition Fish wants to draw between adhering viscerally, even blindly, to righteous obedience and trusting in reason, a trust that Fish calls a temptation insofar as it grants "independence to values other than . . . obedience."[38] When he shows Satan and Eve applying contractual language to a noncontractual prohibition, Milton invites readers to use their reason to see the fundamentally flawed nature of the resulting legal argument. Thus his depiction of wrong-headed legal reasoning in books 9 and 10 of *Paradise Lost* complements his method in a work such as *Doctrine and Discipline of Divorce*. There, in his discussion of the Mosaic law of divorce, Milton gives his chapters headings such as "The Second Reason for this Law" and "The Third Reason for this Law." In his view, it is not enough simply to know the law and obey it blindly. Milton also wants readers to understand the law.

Ownership in Paradise

Early modern England did not categorically separate contract law from issues of commercial exchange, and as a result, conversations

38. Fish, *How Milton Works*, 53.

about contract were also conversations about the ownership of things.[39] The blurring of the language of contract and the language of ownership is a strategic asset from Satan's point of view. By emphasizing Eve's bargain with God, Satan can simultaneously direct her view toward how this bargain regulates the use and possession of a material good: the Edenic tree and the knowledge it putatively contains. Satan's temptation of Eve consistently invokes ideas of ownership to characterize God as the ultimate "have" and Eve as the victimized "have-not." For example, earlier in this chapter I discussed the phrase "petty trespass" (9.693) to show how Satan characterizes eating from the tree as a mere civil offense. The label "trespass" has another strategic advantage from Satan's point of view. There were generally three types of trespass: trespass to land (the form of trespass most familiar today), to persons, and to chattels. Eve is not committing trespass to land, since she can go where she wishes in the Garden, and the issue is clearly not one of trespass to persons. Satan's implication is that she would be committing trespass to chattels, an action that included interfering with, relocating, or even touching chattels in the possession of another. As legal historian Theodore Plucknett points out, trespass in early modern England was akin to a crime like larceny in that it was "a violation of possession."[40] By suggesting that Eve will commit petty trespass, Satan implies that God has things that Eve lacks and that she might want them enough to commit a minor property offense.

Satan draws on this same idea of God as a property owner when he says that God "enclosed/Knowledge of good and evil in this Tree" (9.722–23). The word "enclosed" characterizes the fruit as a miniature enclosure, and so Satan tacitly reminds Eve that while she has unrestricted access to the "enclosure green" and the "enclosure wild" of Paradise, her rights stop at the fruit's skin (4.133, 9.543). Satan sounds like the Digger Gerrard Winstanley lamenting the results of the fall: man became "an incloser, not

39. Berman, *Faith and Order*, 205.
40. Plucknett, *Concise History*, 469.

content that another should enjoy the same priviledge as himself, but incloseth all from his Brother."[41] But whereas the Diggers breached enclosures as part of an attack on private property itself, Satan has a different end in view. According to his insinuation, the problem is simply that the private property in question is God's when it should be Eve's. Satan plays to this incipient idea of possession when he says that "whoso eats thereof, forthwith attains/Wisdom" and asks, "Wherein lies/Th'offense, that man should thus attain to know?" (9.724–26). The verb "attain" meant both to reach and also to come into possession of something, and so Satan links the act of attaining in its upward, aspirational sense to attaining in its ownership sense.[42] According to him, aspiring is inseparable from acquiring. Significantly, Milton's contemporary John Dryden noticed the possessory overtones in this passage and used them in *The State of Innocence*, his stage version of *Paradise Lost*. Dryden's Satan claims that the ban on the tree attests to God's greed. God "does possession keep," and he forbids Adam and Eve the use of the tree "for his own int'rest," drawing on the sense of "interest" as a legal concern in a thing and especially a "right or title to property."[43]

Satan's language of possession may have escaped critical attention in part because he is not talking about land. Like many others who study the early modern period, Milton scholars are quick to equate property with real estate. While this assumption has produced many good studies of Milton's awareness of land and the importance of place, it limits our gaze to only one part of the property spectrum.[44] Chattels were property too. Indeed,

41. Winstanley, *Works of Gerrard Winstanley*, 612. This is a prime example of Loewenstein's point that Satan often uses the rhetoric of the early modern religious radicals. Loewenstein, *Representing Revolution*, 202–41.

42. "Attain," v., def. 8, *OED Online*.

43. Dryden, "State of Innocence," 4.2.99, 97; "interest," n., def. I.1a, *OED Online*.

44. We see this property-land connection in works like Greenberg, "Paradise Enclosed"; Attie, "Enclosure Polemics and the Garden"; Fenton, *Milton's Places of Hope*; and Hiltner, *Milton and Ecology*. As Seipp points out, English ideas of possession were first hammered out in relationship to animals and objects, and once refined in these areas, they were later transferred to real estate. Seipp, "Concept of Property."

since Milton usually rented houses in London rather than buying them and since leased property was known as "chattels real," chattels were the kind of property with which he was most familiar. Owning chattels had a different kind of significance than owning land did. As Katherine Eisaman Maus observes, land was generally associated with permanence and genealogical stability, while chattels were associated with the quirks and whims of individual desire. These associations stemmed from the way in which each form of property could be transmitted. Laws tightly regulated the terms on which land could be handed down between generations, but the transmission of chattels lay entirely at the individual owner's discretion.[45] This link between chattel ownership and personal desire or fulfillment is at the heart of Satan's temptation of Eve. He directs Eve's attention away from her familial connection to Adam and toward her own personal desires,[46] and at the same time he also directs her gaze toward a material chattel that she could make uniquely her own. Eve takes Satan's appeal to chattel ownership one step further when she actually breaks off a branch from the tree and approaches Adam holding "a bough of fairest fruit that downy smiled" (9.851). When the fruit was still connected to the living tree, it was part of the Garden's real estate. When she breaks the branch, however, Eve turns the fruit into a "moveable" and a "consumable," early modern synonyms for chattels that capture the essentially mobile and transient nature of chattel properties.[47] Once the fruit is converted into a piece of personal chattel, it can be transmitted to Adam once Eve concludes that this transmission benefits her.

In tempting Eve with ownership of the fruit, Satan also manipulates her link to the Garden's vegetable resources, a link Milton stresses earlier when he says that Eve's hair curls "as the vine curls her tendrils" (4.307). We also see this Eve-nature connection in

45. Maus, *Being and Having in Shakespeare*, 46–47.

46. On the way that Satan directs Eve's attention outward toward the social and political realms, see Miller, *Engendering the Fall*, 66–72.

47. "Moveable," adj. and n., def. B1a, *OED Online*; "Consumable," adj. and n., defs. 2 and B, *OED Online*.

Milton's use of possessive adjectives. In general, he is careful with these words. For example, the word "her" as an adjective is applied primarily to the landscape: Eden stretches "her line"; Nature paints "her colors"; an "irriguous valley" spreads "her store"; and the soil of Hell has "her hidden luster, gems and gold" (4.210, 5.24, 4.255, 2.271). Occasionally Milton uses "his" and "her" to indicate Adam and Eve's possessory use of things—although, to be clear, he does not mean absolute legal ownership but rather what we might think of as use rights, as in the case of a theater seat that might be "mine" or "yours" even though neither of us actually owns it.[48] In these few cases, Adam appears in connection with forms of real estate, as when he sits before "his cool bow'r" and invites the angel to "his lodge" (5.300, 5.arg.). Eve, however, is more likely to appear in a quasi-possessory relationship to the Garden's botanical things, as when she uses "her fit vessels" to prepare a meal for Raphael, or when she rises to tend "her fruits and flow'rs" in what Milton calls "her nursery" (5.348, 8.44, 8.46). In his temptation of her, Satan exaggerates Eve's natural connection to the Garden's flora by suggesting that the fruit—and the knowledge within it—should be "hers" in a more exclusionary and more fully proprietary sense. Not surprisingly, Satan applies the pronoun "your" to Eve five times in quick succession: "your dauntless virtue"; "your fear"; "your eyes"; "your knowledge"; and "your need of this fair fruit" (9.694, 702, 706, 727, 731). These are the first times in the epic that this possessive adjective is used in relationship to Eve, and so she is newly being addressed as an independent being who can have an independent ownership of the things around her. Previously, Milton prefers the plural, particularly in book 4 where Adam refers to "our obedience"; "our delightful task"; "our pleasant labor"; "our walk at noon"; and "our scant manuring" (4.428, 437, 625, 627, 628). While outside the sole propriety of marriage, Adam and Eve have a communal relationship to everything in Paradise, Satan pushes Eve into a conceptual world dominated by more modern ideas of

48. For a discussion of the concept of use rights as part of Natural Law, see Buckle, *Natural Law.*

meum and *tuum*, in which one person can own a thing to the utter exclusion of all others.[49]

Milton was not the first poet to show Satan luring Eve with the prospect of gain. Hugo Grotius, in his 1601 dramatic poem *Adamus exul*, tells the story of the fall of Adam and Eve, and his work was a "probable model" for Milton's own.[50] In *Adamus exul*, Satan suggests that Adam and Eve are parties to an unfair contract. Since God did not impose the restraint on the tree until after Adam and Eve had been given sovereignty, the restraint on the tree is void ("irrita"), and Grotius's Satan tells Eve that God is just jealous: he "grudges you the good that hides within the fruit" (Invidit illud, quod latet fructu, bonum).[51] Milton's Satan similarly asks, "Is [God's motive] envy, and can envy dwell/In heav'nly breasts?" (9.729–30). In both *Paradise Lost* and *Adamus exul*, Satan's ascription of envy suggests either that Eve has things that God wants and can't get or that God will jealously protect the things he has by unfairly blocking Eve's access to them. In *Adamus exul*, Satan urges Eve to break the bargain with God ("arripite pacti jura") because it does not provide equal rights to both sides. According to Satan, "there is never a good reason not to defend one's own rights" (nulla ad jus sui/ Sibi vindicandum negligenda occasio est).[52] The vaguely contractual language of rights quickly takes on a commercial edge. Eve should seek to acquire more in order to insure against future loss ("Quod non habes tibi quaere, ne perdas tua"), and when he tells her, "To seize profit is to reduce potential loss" (captare lucrum, maxima est damni fuga), Satan sounds like a merchant

49. What we might think of as Eve's fall into individual ownership resonates with Miller's point that, unlike Adam, Eve has a proclivity to want to be alone. Miller, *Engendering the Fall*, 35–36.

50. Poole, *Milton*, 189; for Poole's discussion of Grotius's idea of the fall in relation to Milton's, see 101–7. Evans argues that Grotius's play had a decisive impact on how Milton chose to structure *Paradise Lost*. Evans, *Paradise Lost*, 207–16.

51. Grotius, *Adamus exul*, ll. 1122, 1130.

52. Ibid., ll. 1195, 1206–7.

adventurer counseling an apprentice on how to maximize one's financial position.[53]

Like Grotius, Milton makes his Satan into the epic's spokesman for private ownership, and his use of the word "right"—like Grotius's "jus" in "nulla ad jus sui"—embraces both the broader idea of justice and the more focused idea of proprietary rights. Sometimes Milton uses "right" in the general sense of that which is true and reasonable, as when, in serpent form, Satan tells Eve, "[It is] right thou shouldst be obeyed" and calls her "of right declared/Sov'reign of creatures" (9.570, 611–12). Sometimes, however, it expresses a wider range of meanings. As Satan summons up his oratorical powers, Milton says that he is filled with "zeal of right," and here Milton also calls on the sense of a right as a privilege to which one is legally entitled (9.676). "Right" also meant specifically "a title or claim to the possession of property or authority," and most of the early modern examples the *OED* furnishes in support of this definition come from legal and testamentary contexts.[54] This link between "right" and issues of legal ownership is visible in the common law action called the writ of right, which restored property to its original owner.[55] When Milton describes Satan as filled with the "zeal of right," he offers a multilayered pun. Satan is like one eager to do the "right" thing. Like a good lawyer, he is also zealous to protect Eve's property rights; he feels what Milton calls "indignation" at the "wrong" done to Eve and is determined to help restore that which is rightfully hers (9.666). And finally, since Satan himself aims to gain ownership of Earth and thus to found his empire, his "zeal of right" points darkly toward his own possessive

53. Ibid., ll. 1208, 1216.

54. "Right," n., def. 9a, *OED Online*.

55. Smith writes that the "writ of right" (which he calls an action "in *rem*," literally "in the thing") is used in actions "possessorie to aske, or to keep the possession." Smith, *De republica anglorum*, 67. This action generally died out by the end of the sixteenth century, and its function was taken over by other actions.

impulses.[56] The stress on legal rights in book 9 is mirrored by the increased emphasis on "thing." This word appears more times in this book than anywhere else in the poem, and Milton's usages draw not only on the sense of a thing as an entity with a separate ontological status but also on "thing" as the English translation of the common legal term *res* or *rem*, meaning generally "any thing in respect of which a person may claim a right."[57] Strolling through Eden, Satan is like one who "from each thing met conceives delight," and since he is planning to seize possession of this terrain, the "things" he sees point toward his imagined possession (9.449). Lying to Eve in serpent form, he says that he "considered all things"; he sees in the Garden "all things fair and good"; he dismissively says of death, "whatever thing death be" (9.604, 605, 695). Once she falls, Eve begins using this same vocabulary: she is now aware of "each thing on Earth," and she imagines superiority over Adam as "a thing not undesireable" (9.813, 824). Like Satan, she looks out at the world and assesses the thingness of persons and objects, and she is newly aware both of how these entities are estranged or distanced from her and of new possibilities for ownership and dominance.

We see Eve's new proprietary impulse clearly when, considering the promise of knowledge implicit in the fruit, she reasons, "For good unknown, sure is not had, or had / And yet unknown, is as not had at all" (9.756–57). She equates not knowing things with not owning things, and her new desire for ownership is indicated by the appearance of the verb "to have" three times in these two lines. Knowledge has become a possession that Eve desires, in Satan's words, to "attain," and she is newly aware of her own "want" (9.755). She now thinks of God primarily in terms of what he has and she does not have, for after she eats, she tells herself,

56. This image supports Fenton's claim that Satan "bases his hopes for the future in the division of property and on his fallacious argument about property rights." Fenton, *Milton's Places of Hope*, 57.

57. "Res," n. 1, def. 1, *OED Online*.

> Others [i.e., God] envy what they cannot give;
> For had the gift been theirs, it had not here
> Thus grown. (9.806–808)

God cannot "give" the tree and the knowledge it contains because he does not own them, and Eve's evidence for this claim is that if God actually owned the tree, it would not have "here/ Thus grown" in the Garden. She is thinking like a private property owner. If I say that the mature trees already growing on your land are really my property that I am now generously giving to you (with the exception of that one fruit tree which you may not touch), I am both trying to con you into a false sense of obligation by pretending to give that which is not mine and trying to block you from the rightful use of what is yours. Eve reduces the tree into a token in a power struggle between a distant lord and a local tenant farmer. Here Milton suggestively rewrites the terms of his youthful poem "The Fable of the Peasant and the Landlord." In that brief Latin fable, the greedy landlord transplants an apple tree from the garden where it has thrived for years under the peasant gardener's care, and when it dies, the landlord learns too late that he should have left the tree where it grew and checked his own appetite. According to Eve's logic, God in *Paradise Lost* is acting like a wiser but more miserly version of this landlord: since he cannot transplant the tree, he simply bans the locals from its use.

All of this language of ownership shows Eve exchanging an erected form of private property for a debased one. As I suggested in the previous chapter, Eve already participates in a righteous system of co-ownership within the sole propriety model of marriage. Satan simply redirects these proprietary impulses so that instead of resting content with her reciprocal rights in wedded love and in Adam's body, Eve wants to own things around her. We see this exchange of marital sole propriety for other kinds of property when Eve considers whether she should share the fruit with Adam:

Shall I to him make known
As yet my change, and give him to partake
Full happiness with me, or rather not,
But keep the odds of knowledge in my power
Without copartner? (9.817–21)

"Knowledge" and "full happiness" are now things in Eve's "power," entities that she has and Adam does not. Earlier, she told the tree, "Thy full branches [are] offered free to *all*," but her possessive language in this passage indicates that she thinks of the fruit as private rather than communal property (9.802, emphasis added). She possesses the "odds" on these commodities, and they are in what she calls "my power." As I noted in chapter 5, the word "partner" was cognate with "parcener," which designated a legal owner or heir. When she considers the option of remaining without "copartner," Eve imagines herself as the sole proprietor of the fruit and its gift of knowledge.

Milton's choice of the word "extinct" also indicates the degree to which Eve is thinking about systems of ownership. In a legal register, "extinct" was used to describe a legal right that had died out.[58] It appears most often in discussions of testamentary arrangements and transferals of property, as when Richard Brownlow, in his *Reports of Diverse Choice Cases in Law*, examines the rights of tenants "after possibility of Issue extinct" and the conditions under which a copyhold having "being granted to three successively" becomes "extinct."[59] When she fears that she might be "extinct" and Adam would thereby enjoy "another Eve," Eve not only thinks of herself as physically dead; she also imagines herself as legally canceled out (9.829–30), and she chooses to have a "copartner" in order to retain at least partial ownership of her new knowledge. Ironically, when she in effect prefers Satan's offer of private chattel ownership to God's system of mutual marital ownership, Eve erases all of her legal agency. Although scholars debate to what degree early modern wives could retain some con-

58. "Extinct," adj., def. 5d, *OED Online*.

59. Brownlow, *Reports*, 88, 157.

trol of landed interests under common law, it is clear that married women had virtually no control over chattel property, all of which passed to the husband.[60] While Eve is not extinct in a physical sense, at the moment of sin, she becomes extinct in a legal one.

In this chapter, I have tried to show various ways in which the law gets manipulated. Satan applies the principle of legal interpretation to a law that does not need it. Adam and Eve live in the Garden under the terms of an outright law, not a contract, and so when Satan draws the ban on the tree out of the realm of "thou shalt not" and into the realm of reciprocal bargains, he can begin unraveling Eve's sense of its binding force. Eve has already been endowed with a form of sacramental property that exists only within the confines of her marriage, but Satan persuades her that she should also have possession of the things around her. Adam knows that he is guilty of a crime, but he uses the language of contract and then the language of equity to try to mitigate his guilt. Legal ideas or principles are being transferred out of their proper sphere and applied in ways that they were never intended to be. These corruptions of law and of forms of judicial thinking indicate that the fall is aided and abetted not so much by the law itself as by misunderstandings and misuses of the law. The presence of the law in *Paradise Lost* works much like the Tree of Knowledge itself: what should have been the "sole pledge of . . . obedience" becomes the instrument of sin (3.95). Like Satan using the Tree of Life as a mere perch, when Adam and Eve regard the law as both an obstacle in the path of their desires and an incitement to sin, they pervert "best things / To worse abuse" (4.203–4).

60. For an example of opposing views of early modern women's ability to control land, see Spring, *Law, Land, and Family*; Erickson, *Women and Property*.

7

The Mortal Sentence

In 2003 the American Civil Liberties Union and the Southern Poverty Law Center filed suit in a US District Court against Roy Moore, then chief justice of the Alabama Supreme Court. Moore had commissioned a massive granite monument of the Ten Commandments and had had it installed in the entrance of the Alabama Judiciary Building, and the plaintiffs claimed that Moore's actions violated the Establishment Clause of the US Constitution, separating church and state. During arguments in the case, Moore reasoned that since God was sovereign in the state of Alabama (the preamble to the Alabama Constitution invokes the "favor and guidance of Almighty God"), God's laws were therefore the basis for all human law, making his actions both moral and legal. The district judge, however, ruled in favor of the plaintiffs, and when Moore appealed the case, a federal circuit court judge backed the lower court's findings: the Ten Commandments had to go. But several days before the late August deadline for the monument's removal, in an action that made national headlines, Moore publicly proclaimed his intention to defy the federal ruling. When the deadline passed with the Ten Commandments still in place under the high rotunda, Moore was suspended from office on charges of an ethics violation and, in the wake of a Court of the Judiciary hearing, expelled from office. Asked why he had risked his career over a sculpture of the Decalogue, Moore replied, "I cannot forsake my conscience. . . . And I will never, never deny the God upon whom our laws are based."[1]

Roy Moore's abbreviated first term as the state's chief justice provides us with a textbook example of how the mingling of law and Law that was so pervasive a feature of Milton's world can sometimes persist into our own, although the general outcry against Moore also shows how distant that world's juridical ideas can seem to us now. It also has something important to tell us about earlier attitudes toward judges. As chief justice, Moore saw himself not only as an agent of the law but also as a custodian of the Law. For him, those roles were inseparable. If the law being administered in the courtroom is a version of God's Law, then the people who implement that law from the bench speak with God's voice, in much the same way that Catholic priests are believed to speak and act with divine authority at the elevation of the Host. Moore's view provides us with a good window on seventeenth-century attitudes toward acts of legal judgment. For example, in a 1697 sermon preached before Assize judges in York, the minister Christopher Wyville claimed that since Christian magistrates would one day judge the angels (a claim based on 1 Corinthians 6:3), God called them to practice this same faculty of righteous judgment in "smaller Judicatures" on Earth. Naturally, the period knew perfectly well that judges could abuse their positions. In *An Appeal to God and the King*, the merchant Benjamin Albyn offers a highly conventional (and sadly plausible) complaint about a biased judge who manipulated the evidence against him, and Milton himself makes a similar point in *Of True Religion*, likening those who try to "bribe" God with Catholic indulgences to those who slip money to a "corrupt judge" to buy a favorable verdict (*CPW* 8:439).[2] And yet, just as writers could criticize the

1. Quoted in "God, Law, and Alabama," 78.
2. Wyville, *Of Christian Magistracy*, 3; Albyn, *Appeal to God*, 18.

injustice of specific laws—as when Milton refers to the nation's laws forbidding divorce as "mans unjust laws" (*CPW* 2:339)—and still regard the law itself as an expression of God's will, they could also accommodate the reality of venal human judges to the theory that judges in the abstract acted at God's direction. Indeed, so strong was the cultural assumption that God's will was at work in the courtroom that seventeenth-century judges and juries "were almost invariably treated as the mere instruments or conduits in the supernatural accomplishment" of justice.[3]

Whereas in previous chapters, I have been primarily concerned with what we might think of as the law's substance, here I turn to the law's procedural side, to the protocols and practices by which legal customs, cases, and statutes were implemented. This chapter argues that in book 10 of *Paradise Lost*, Milton relies on the widespread early modern association between human judgment and divine judgment. He creates continuities between the kind of justice the Son administers and that administered in early modern English courtrooms, and he thereby invites readers to assess the Son's judgment by comparing it to the judicial practices they already know. Adam's arguments to the Son also have a familiar judicial ring. By using both legal terms and allusions to contemporary judicial and law enforcement practices, Milton casts Adam as a defendant trying to mitigate his guilt by any available means, however unsavory. As with so many other appearances of legal justice in *Paradise Lost*, the judgment scene of book 10 points readers in two directions at once. By showing his readers recognizable judicial protocols, Milton suggests that the administration of temporal justice—if done with kindness, intelligence, and impartiality—is an area where the principles of Heaven can be still be seen working actively in a fallen social order. Along this axis, Milton's depictions of the Son and of Adam work to justify the law. In another direction, this scene justifies

3. Rosenberg, "Sanctifying the Robe," 166. For discussion of how the punishment of crime fit into a Protestant providential mind-set, see Walsham, *Providence in Early Modern England.*

God, for while the Son conforms to early modern ideas of the good judge, he also transcends them by administering a perfect form of "justice [and] mercy" (10.78).

The Assizes of Paradise

God says that Adam "soon shall find/Forbearance no acquittance ere day end," and before nightfall in Paradise, the Son will have pronounced "the mortal sentence" on the fallen pair (10.52–53, 48). While this is the most prominent judgment scene in book 10, it is not the first. Near the beginning of the book, Milton shows the angels who had charge of Paradise hurrying toward God:

> They towards the throne supreme
> Accountable made haste to make appear
> With righteous plea, their utmost vigilance,
> And easily approved. (10.28–31)

The angels are "accountable," or liable to answer to a higher authority for their conduct, and so they must make a formal "plea." The outcome of this plea is a quick and easy acquittal, for unlike Adam and Eve, the angels can make the "righteous" excuse of "utmost vigilance." Whereas this first judgment in book 10 occurs before the throne of God, the second one requires that the judge travel out to the edges of his realm. God asks, "But whom shall I send to judge them?" and then answers his own question: "Whom but thee/Vicegerent Son" (10.55–56). If the acquittal of the angels is reminiscent of a trial at Westminster Hall, the second hearing is more akin to the early modern Assizes. In our modern world, legal justice tends to be associated with a courthouse on a busy city street. Judges have paneled courtrooms with private chambers, and those men and women moving through the judicial system come to this central place of justice to hear and be heard. But given the rural and remote nature of most of England, legal justice in the seventeenth century had a different, more peripatetic set of associations. Although sometimes plaintiffs and defendants had to suspend their ordinary lives and make the long, expensive trek to London, in the majority of significant criminal cases and many civil ones, law was administered at the regional Assizes. Judges from the central courts were appointed to travel a long, looping circuit through various towns. They set up temporary courts in provincial buildings or in open spaces and tried those cases deemed too serious for the county Quarter Sessions. Milton was clearly familiar with circuit justice. In *Doctrine and Discipline of Divorce*, he likens the man who condones injustice out of cowardice to "some wretched itinerary Judge" who fears to pronounce an impartial verdict lest those convicted "break his head," an image that glances at the notorious rowdiness of Assize courtrooms (*CPW* 2:323). He provides a more complimentary description in *The History of Britain*, when he says that King Edgar often "rode the Circuit as a Judge Itinerant through all his Provinces, to see justice well administered" (*CPW* 5:322).

Perhaps because of their familiarity and their sheer importance to the regular maintenance of law and order in England, the circuit courts became a common metaphor for God's judgment. This metaphorical relation appears in literally hundreds of devotional works and Assize sermons in the period. For example, in *Christ Inviting Sinners to Come to Him for Rest*, Jeremiah Burroughs likens the man who must "answer to Gods justice upon the breach of it" to the "man that is bound over to the assize and session to answer." Similarly, in a 1617 Waterford Assize sermon, Robert Daborne urged his listeners to be so virtuous and mild "that these Judges which are sent of God, may finde us such in their Circuit, as we would be found at the general Assize by the Judge of Judges Christ Jesus."[4] Milton participates in this same tradition in "On the Morning of Christ's Nativity," for he calls Christ the "dreadful judge" who ventures out into "middle Air" to preside at "the world's last session" (163–64). Sometimes the Christ–Assize judge parallel was drawn out in remarkable detail.

4. Burroughs, *Christ Inviting Sinners*, 232; Daborne, *Sermon Preached*, 5–6. On the ideological importance of Assize sermons, see Brooks, *Law, Politics, and Society*, 211–14.

For example, the nonconformist writer Thomas De Laune, in his *Tropologia, or, A Key to Open Scripture Metaphors*, systematically plots Christ's actions as a judge against those of human judges in the fulfillment of their duty. For example, like a responsible judge, Christ "acts not of himself, but by Commission from the great and mighty Potentate of the whole Universe"; he observes the proper calendar of judgment, for "in like manner" to human courts, there is "a set Time, a certain Day limited, for the Lord Jesus, the great Judg, to keep a general Sessions, and hold a solemn Assize."[5] Just as a good judge should, Christ also opens his "great Law-Books." He even calls for the presentation of evidence, including the testimony of "witnesses [who are] sufficient to prove Matter of Fact, both in Number and Capacity" (i.e., God, conscience, and, depending on the soul in question, the good or evil angels).[6]

In his depiction of the Son in book 10, Milton similarly aligns what the Son does with what circuit judges were expected to do. Before the Son descends to Paradise, God says to him, "To thee I have transferred/All judgment" (10.56–57), and this brief exchange recalls the fact that, before beginning their circuits, judges were summoned before the king or the lord keeper and formally invested with the commission of jail delivery and *oyer et terminer* (literally "to hear and determine"). After the trial, the Son leaves Paradise "with swift ascent" (10.224), a speed that resembles that of the judges who "arrived, presided, and then immediately departed"; the procedure "lent an air of mystery and finality" to the Assize proceedings.[7] And once he returns to God's "blissful bosom," the Son relates what has happened ("what had passed with man/[He] Recounted") (10.225, 227–28), a detail reminiscent of the postcircuit reports that each judge made to the king or lord keeper. The king was often said to "send down" his judges to administer the law, a phrase that captures in spatial

5. De Laune, *Tropologia*, 282.
6. Ibid., 283.
7. Herrup, *Common Peace*, 51.

terms the royalist idea that the law derived from the monarch.[8] Milton both alludes to this idiom and trumps it. God literally sends down a perfect judge, and so all agents of human justice should regard Heaven, not the monarch or the central state, as the ultimate source of their professional authority. While contemporary judicial practices provide Milton with a descriptive framework for his account of the Son's judgment, this does not mean that England's circuit judges serve as a model for the Son of God's actions. To capture early modern attitudes, we need to come at the justice-Justice likeness from the other direction: human judicial practices—even down to the details of how circuit court judges were commissioned—could be studied for evidence of God's will precisely because God was, as Milton wrote in "Psalm 7," the ultimate "just judge" and thus the source of all juridical norms (43). The general cultural assumption that human judgment should mirror divine judgment also allows Milton to highlight those points where human justice goes astray. For instance, England's judges were escorted in and out of each town on their circuit by elaborate ceremonial processions, and circuit courtrooms were so crowded and chaotic that one eighteenth-century observer likened them to the "noise of a wild elephant [crashing] through a sugar plantation."[9] Milton seems to rebuke precisely such forms of judicial fanfare when the Son, before descending to Earth, says flatly that he "attendance none shall need, nor train" (10.80).

When God says that the Son will act both as "man's friend" and "judge" (10.60, 62), Milton matches contemporary ideas about how England's judges were supposed to act toward defendants.

8. For an example of this idiom, see Smith, *De republica anglorum*, 95.

9. One French visitor described an Assize processional pageant where there were "bells ringing and trumpets playing" and where the judge was "preceded by the sheriff's men, to the number of twelve or twenty, in full dress, armed with javelins." Beattie, *Crime and the Courts*, 317. For the "wild elephant" quote, see Cockburn, *History of English Assizes*, 122.

To appreciate the judge-friend link, we have to shed our modern idea of what a judge does in the courtroom. In the modern trial, proceedings are dominated by lawyers, and so the judge's role is to act as the impartial supervisor and umpire. In the early modern legal system, however, the typical criminal trial was conducted without the use of counsel. If a lawyer was present, he was there on behalf of the plaintiff (defense counsel did not become a regular part of criminal trials until the eighteenth century).[10] Sir Thomas Smith, in his description of the early modern legal system, puts the matter succinctly: in criminal cases, "procurer or advocate he [the accused] gets none."[11] The absence of lawyers for the defense meant that the role of assisting the accused fell to the judge, who was "thought to be counsel for the prisoner as well as for the king."[12] While there were certainly instances of sarcasm and bullying from the bench, English judges were generally distinguished by their humanity. The magistrate Sir Thomas de Veil wrote that English judges were characterized by the "utmost mildness and decency" and that they displayed "that tenderness which humanity requires for those that, however bad they may be, are still our fellow creatures."[13] While high-profile trials had shown that this stereotype did not always hold true at Westminster, the regional circuit courts were seen as enacting a gentler brand of justice.[14] Indeed, so customary was the paternal

10. Beattie, *Crime and the Courts*, 343. Trials began with the prosecutor (usually the plaintiff) telling his version of events to the jury. Then witnesses for the Crown and any public officials such as constables spoke, and finally the accused could reply to the evidence presented. The role played by lawyers in modern trials—setting the pace, managing the order of witnesses, and introducing evidence—was played by the early modern judge.

11. Smith contrasts this absence of lawyers in criminal trials with that in the case of "civill and pecuniare matters . . . be it for land, rent, right, or possession," where the need for lawyers "is never denied." Civil courtrooms were noteworthy for the continual "declaration and altercation of the advocates." Smith, *De republica anglorum*, 67, 72.

12. Beattie, *Crime and the Courts*, 345.

13. Cited in Beattie, *Crime and the Courts*, 345.

14. Cockburn, *Assizes*, 125.

kindness of the Assize bench that its absence—that is, a judge's sharpness toward an offender—could serve as sufficient grounds for a pardon.[15] Milton's Son displays all the tender humanity of the ideal judge. He is "gracious" and speaks to the accused "without revile" even though they have become his "enemies" (10.118, 219). This same graciousness continues after he has passed sentence, for, "pitying how they stood/Before him naked to the air," the Son provides them with clothing (10.211–12). Measured against modern ideas, the Son seems to have stepped well outside of his capacity as judge at this point. Measured against early modern ideas, however, he is acting exactly as a good judge ought to. A judge at Southwark Assizes in March 1605 loaned a convicted man his spectacles so that he could read the neck verse, and one bitter observer complained in a letter to Burghley that justice in England was marred by the fact that judges showed too much "pity and mercy, or favouring life (as they miscall it)" to those who had been convicted.[16]

The figure of the circuit judge may have appealed to Milton because of the decentralized nature of Assize justice. While all judges were appointed by the king and thus in theory—and sometimes in practice—spoke in the interests of monarchical power, English judges were not simply royal yes-men, and the Stuart bench showed striking instances of judicial independence.[17] Moreover, the close association between the workings of justice and the will of God made it easy for the Assizes, like the law as a whole, to seem operationally independent from the nation's center. As Phillippe Rosenberg points out, in the writings of the early modern period, "justice, whether it was imagined to be tran-

15. Hay, "Property, Authority," 32.

16. Cockburn, *History of English Assizes*, 125–26.

17. For example, some judges continued using writs of prohibition to move cases out of the royal prerogative courts into the common law courts (an action that construed the common law as the higher jurisdiction), and other judges refused to endorse the forced loan even when Charles I threatened to restock the bench with men willing to interpret the law as the king wished. Sharpe, *Personal Rule of Charles I*, 661–64.

scendent or immanent, was portrayed as a process independent, in important respects, from the agency of . . . the state." Sir Francis Bacon demonstrates—although probably unwittingly—how readily the law could seem detached from the king. In a 1617 speech to circuit judges, Bacon likened them to orbiting planets, a clearly centralizing metaphor that figures James I as the sun. But Bacon also called their circuits "rivers in Paradise that go to water the whole kingdom."[18] When he says that these rivers "go," he implies that justice flows from some main (royal) reservoir into smaller waterways and rivulets and that justice is thereby infused outward from the center into the farthest corners of the land. Bacon would have carried his point better if his metaphor had been the human heart, for rivers work in precisely the opposite way. Water flows down from small local sources into larger central ones, and so Bacon's river analogy—which is meant to underscore the king's role as the fount of justice—ends up calling attention to the idea that the nation's margins, its local Quarter Sessions and manorial courts, could be the true wellsprings of law and order. Bacon's uneasy idea of justice as rivers (which way do they flow?) epitomizes the debate over the law in the early modern period. Was it an extension and derivative of the king, an idea epitomized in the aphorism *rex lex*, "the king is law"? Or was it the will of the people, as epitomized in Samuel Rutherford's famous Civil War pamphlet *Lex Rex*, "the law is king"?

Unlike Bacon, Milton saw local communities as the ultimate source of the nation's justice, for he supports a decentralized judiciary in five of the six political pamphlets he wrote on the eve of the Restoration. In works like *A Readie and Easie Way*, *A Letter to a Friend*, and *Proposalls of Certaine Expedients*, he argues for the establishment of permanent local courts of justice presided over by locally elected judges, and his position throughout is that

18. Rosenberg, "Sanctifying the Robe," 166; Bacon, *Letters and the Life*, 6:303. On Bacon's speech in the context of the Stuart undermining of judicial independence, see Cockburn, *History of English Assizes*, 230.

justice can be best achieved not in London's main courts but rather in England's smaller towns. We see a hint of this stance in the earlier *History of Britain*, when Milton praises "Itinerant" King Edgar for doing justice in "all his Provinces." He pushes the idea even further in the first edition of *Proposalls of Certain Expedients*. Here he claims that an "elected judicature" is urgently needed because communities should "have justice in thir own hands" (*CPW* 7:338). Similar arguments appear in *A Readie and Easie Way*. In the first edition, Milton hopes that "civill Justice may be in the City or chief towne of every county without appeal, Judges and all such officers by themselves chosen," and he goes as far as to say that "nothing can be more essential to the freedom of a people" than to have "the administration of justice . . . in thir own election and within thir own bounds" (*CPW* 7:383, 384). In the second edition, he argues for a judicial system in which "law [is] executed fully and finally in [the people's] own counties and precincts, long wishd and spoken of, but never yet obtaind" (*CPW* 7:459).[19] His reasoning reminds us that in the highly participatory early modern English system, legal justice was not simply what the state did. It was also what communities did. For Milton, the ongoing work of remaking the nation in God's image required that the administration of law and order be fully diffused throughout the land. This same vision informs the judgment scene of *Paradise Lost*. Genesis 3:8 says that God comes "walking in the garden in the cool of the day" to judge Adam and Eve, and Milton elaborates this image of the heavenly judge coming down to Earth to show that God himself practices a form of attentive local justice. Whereas the angels are summoned before the awesome judgment seat of God, Adam and Eve experience a justice that comes to them. Milton not only points to the Son's inimitable perfections as a judge; he also tacitly reminds readers of the need to bring both law and mercy directly into the communities.

19. For a fuller discussion of Milton's recommendations for judicial reform in these works, see Chapman, "Milton and Legal Reform."

Arraignment and Plea

Although he strips away all the ritualistic elements characteristic of the early modern courtroom (as when the judge donned a black cap before passing a capital sentence), Milton leaves the basic procedures intact, and so we can see in the Son's judgment of Adam and Eve the same general structure of English criminal trials.[20] He thereby echoes the contemporary idea that even the nuts-and-bolts procedures of the early modern courtroom were to some degree modeled on the will of God. In a 1614 Assize sermon, the minister William Est explains the parallels between the "order to be observed in judgement" and God's own model. For example, instructing judges and juries in the need to listen carefully to the testimony of the accused before arriving at a verdict, Est cites God's practice in Genesis: "For the first, that inquirie must goe before judgement; God himself hath put it out of all question, in conventing *Adam* to knowe what he had done, before he pronounced sentence upon him. Gods eyes cannot be blinded, for he beholdeth all things, yet herein he dealeth with man, as if he himselfe were not God; to teach the Gods on earth, which see but in part, how they should proceed in judgement."[21] Since an omniscient God clearly did not need to ask Adam, "Hast thou eaten of the tree, whereof I commanded thee that thou shouldest not eat?" (Gen. 3:11), he does so purely to show human judges—whom Est calls "Gods on earth"—how they should hold a courtroom inquiry. Similarly, Est says that God conducts a careful examination of the physical evidence as part of his due process: "This God taught in comming downe to see *Gomorah* before he destroyed it."[22] By implication, judges and juries that pore over the evidence are acting just like their Creator.

20. Milton is offering a powerful contrast to the way in which early modern legal proceedings had become forms of political theater. On this phenomenon, see Sauer, *"Paper Contestations" and Textual Communities*.

21. Est, *Judges and Juries Instruction*, 16.

22. Ibid., 18.

The stages of the Son's judgment in book 10 also mirror those in an early modern criminal trial. In *De republica anglorum*, Smith explains that after the prisoners were led into the courtroom, the hearing began with a formal act of identification: "Then the prisoners are called for by name, and bidden to aunswere to their names." Early modern jurists saw this important opening stage of the trial—known as the citation—as authorized by Genesis, for God issued a summons to Adam and Eve before judging them.[23] Milton provides his own version of the judicial citation when the Son calls the first defendant by name: "Approaching, thus to Adam [he] called aloud./'Where art thou Adam[?]'" (10.102–3). Once the names of the accused had been read aloud and each man or woman had responded, the first prisoner to be indicted was instructed to step forward and stand at the bar. As Smith describes it, the court clerk instructs the prisoner, "Come to the barre, hold up thy hand."[24] Milton shows a similar summoning forth of Adam and Eve to face their judge and hear the charges against them. The Son says "Come forth," and they step to the bar: "He came, and with him Eve, more loath, though first/To offend" (10.108–10). Milton emphasizes that Adam and Eve's guilt is legible on their faces. They are

> discount'nanced both, and discomposed;
> Love was not in their looks, either to God
> Or to each other, but apparent guilt,
> And shame, and perturbation, and despair,
> Anger, and obstinacy, and hate, and guile. (10.110–14)

Milton echoes the early modern belief that guilt was legible from the outside. This assumption had a direct impact on courtroom practice, for the way in which people conducted themselves before judges and juries was often as important as the objective evidence. "Innocent people were supposed to submit to legal questioning without either fear or discomfort," and actions such as

23. Helmholz, *Canon Law and Ecclesiastical Jurisdiction*, 318.
24. Smith, *De republica anglorum*, 97.

blushing, looking away, and hesitancy in answering were all seen as signs of culpability.[25] Adam and Eve look precisely like guilty criminals at the bar were supposed to look.

However open to criticism Adam and Eve are at this point in *Paradise Lost*, they are at least willing to stand before their judge and undergo the process of sentencing. Satan, in contrast, has fled the scene. Genesis 3 does not specify whether the serpent remains at the scene of judgment, but Milton leaves no doubt about the matter. In book 9 Satan hides at the moment Eve reaches for the fruit ("Back to the thicket slunk/The guilty serpent" [9.784–85]), and then he runs away at the sight of the Son descending:

> But when he saw descend
> The Son of God to judge them, terrified
> He fled, not hoping to escape, but shun
> The present, fearing guilty what his wrath
> Might suddenly inflict. (10.337–41)

Satan's absence, however, does not prevent the Son from passing judgment on him. Speaking to God before his descent to Paradise, the Son says he will confront only two offenders, Adam and Eve. The third offender, Satan, "best absent is condemned,/ Convict by flight, and rebel to all law" (10.82–3). Milton has repeatedly emphasized Satan's impulse to run from justice. Satan has earlier been called the "false fugitive" and the "sole fugitive" (2.700, 4.923), and at the end of book 4, when he sees the scales of justice hanging in the sky, he "fled/Murmuring" (4.1014–15). The fact that the Son judges Satan even in his absence echoes early modern procedures against those who fled from the law. Smith explains that if a man named in a criminal trial refused to appear in court, "process is made out against him, to render himself prisoner, or else hee shalbe outlawed." The missing person was called "three times in diverse countie daies to render himself to the lawe," and on the fourth day, he was declared an outlaw,

25. Herrup, *Common Peace*, 198.

convicted in absentia, and his goods appropriated.[26] The outlaw could be hanged if the outlawry was proved true, regardless of the original offense, and he could be legally killed by anyone if he resisted arrest. When the Son says that Satan "best absent is condemned," he echoes the early modern assumption that those who refused to present themselves before the law were "convict by flight," and when he calls Satan a "rebel to all law," the Son effectively pronounces the verdict of outlawry upon Satan.

The next stage of the trial was the arraignment or reading of charges, followed immediately by the request for a plea. Smith gives an example of a court clerk reading an indictment for horse stealing to a prisoner known as A.B: "*A.B.* . . . of such a towne, in such a countie, art endicted, that such a day, in such a place, thou hast stolen with force and armes an horse, which was such ones, of such a colour, to such a valor [value], and carried him away feloniouslie, and contrarie to the peace of our soveraigne Ladie the Queene. What sayest thou to it, art thou guiltie or not guiltie?"[27] In Milton's version, the arraignment is characteristically brief and devoid of formality. The Son asks. "Hast thou eaten of the tree/Whereof I gave thee charge thou shouldst not eat?" (10.122–23). The *allocutus* or allocution (from the Latin *eloqui*, to speak out) was the portion of the trial where the accused entered a plea and made any formal statements about why the court should not bring an adverse charge, and Milton may have this etymology in mind when he says that at the moment of entering her plea, Eve is not "loquacious" before her judge (10.161).

Unlike Eve, Adam does not enter a straightforward guilty plea; instead, he cavils about the dilemma he faces:

> To whom thus Adam sore beset replied.
> "O Heav'n! In evil strait this day I stand
> Before my Judge, either to undergo

26. Smith, *De republica anglorum*, 87.
27. Ibid., 97.

> Myself the total crime, or to accuse
> My other self, the partner of my life." (10.124–28)

At this moment, Milton alludes to one of the most dramatic moments in any early modern courtroom: when the prisoner refused to plead at all, a refusal that was known as standing mute. As Sir Matthew Hale notes in his *Pleas of the Crown*, standing mute included more than mere silence and could apply when the accused pleads, "but not effectually; as when he answers not directly to the Fact."[28] Although the period's most famous example of standing mute was Charles I, who had refused to plead on the grounds that Parliament had no jurisdiction over him, the majority of those who stood mute in the early modern courts did so to protect their families. Since a capital conviction meant that the felon's chattels were forfeit to the Crown and his real possessions to his landlord, the only way for a man to prevent his family from being disinherited was to refuse to plead at all. Doing so brought dreadful penalties. Because the early modern courts did not presume either innocence or guilt, a refusal to plead was a threat to the whole system, and those who stood mute suffered what was called the *peine forte et dure*. The accused was chained to the floor and his chest increasingly piled with weight until he either entered a plea or his rib cage collapsed. Milton makes this fate the subject of a grim witticism in his youthful poem "Another on the Same," about the death of Hobson, the Cambridge carrier, for he likens Hobson to the man "pressed to death" who "cried 'More weight'" (26). Whereas men standing mute sometimes begged for more weight to hasten death, Hobson wants more weight because carrying things was his employment and "lack of load," or idleness, paradoxically "made his life burdensome" (24).

When Adam in book 10 fears lest "both sin and punishment,/ However insupportable" should be "devolved" upon him, Milton glances at the penalties of standing mute (10.133–35). The image

28. Hale, *Pleas of the Crown*, 185.

here is of a heavy burden being piled atop him, one that he would find "insupportable." In its general sense, to "devolve" meant "to roll down; to cause to descend with rolling motion," and so it, too, summons up the image of something heavy being heaved or rolled onto a victim.[29] But having alluded to the possibility of standing mute, Adam chooses to plead. In part, he recognizes the futility of standing mute before an omniscient judge: "Though should I hold my peace, yet thou/Wouldst easily detect what I conceal" (10.135–36). Mainly, however, he refuses to "undergo/[Himself] the total crime" (10.126–27). Strictly speaking, one could commit a crime but not undergo it, and since available early modern meanings of "undergo" include "to go or pass under" and "to bear, sustain (a burden, etc.)," Milton again seems to have one eye on the world of legal pleadings.[30] Unlike those men who chose to have their bodies broken in order to protect their loved ones, Adam will not "undergo" the double burden of "sin and punishment" in order to protect Eve (10.133). He thereby undoes the loyalty he earlier boasted of when he told Eve that while he "might have lived and joyed immortal bliss," he instead "willingly chose rather death with [her]" (9.1166–67).

The Informant

While readers have traditionally found little to admire in Adam's conduct before his judge in book 10, a consideration of early modern legal norms makes his actions seem even worse. Adam's decision to point his finger at his coconspirator, Eve, echoes new developments in the early modern law. Before the early modern period, those arraigned for capital crimes received no benefits for revealing their accomplices. In a series of attempts to control the nation's growing crime problem, seventeenth-century officials began experimenting with reduced penalties for offenders willing to name their collaborators. At first, the arrangement was merely

29. "Devolve," v., def. 1a, *OED Online*.
30. "Undergo," v., defs. 3a, 5b, *OED Online*.

tacit: while the accomplice was not guaranteed a pardon, there was an "implied confidence" that the person would have "an equitable title to a recommendation for the king's mercy."[31] By the middle of the seventeenth century, this informal practice had been codified into law. For example, *A Proclamation for Discovery of Robberies and Burglaries, and for a Reward to the Discoverers* provides both a pardon and a ten-pound reward to the felon willing to "discover his or their fellow-Offenders, or any of them, so as to cause them to be apprehendeth."[32] This context provides us with a new angle on Adam's actions. Implicitly, he hopes that if he construes Eve as the more serious offender, he will get off with some form of reduced penalty. He may even imagine that Eve alone could receive a capital sentence, leaving him free to resume his life in Paradise, a hypothetical outcome that ironically revisits Eve's earlier fear that if she alone sins, Adam might get "another Eve" (9.828).

Milton also shows Adam doing the very thing that he earlier reproached Eve for: turning accuser. When Eve points out Adam's complicity in the fall at the end of book 9, Adam lashes out at her:

> And perhaps
> I also erred in overmuch admiring
> What seemed in thee so perfect, that I thought
> No evil durst attempt thee, but I rue
> That error now, which is become my crime,
> And thou th' accuser. (9.1177–82)

Adam is trying to think his way out of full criminal culpability. He says that by "overmuch admiring" Eve, he has committed an "error," and he adds that this error "is become my crime." The passive voice construction "is become" suggests that the error has transformed into a crime more or less without his knowledge, in much the same way that an error of judgment such as following

31. Baker, "Criminal Courts and Procedure," 40.
32. Charles II, *Proclamation for Discovery*.

a tip from a stock broker could inveigle one unwittingly in the crime of insider trading. In short, he simply made a mistake; he never had any criminal intent. Adam also accuses Eve of accusing him. Like Satan who is "the Tempter ere th' Accuser of mankind," Eve has first tempted Adam and then accused him (4.10). But Milton tacitly draws our attention to the fact that an accusation could take two different forms: caustic words bandied in private between aggrieved parties versus formal charges brought before a judge or magistrate. In book 9 Eve levels the former kind of accusation when she blames Adam for her sin. In book 10 Adam brings the latter, accusing Eve before the Son of God.

Speaking to the Son, Adam refers to Eve as her "whose failing, while her faith to me remains,/I should conceal, and not expose to blame/By my complaint" (10.129–31). His use of the word "complaint" suggests that he is working to reduce his own exposure before the law. In its legal sense, a complaint was "a statement of injury or grievance laid before a court or judicial authority (esp. and properly a Court of Equity) for purposes of prosecution or of redress; a formal accusation or charge."[33] The *OED*'s parenthetical reference, "esp. and properly a Court of Equity," illustrates an important fact about the complaint: it was a technical term associated with civil actions. As I noted in the previous chapter, equity courts did not generally hear criminal matters, so by suggesting that he is filing the metaphorical version of a Chancery complaint against Eve, Adam reduces the severity of the offense. The idea of Adam's presenting a complaint also subtly reframes the Son's role, for Adam implies that the Son has come down to Earth not to enforce the law but rather to adjudicate between private parties to a civil dispute.

Adam's adversarial stance toward his codefendant also leads him to an adversarial stance toward his judge. Having piously considered the possibility of not lodging a complaint against his wife, Adam says that were he to hold his peace, the Son "wouldst

33. "Complaint," n., def. 4b, *OED Online*.

easily detect what I conceal" (10.135–36). His use of the verb "detect" contains a veiled critique. The modern sense of detecting as examining clues was not available in Milton's day. Instead "to detect" carried the meaning of uncovering or exposing something hidden, and it was used in a judicial sense to mean "to inform against." For example, early modern churchwardens were expected to submit "bills of detection" in which they identified the moral lapses of parishioners, and the author of *Heresiography* tells of a villainous Anabaptist who, having killed his wife, "also cut a young wenches throat lest shee should detect him."[34] If I walk into a room today and say, "I detect someone," I mean that I can tell by a series of clues—a door ajar, a faint odor on the air, the sound of a footfall—that someone is nearby. If I walked a room in the seventeenth century and said "I detect someone," I would mean that I know that someone is guilty and that I am planning to reveal or have already revealed her or his crime to the authorities. When he says that the Son will "detect" him, Adam does not mean just that the Son knows what he has done. He also means that the Son knows and will inform on him. Even if Adam remains silent and protects Eve, the Son will bear tales to the divine lawgiver. Therefore, since the Son is going to inform on him no matter what he does, Adam might as well inform on Eve, a line of reasoning that lays the primary fault for exposing Eve at the Son's feet.

In attempting to make what looks like a plea bargain with the Son, Adam construes Eve as an independent legal entity more deserving of punishment than himself. We first see this idea arising in him when he hopes that punishment will not be "devolved" solely onto him. In its most common legal sense, "devolve" meant "to cause to pass down by inheritance or legal succession" and especially "to cause to pass (*to* or *into* the hands of another); especially

34. Helmholz, *Roman Canon Law*, 106; Pagitt, *Heresiography*, 9; "detect," v., defs. 2a, 2b, *OED Online*.

through the failure or forfeiture of the previous holders."[35] When Adam fears lest sin and punishment should "devolv[e]" onto him, he casts Eve as the one who has failed and himself as the miserable recipient of her forfeiture, like a son who must shoulder the noxious burden of a father's debts. In construing Eve as the rightful owner of sin and punishment and himself as the unfortunate successor owner, Adam tries to undo the legal subjection of Eve that he himself created in book 9. One of the first symptoms of sin is that Adam claims a greater dominance over Eve and thereby makes her into the prototype of the feme covert. Here, however, Adam tries to reverse that action, to put Eve back on the legal radar, so to speak, in order to mitigate his own liability. When Adam wonders whether he should "accuse/ . . . the partner of my life," he seems to be doing much the same thing (10.127–28). Since "partner" is cognate with "parcener," a common legal term for a co-owner or coheir (see chapter 3), by calling Eve his "partner," Adam does more than just point to the connection between them. He also subtly reminds the Son of Eve's status as an independent, coordinate legal agent. In his implied logic, if she shares in ownership, then by rights she should share in the blame and punishment.

Adam's argument contravenes a fundamental assumption of the English common law. Early modern legal proceedings operated on the principle that "a married woman could not be held responsible for illegal acts done in the company of her husband (unless he could be shown to be blameless)."[36] Since women were under the legal umbrella of the husband, the common law assumed that if a wife cooperated with her husband in a crime, then she must have been operating under his coercion or at his direction. The legal realities are laid out clearly in Thomas Edgar's *The Lawes Resolutions of Womens Rights*: "If a man and his wife commit felonie jointly, it seemeth the wife is no felon, but it

35. "Devolve," v., defs. 3a, 3b, *OED Online*.

36. Beattie, *Crime and the Courts*, 238.

shall be wholly judged the Husbands fact." Adam tries to point out that Eve sinned first, but even this defense would not excuse him under the common law. Edgar explains that if a wife commits a felony, the husband who wishes to escape guilt "so soone as hee perceive it" must "waive and forsake [his wife's] company, and his owne house."[37] Far from departing from Eve when he realizes she has committed a crime, Adam willingly participates with her in a reiteration of the act. When faced with a husband and wife who had collaborated in a crime, the courts typically convicted both of them and then either discharged or pardoned the wife on the grounds that she acted at her husband's direction and was fulfilling her role as an obedient wife, one of the few ways in which the gender inequities of the early modern legal system actually worked in a woman's favor. Adam seems to be trying to prevent just this outcome by making a case for his own blamelessness. When he says that he "could suspect no ill" from Eve, he is trying to make it clear that his wife is the guilty party and that, like those angels who are exonerated from blame earlier because they have exercised "utmost vigilance," he too should be "easily approved" (10.140). Ironically, Adam makes a version of the same legal argument that early modern wives did: they were not responsible under the law because they had acted at the direction of their husbands. In effect, he construes himself as an "homme covert."

Ultimately, underneath the veneer of Edenic strangeness, much about the judgment scene of book 10 may have seemed quite ordinary to those early modern readers who had even a passing experience with the contemporary judicial system. In contrast, many of God's judgments in the Bible are puzzling or even confounding. When God sentences Moses to die in exile for what looks like the petty offense of striking a rock or when he proves Job's innocence through tremendous suffering, readers have often wondered how and why these actions are just. The

37. Edgar, *Lawes Resolutions*, 206.

ambiguous ending of *Samson Agonistes*, in which Samson brings a temple down around the heads of ostensibly innocent civilians, suggests that Milton well understood the difficulty of distinguishing between biblical justice and biblical injustice. Sometimes, too, the biblical God practices a form of due process that is simply unavailable to human beings. When the psalmist asks, "Search me, O God, and know my heart: try me, and know my thoughts" (Ps. 139:23), he is asking for the kind of trial that only God can provide. From at least the fifteenth century onward, jurists were concerned with the role of intent or motive (or mens rea, the guilty mind) as a crucial component in crimes, and early modern changes in the role of the judge and jury and the growing emphasis on witness testimony had made evidence of intention an increasingly important judicial criterion. However, jurists were also uneasily aware that in trying to gauge intent, they were attempting to do what human beings simply could not: know the truth of the human heart. Milton's response in book 10 of *Paradise Lost* to the inscrutability and inimitability of so many of God's judgments is to make at least this one primal scene of judgment as legible and as familiar as possible. Adam and Eve act like seventeenth-century defendants. The Son acts like the best kind of seventeenth-century judge. The upshot is that the Son's justice as depicted in book 10 is one that even a fallen human society could try to replicate. After Adam and Eve's "trial," the Son clothes Adam and Eve with the skins of animals, and by doing so, he provides them with an example of how they might array themselves. Similarly, when he comes down in person to question the accused, when he asks them how they plead, and above all when he passes a verdict that mingles justice and mercy, Milton's Son gives human beings an example of how they can do justice among themselves.

Judges of Fact

While most critics who have discussed empirical forms of knowledge in *Paradise Lost* have situated empiricism within a context of science and scientific inquiry, the increasingly legal language of books 9 and 10 reminds us that empiricism is equally constitutive of judicial inquiry.[38] The majority of what we might think of as the poem's "scientific moments" (Eve's question about the stars, Satan's space exploration, Raphael's account of the cosmic food chain, his description of the creation of the animals, etc.) appear in the prelapsarian books, but once the fall occurs, the poem's empirical language tends to be more reminiscent of the courtroom. For instance, the word "evidence" and its cognate "evident" appear in the poem only in sinful contexts. Eve says that Adam's decision to sin with her provides "illustrious evidence" of his superiority and his love, and Adam worries that the "signs" of their fallenness are "evident" in their faces (9.962, 1077). Encountering Satan on the bridge across Chaos, Sin says that his "looks" give "evidence" of his success (10.360–61). Other legal, empirical words crop up more frequently in the wake of sin, as when Eve rejoices that Adam's decision to sin with her gives "good proof" of their marital union, when Adam finally consents to Eve's request to work alone because "he is desirous to make trial of her strength," and when he says that he could not "suspect" Eve (10.967, 9.arg., 10.140). The rise of legal terms such as "evidence" and "proof" reminds us that the epistemological changes wrought by the fall also have profound judicial consequences. Unlike God, who knows the human heart, human beings can only consider the evidence, and after the fall, this evidence-driven thinking—whether in a courtroom or in a laboratory—becomes the primary means of assessing what is really happening in the world. It is no coincidence that words like "proof" and "evidence" are also part of the rhetorical tradition. While rhetoric, like its subset law, is not an intrinsically fallen endeavor (Adam's book 4 marriage proposal and his book 8 colloquy with the Son point to the prelapsarian role of rhetoric),

38. For example, Harinder Singh Marjara discusses the empirical method solely in the context of scientists like Galileo and Copernicus. Marjara, *Contemplation of Created Things*, 54–68.

both rhetoric and law are applied in new ways after the fall. Adam and Eve use evidentiary reasoning and forensic forms of argument to persuade themselves, each other, and God of their mitigated guilt.

Milton's legal language also issues a specific kind of invitation to readers to participate in the juridical work of the poem. We can see the nature of this invitation best by considering the way Adam and Eve both use the word "fact," which appears in the poem only after the fall. Before Adam eats, Eve tells him that she would "rather die/Deserted, than oblige thee with a fact/ Pernicious to thy peace" (9.979–81). In contrast to the dominant modern sense of "fact" as that which is ontologically true, the *OED* notes that "the commonest sense" of the word in the sixteenth and seventeenth centuries remained "an evil deed, a crime."[39] Milton, in his *History of Britain*, uses "fact" in precisely this way: the murder of Oswin is a "detestable" "fact"; Athelstan's reported fratricide is "so foul a fact"; a cup-bearer who brings a false charge of treason is an "adviser of that fact"; a man who finds a body pierced by an arrow is said to have been "coming by upon the fact"; and two men commit a "fact" when they kill King Edward by "thrusting a sharp Iron into his hinder parts" (*CPW* 5.209, 309, 314, 326, 358). When Eve claims that she is not "oblig[ing]" Adam with a "fact," she is saying that the action of eating does not rise to the level of a criminal offense. As Barbara Shapiro argues in her *Culture of Fact*, during the early modern period, the concept of fact was first developed and refined in legal contexts, and then it was picked up by discourses like natural philosophy to express those things that seemed beyond dispute.[40] The widespread use of "fact" in association with courtroom proceedings had also given it another shade of meaning, for "fact" was often used to denote "an unproved assertion," that which had been alleged but not supported with evidence.[41] In this sec-

39. "Fact," n., def. 2, *OED Online*.
40. Shapiro, *Culture of Fact*.
41. "Fact," n., def. 9, *OED Online*.

ond sense, Eve suggests to Adam that even if the action of eating is a criminal "fact," they might escape conviction owing to lack of proof. Eve earlier thinks along precisely these lines when, worried that God might have seen her sin, she reassures herself,

> I perhaps am secret; Heav'n is high,
> High and remote to see from thence distinct
> Each thing on Earth. (9.811–13)

Sin's first effect is to push Eve into an adversarial relationship to the law, in which she immediately thinks about the presence of incriminating witnesses and evidence.

Adam picks up Eve's language of fact, although he uses it in a subtly different way and with a different end in view. Having eaten, he says to Eve,

> Perhaps the fact
> Is not so heinous now, foretasted fruit,
> Profaned first by the serpent, by him first
> Made common and unhallowed ere our taste. (9.928–31)

Unlike Eve, who denies either that there has been a criminal fact or that it can be proven, Adam admits the fact's existence. His strategy is to mitigate its seriousness by imagining it as "not so heinous." As in his soliloquy when he wants a "more equal" judgment, Adam's characteristic habit is simultaneously to half-admit wrongdoing and to look for a means to reduce the severity of the crime and thus the rigor of penalty. In this passage, Adam tries to exculpate himself in a theological sense by arguing that once the fruit has been touched, it loses its sacrosanct quality, as if the fruit discharges a static shock into the first one who touches it. Implicit in the theological argument is a judicial one. Significantly, Milton was one of only two commentators on Genesis who saw the fall as including the crime of theft, a point he makes clear when he refers to Adam and Eve's "stol'n fruit" (11.125).[42] Admitting that he has committed a "fact," Adam seems to be thinking about how

42. Almond, *Adam and Eve*, 194.

guilt should be apportioned between the principal and the accessory. His implicit logic is that he was not a principal in this case since he received the stolen goods from Eve, who received them from the serpent. Considering how different circumstances alter the penalties for theft, Sir Matthew Hale writes in his *Pleas of the Crown* that "a receipt of stolen Goods makes not Accessary." But Adam's legal hairsplitting runs into an obstacle, for Hale adds in a crucial disclaimer that the receiver of stolen goods is innocent only so long as he refuses to "receive [the] Thief." Since Adam clearly receives Eve, and since Eve has listened to and approved the serpent, neither one of them can dodge the full brunt of guilt. Readers are invited to watch both Adam and Eve speciously considering the nature of their "fact" and to make their own judicial assessments about the crime and its resulting punishment. Picciotto argues that "as readers we have been both the objects and co-curators of Adam's labor of paradisal construction, a labor that begins with diagnostic self-scrutiny." She focuses on Adam and Eve's labors to tame the garden, stating that Milton "invites us to identify the vegetation's recalcitrance with our own resistance to taking these steps" to reform a fallen world along Edenic lines.[43] Picciotto's point can be extended to the judicial labor of reading *Paradise Lost*, for by asking readers to serve as judges of Adam and Eve, Milton implicitly also asks them to apply these same legal and epistemological tools to their own world.

This invitation to readers to participate in the juridical work of the poem acquires new urgency when we consider early modern changes associated with words like "fact" and "evidence." Unlike the Romano-canon legal system, which put all judicial determinations in the hands of trained jurists, the English common law located laypeople at the center of the judicial process. By the early modern period, the work of trying a case and rendering a verdict had been divided into "matters of law," which were in the hands of judges and lawyers, and "matters of fact," which were in the hands of lay jurors. As a result of this division

43. Hale, *Pleas of the Crown*, 180; Picciotto, *Labors of Innocence*, 490.

of labor, "experience with 'fact' and fact determination became familiar to that quite substantial group of ordinary individuals eligible to serve on juries."[44] Like "fact," "evidence" was also a newly important word, for rules of evidence were being hammered out in front of seventeenth-century juries. The feature of the modern courtroom that moderns probably take most for granted—that a trial should center on the impartial, systematic production and evaluation of evidence—was generally speaking an invention of the sixteenth and seventeenth centuries, and by Milton's day the presentation of evidence had newly become the axis around which courtroom proceedings revolved. This judicial change, in turn, had generated questions about what actually counted as evidence: Was the testimony of a child reliable? What could be defined as circumstantial evidence? When should evidence provided by paid informers be trusted? In response, the common law courts rapidly developed rules of evidence, rules that still form the basis of Anglo-American practice.

Changes in contemporary writings about law and legal offenses suggest that this interest in weighing facts and evidence had spilled over into English culture at large, with striking results. While the spike in the numbers of seventeenth-century crime pamphlets bespeaks a general national obsession with criminal wrongdoing, the way many of these pamphlets present their material suggests a new, more active engagement among readers. John Quick's *Hell Open'd, or, The Infernal Sin of Murther Punished* epitomizes this change. Quick tells the story of Anne Evans, executed in 1676 for poisoning a family in Plymouth. Instead of simply providing a narrative of Evans's crime and death, Quick also supplies verbatim copies of the depositions taken from the doctor, the coroner, the apothecary, and various neighbors, as well as statements taken from Evans herself and her alleged accomplice, Nurse Cary. Quick gives readers not just his story of Evans's crime but also a reasonable approximation of the actual evidence that was presented to the jury in the Evans trial.

44. Shapiro, *Culture of Fact*, 9.

Readers are thereby invited to decide for themselves whether, say, the apothecary's testimony is reliable and whether Nurse Cary should be convicted as an accessory. Pamphlets like Quick's—and there were many of them—speak to a more active seventeenth-century readership, one in which debate about printed crime stories reinforced the public's role in the actual administration of legal justice.[45]

The crucial point in all of this is that fact and evidence were at the center of the juror's expertise. If the issue in question was about law, then laypeople were expected to fall quiet and listen to the real legal experts. But when the issue was about fact or evidence, those same legal experts sat back and waited patiently on the lay jury. Zachary Babington, in his *Advice to Grand Jurors in Cases of Blood*, pervasively uses phrases like "every Fact," "the single Fact," "the whole matter of Fact," a language that indicates just how central the whole business of fact-determination was to the jury's mission.[46] As a result of this fact-jury association in the early modern consciousness, words like "fact" and "evidence" in *Paradise Lost* work like trip wires: they signal that the issues at hand are judicial ones and that they are specifically the kinds of issues that readers can weigh in on. The early modern "fit audience" is tacitly invited to roll up its collective sleeves and get to work. When God refers to his foreknowledge in book 3, Milton assumes that readers will muster up what they know of Calvinism. When Milton uses "fact" and "evidence" in books 9 and 10, he similarly assumes that readers will bring to bear familiar forms of juridical evaluation. Those readers have both the theological expertise to understand Milton's Arminianism and the juridical expertise to weigh Adam's assertion that his "fact" is not heinous and Eve's claim that her "fact" is not really a fact at all. Babington reminds his readers that as jurors they will often face "doubtful and perplex Evidence" that will tax their ability to

45. Martin, *Women, Murder, and Equity*.
46. Babington, *Advice to Grand Jurors*, B.

render a right verdict, for "there [was] much more of Black-art used to darken and obscure the truth of the fact." Each juror must try carefully to see beyond those things that, in Babington's words, "falsifie his clear sight" in order to reach a proper verdict—*ver-dict*, literally a true speaking.[47]

47. Ibid., C6v.

8

Begging Pardon

God's willingness to pardon is a mainspring of *Paradise Lost*, transforming the epic from bleak to hopeful. The poem's opening lines express Milton's trust that the Son—the "greater man"—will one day "restore" fallen men and women (1.4–5), and the merciful restoration planned by God and the Son in book 3 is initiated at the end of book 10, when Adam and Eve, their hearts softened, fall prostrate and beg pardon in "sorrow unfeigned and humiliation meek" (10.1104). Milton also gives a surprising amount of attention to the possibility of Satan's pardon. Chronologically speaking, the earliest reference appears in book 5, when Abdiel urges Satan,

> Hasten to appease
> Th' incensèd Father, and th' incensèd Son,
> While pardon may be found in time besought. (5.846–48)

In book 1 Satan entertains the hypothetical idea of mercy even as he refuses "to bow and sue for grace/With suppliant knee," and Mammon revisits this subject during the epic debate when he allows that even if God were to "relent/And publish grace to all, on promise made/Of new subjection," the fallen angels would refuse to rejoin Heaven's polity (1.111–12, 2.237–39). In book 3 we see this issue from Heaven's point of view, for God proclaims that the fallen angels are not eligible for mercy because they are "self-tempted, self-depraved" (3.130). Finally, the idea of pardon centrally occupies Satan during his soliloquy at the beginning of book 4. Reflecting on his own rebellion and punishment, he asks, "Is there no place/Left for repentance, none for pardon left?," and he wonders whether he "could repent and could obtain/By act of grace [his] former state" (4.79–80, 93–94).

While critical discussions of the way pardons work in *Paradise Lost* have been conducted almost entirely within the framework of Milton's Arminian theology, I argue in this chapter that Milton isn't just thinking theologically when he depicts scenes of pardon.[1] He is also thinking juridically and culturally. Pardons were at an all-time high in Milton's world, and, as I explain in the next section, Milton himself had been the beneficiary of two of them. By the middle of the seventeenth century, pardoning had evolved into an elaborate set of symbolic conventions with its own forms of address, gestures, procedures, preconditions, and contingencies.[2] Especially in the case of the special or individual pardon, one obtained mercy (if at all) only after playing a usually long and complex role as a pardon seeker, and those who did not play by the unspoken rules of pardoning were less successful than those who did. As historians have shown, early modern men and women across the social spectrum were remarkably well versed in these rules. They understood the details regarding how, where, and when different kinds of pardons should be sought under differing circumstances (Was it a collective offense or an individual one? Who were the victim's family, and were they alive? Had the

1. The classic treatments of Milton's Arminian views are provided by Kelley, *This Great Argument*; and Danielson, *Milton's Good God*. See also Fallon, "Milton's Arminianism." For a discussion of how Milton uses early modern pardoning practices in *Samson Agonistes*, see Greenberg, "Dalila's 'Feminine Assaults.'" Brittan and Posner glance very briefly at pardons in "Penal Theory in *Paradise Lost*."

2. For the highly symbolic nature of medieval pardons, see Koziol, *Begging Pardon and Favor*. Early modern pardon petitions indicate that many of the core features of this quasi-ritualized social discourse remained the same.

accused initially fled the scene or not? Was there provocation? Had the crime happened in another county? Etc.). As a result, Milton could rely on a readership conversant in what kinds of actions and claims would best serve the petitioner's end.[3]

In *Paradise Lost*, Satan and the other fallen angels systematically snub many of the practices that led to successful pardons in the early modern world. Conversely, Adam and Eve conform to them. For instance, the period assumed that pardons should, whenever possible, be sought in the same place where the accused had been judged or where the crime had been committed, and care in choosing one's pardoning ground was seen as an important indicator of penitence.[4] Milton takes pains to show Adam and Eve observing this feature of contemporary pardoning practice. Eve says that she will return "to the place of judgment" to ask pardon, and Adam says they should beg pardon at "the place/ . . . where he judged us" (10.932, 1086–87). Milton's narrator describes Adam and Eve's actions in the same terms:

> They forthwith to the place
> Repairing where he judged them prostrate fell
> Before him reverent. (10.1098–1100)

By this same cultural logic, Satan should have taken the opportunity to beg pardon when he stood at the foot of the ladder to Heaven in book 3. Instead, he considers the possibility of asking

3. Kesselring, *Mercy and Authority*; Davis, *Fiction in the Archives*.

4. For instance, men and women who had been convicted in the Star Chamber often waited until the next time that the king was present there before coming in and begging for mercy. There are many instances of this attention to what we might call the symbolic geography of pardons. For example, in 1579 Thomas Appletree was standing on the banks of the Thames showing off his new gun to a friend when he sportively pulled the trigger. The bullet narrowly missed Queen Elizabeth and the French ambassador, who happened to be traveling by in the royal barge, and hit one of her bargemen in the leg. Authorities expended some effort to erect a gibbet for Appletree's execution on the precise place "betwixt Detforde and Greenwitch," where the crime had been committed (see *Brief Discourse*, A2v). As a result, when a last-minute pardon arrived from the queen as Appletree stood with the noose around his neck, the place of the crime, the place of the execution, and the place of the pardon were all in perfect alignment.

forgiveness only after he has turned his back on God and descended to Eden in book 4, and so his choice of terrain signals his insincerity well before he asks, "Is there no place/ . . . for pardon left?" (4.79–80). Such scenes suggest that mercy in *Paradise Lost* is more than just a divine "yes/no" option, a gift given irrespective of the petitioner's actions. Adam and Eve actively and intelligently participate in the forgiveness given to them, and so the contemporary vocabulary of pardons helps Milton make sense of why some beings in *Paradise Lost* receive mercy and others do not.

Milton's Pardon

While, technically speaking, pardons were extralegal phenomena that happened after the courts had done their job, over the course of the early modern period, pardons came to occupy an increasingly important role within the judicial process itself. As social historians such as Beattie and Herrup show, those men who served as judges and juries understood perfectly well that crimes that were capital in theory should not always be capital in practice.[5] This awareness had led to a series of collectively agreed-upon jurisprudential fictions, which allowed judges and juries to pronounce guilty verdicts without thereby sending men and women to their deaths. For example, convicted felons under certain circumstances could plead benefit of clergy (as Ben Jonson did in 1598 after killing Gabriel Spenser), even when everyone involved knew that those accused were not men of the cloth. Similarly in theft cases, juries regularly devalued stolen goods so that the crime qualified as petty larceny, which was not a capital offense. But the most common means of preserving the integrity of the judicial process without overusing the scaffold was the pardon. Pardons acquired an even more heightened visibility during the second half of the seventeenth century. Beginning in

5. Beattie, *Crime and the Courts*; Herrup, *Common Peace*. See also Potter, *Hanging in Judgment*; Sharpe, *Crime in Early Modern England*.

the Civil War years, Parliament increasingly claimed the right to determine who should and should not receive mercy, thereby challenging the king's traditional role as the sole fount of mercy. The Stuarts pushed back, especially after the Restoration, insisting that they alone had the right to issue pardons and dispensations and that they could do so irrespective of the crime involved. As a result, by the late 1670s, pardons had become a politically supercharged symbol of the struggle over executive privilege.[6]

Broadly speaking, there were two different kinds of pardons available in early modern England: the individual or special pardon and the collective pardon, which was also called an act of grace. The individual or special pardon was, as its name indicates, granted to a single person or small group of persons who had broken the law and to whom the king chose to extend mercy. Collective pardons were more impersonal. They usually targeted whole groups of offenders and resulted from broadly social and political concerns. For instance, Henry VIII and Elizabeth I issued acts of grace as often as every four to six years for a variety of reasons. Sometimes prison overcrowding had reached the critical point, and these blanket pardons were used to ease the strain on a literally crumbling judicial system. Sometimes acts of grace were issued in tacit recompense to Parliament for having levied new taxes.[7] Sometimes acts of grace responded to perceived inequities in the law. For instance, the seventeenth century witnessed a rising imprisonment for debt. The rogue John Hall, in his lurid description of Newgate prison, describes debtors who talk "altogether of an *Act of Grace*," hoping for a royal pardon that

6. We see this concern over the abuse of pardoning power in the *Heads of the Proposals Offered by the Army*, which asks that no one "may be capable of protection or pardon from the King" without the consent of Parliament. Gardiner, *Constitutional Documents*, 318. The monarch's pardoning prerogative erupted into a truly national debate in 1679. Parliament impeached the Earl of Danby for treason, and in response, James II offered him a special pardon. Renfrow provides a detailed discussion of the Danby impeachment and the many issues it raised. See her "Tudor and Stuart Theories," 380–94.

7. Kesselring provides a general survey of acts of grace in *Mercy and Authority*, 57–73. On Parliamentary involvement in these acts of grace, see Dean, *Law-Making and Society*, 55–62.

would protect them from their creditors.[8] Sometimes acts of grace seemed simply intended to foster improved relations between sovereign and people. In April 1582 the Elizabethan justice of the peace William Lambarde wrote that the queen issued "her general and free pardon, thereby not only forgiving us the most part of our offenses that are past but also giving us great cause to use better obedience for the time that is to come."[9] In Lambarde's view, collective pardons helped to mend small tears in the social fabric.

Milton was the beneficiary of both types of pardon. As his early biographers emphasize, Milton was included in the general 1660 Act of Indemnity and Oblivion, a collective pardon drafted by Parliament and ratified by Charles II in the wake of the Restoration. Near the beginning of the eighteenth century, Jonathan Richardson writes that with Charles II's return, Milton's works "were Now Accounted Criminal, Every One of Them" but that Milton had "very Powerful Friends at That time," a claim indicating that Milton had firsthand experience with the importance of intercessors in the pardoning process. As a result, Milton was "screen'd from being Excepted in the General Pardon," and "secur'd by Pardon [he] Appear'd again in Publick."[10] Edward Phillips, arguably a more reliable biographer, describes Milton going into hiding at "a Friends house in *Bartholomew Close* where he liv'd till the Act of Oblivion came forth." This act "prov'd as favourable to [Milton] as could be hop'd or expected," and he took a house in Holborn "not long before his Pardon [had] pass'd the Seal."[11] Milton also received a special pardon that same year. During the period of his concealment, the House of Commons had directed the attorney general to send for Milton "in Custody, by the Serjeant at Arms" to answer an indictment about his antimonarchical books.[12] Because this second order was never rescinded,

8. Hall, *Memoirs of John Hall*, 14.

9. Lambarde, *William Lambarde and Local Government*, 71.

10. Darbishire, *Early Lives of Milton*, 271–75.

11. Ibid., 73–74.

12. This discussion is generally drawn from Campbell and Corns, *John Milton*, 313–17.

Milton was taken into custody after he emerged from hiding and was imprisoned in the Tower, probably in October or November 1660. Sometime around mid-December, he received a special pardon from Parliament remitting this particular offense, although the sergeant still charged him for his jail expenses. The text of this special pardon is not extant, but two contemporary accounts speak briefly of it. A Dutch report notes that Milton was "freed through good promises," and Cyriack Skinner writes that Milton "early sued out his Pardon; and by means of that when the Serjeant of the House of Commons had officiously seisd him, was quickly set at liberty."[13] Milton had to make "good promises," and he "sued out" his pardon (suggesting that he had to "plead, appeal or supplicate"), indicating that he observed the typical forms and protocols of pardon, described in more detail below.[14] He likely made his submission and trusted to an intercessor to speak eloquently on his behalf. And in the manner of so many early modern pardon seekers, he likely offered solemn vows of his future obedience and good behavior.

This image of Milton begging pardon is starkly at odds with claims that he made eleven years earlier in *Eikonoklastes*. In *Eikon basilike*, Charles I had congratulated himself on offering "acts of Indempnity, and Oblivion, to so great a latitude, as may include all, that can but suspect themselves to be any way obnoxious to the Laws."[15] Milton retorts in *Eikonoklastes* that good men will spurn such forms of pardon, for they would never seek to be pardoned for the very actions "which may be justly attributed to thir immortal praise." Accepting a pardon was an admission of guilt, and Milton argues that just men would not "assent ever to the guilty blotting out of those actions before men, by which thir Faith assures them they chiefly stand approv'd, and are had

13. Darbishire, *Early Lives of Milton*, 32. As Campbell and Corns point out, Skinner's account does not clarify matters, since it remains uncertain whether Milton was here claiming pardon under the Act of Oblivion or whether he had already negotiated a special pardon related to the Parliamentary indictment (*John Milton*, 317).

14. "Sue," v., def. 22a, *OED Online*.

15. Charles I, *Eikon basilike*, 224.

in remembrance before the throne of God" (*CPW* 3:577). But when he "early sued out his Pardon" in 1660, Milton did precisely this "guilty blotting out" of his earlier actions. We can only speculate about the reasons for Milton's change of heart. Perhaps this bitter pill was eased by the fact that both the Act of Oblivion and the indictment against him were at least nominally issued by Parliament and not the king, and so Milton was submitting to a governing body whose authority he accepted. Perhaps long experience and political disillusionment had led him to conclude that it was better to accept a spurious pardon than to face criminal prosecution. Most of those exempted from the Act of Oblivion were gruesomely drawn and quartered, as Milton knew well.[16] Although we cannot know precisely what Milton's punishment would have been for the lesser indictment for writing against the king, the case of Alexander Leighton, convicted in 1630 for writing a pamphlet against prelacy, provides a possible point of comparison. Leighton was pilloried, whipped, pilloried again, had one ear cut off and then one nostril slit, had his forehead branded with "SS" (for "Sower of Sedition"), pilloried again, whipped again, had the other nostril slit and the other ear cut off, and then was imprisoned for life.[17] Perhaps Milton concluded that begging a pardon, however noxious to his principles, would, in effect, allow him to live to fight another day—in this case, to write a work like *Paradise Lost* that explores how human mercy can be brought into better alignment with the will of God.

Collective Acts of Grace

Satan's soliloquy at the beginning of book 4 revolves centrally around whether he would be eligible for an "act of grace" that might

16. On Milton's familiarity with the execution of the regicides, see Knoppers, *Historicizing Milton.*

17. Veall, *Popular Movement for Law Reform*, 10. Milton glances at the kind of punishment meted out to Leighton and to men like Prynne, Bastwick, and Burton when in *An Apology Against a Pamphlet* he refers to the prelates' practice of "slitting noses" (*CPW* 1:894).

allow him to escape the punishment of Hell and regain "[his] former state" (4.94). In seventeenth-century terms, he has two valid reasons to be asking himself this question. First, collective pardons were commonly issued at the beginning of a reign (witness the 1660 Act of Oblivion), and they played an especially important symbolic role in coronation processions.[18] For instance, in 1603 the new James I pardoned liberally on his journey south from Edinburgh as a way to signal that his reign would be marked by peace and clemency (in fact, London experienced a crime wave as the king neared the city, for the felonious saw an ideal opportunity to commit crimes and escape penalty).[19] In France, coronation pardons were so customary that fugitives from the law strategically surrendered themselves to prisons on the new monarch's processional route.[20] Given this general expectation that the installation of a new ruler would be followed by a celebratory act of grace, it is hardly surprising that Satan thinks in book 4 about his chances of a pardon. The Son's "great vicegerent reign" has only recently begun, and earlier Satan imagines that the Son will "pass triumphant" on a coronation procession through Heaven "and give laws" (5.609, 693). Now a defeated rebel who has been sentenced to a place Milton calls his "prison ordained/In utter darkness" (1.71–72), Satan is in much the same position as those criminals who listened from jail to the ecstatic ringing of London's coronation bells and hoped that the new monarch would remit old offenses.

In a second, related usage, English monarchs often issued acts of grace in the wake of war or insurrection, and since armed rebellion often broke out during the transition from one ruler to the next, inaugural acts of grace frequently included rebels who had submitted. In 1652, near the beginning of the Commonwealth, Parliament "acquitted, Pardoned, Released and Discharged" all

18. Kesselring, *Mercy and Authority*, 90.

19. For a description of the king's procession south, including acts of grace pronounced for towns like Newcastle and York, see T. M., *True Narration*, E2. On the London spike in theft, see Kesselring, *Mercy and Authority*, 67.

20. Davis, *Fiction in the Archives*, 20.

offenses "made, committed, suffered or done before the Third day of September, in the year One thousand six hundred fifty one."[21] Similarly, in 1660, at the beginning of Charles II's reign, the Act of Oblivion pardoned combatants on both sides of the war, exempting from penalty "all Acts of Hostilitie and Injuries, whether between the late King, and the Lords and Commons then in Parliament assembled, or between any of the People of this Nation . . . by reason of the late Troubles or in the late Warrs."[22] As the leader of an insurrection, Satan has "against the throne and monarchy of God/Raised impious war," so when he wonders if he could regain his former position "by act of grace" (4.42–44), he imagines God as acting like the Commonwealth Parliament or Charles II, letting bygones be bygones in order to heal the polity of Heaven. From Satan's standpoint, the collective pardon has another great advantage: recipients did not have to petition for it. Instead, the act of grace was proclaimed by the sovereign, and its provisions were printed in broadside and distributed. Those who wished to avail themselves of the pardon's clemency simply paid a court fee to have their pardons ratified. Given that Satan refuses to "bow and sue for grace/With suppliant knee" (4.111–12), the impersonal mercy characteristic of the act of grace has a definite appeal. In imagining a pardon without personal abjection, Satan tacitly echoes a moment from book 2 when Belial speculates that in time God will "much remit/His anger" and "not mind us not offending, satisfied/With what is punished" (2.210–11, 212–13). Like Satan, Belial hopes that the fallen angels might be the passive beneficiaries of a distant mercy and receive a pardon without having to ask for it.

In one sense, Satan is right: God does issue a formal act of grace. After the Son quells the military threat to his new rule, he and God consider those criminals who have already disobeyed the law (the fallen angels) and those who will do so shortly (Adam

21. Act of General Pardon, 1652, in *Acts and Ordinances of the Interregnum*, 2:565.

22. Act of Free and General Pardon, 1660, in *Statutes of the Realm*, 1 Car. 2, c. 23.

and Eve). God lays out the conditions of the pardon, conditions that exempt Satan and his crew:

> The first sort by their own suggestion fell,
> Self-tempted, self-depraved: man falls deceived
> By the other first: man therefore shall find grace,
> The other none. (3.129–32)

Although Satan's exclusion from grace has disturbed some modern readers, it is a typical feature of acts of grace, for monarchs routinely stipulated that certain more heinous offenses were not open to clemency.[23] For instance, upon entering into Newcastle, the new James I pardoned all city prisoners "except those that lay for treason, murther, and Papistrie."[24] Such exemptions from pardon were frequently made for those who had been the ringleaders of rebellion. While the Act of Oblivion pardoned not only those who had fought against the king but also "all manner of Treasons, Misprisions of Treason, Murthers, Felonies, Offences, Crimes, Contempts, and Misdemeanors," it also stipulated that this general pardon was not extended to those who were "out of this present Act wholly excepted and foreprised," primarily those who had been directly instrumental in the trial and execution of Charles I.[25]

In book 3 God says since Adam has no means to "expiate his treason," the law must run its course: "Die he or justice must" (3.207). He speaks both the language of Protestant atonement and the related language of the early modern law.[26] Joan Bennett argues that since Milton's God is "utterly accountable to a perfect law," there are "things God 'cannot' do." One of these things is to

23. As Kesselring notes, over the course of the sixteenth century, the tendency was for more and more offenses to be excluded from the act of grace. See her *Mercy and Authority*, 73.

24. T. M., *True Narration*, C4v.

25. Act of Free and General Pardon, 1660, in *Statutes of the Realm*, 1 Car. 2, c. 34.

26. As Patrides points out, Protestant works of the period often describe the atonement using legal metaphors of trial, evidence, and acquittal, so the judicial flavor of book 3 is consistent with contemporary theological works. Patrides, "Milton and the Protestant Theory."

grant a pardon in a way that disrupts the workings of justice. As Coke explains in his *Third Institutes*, the king could not pardon an offense in such a way as to prevent reparations. Coke gives an example of a man charged with maintaining a bridge who fails in his duty. If the bridge collapses, the king can remit those punishments that satisfied the Crown's interest (such as fines or whipping), but he cannot absolve the offender from having to repair the bridge, since such an absolution would injure the public good.[27] England's church courts echoed common law practice, for they consistently ruled that pardons did not absolve the accused from making just reparations.[28] Milton clearly held a very similar view about the limits on the monarch's pardoning prerogative. In his discussion of treason in *A Defense of the English People*, he answers Salmasius's argument that the king cannot be a traitor because he has the power to pardon treason (which implies that he is above the laws). Milton emphasizes the limits on the royal pardon, arguing that "at times, though not always, he could pardon other offenders" and that the king has only "on occasion some right to reprieve a wrongdoer" (*CPW* 4:532). Even these limited pardoning powers vanish in the cause of crimes against the commonwealth: "The king, like anyone else, could pardon treason to himself, but not to the kingdom," and the king cannot use his pardoning power "to destroy all good men" (*CPW* 4:532). The same juridical reasoning is at work in *Paradise Lost*. If Adam had committed strictly a personal crime against God, then God could absolve him immediately and utterly. However, as I argued in chapter 3, Milton has taken pains to show that Adam primarily betrays the law. Like Coke's public, which had a right to justice and a working bridge, irrespective of the monarch's willingness to grant a pardon, the entirety of creation—animals, plants, birds, people yet unborn, all of them now subject to death and decay because of Adam's crime—can be considered as interested parties to the criminal version of a class action suit

27. Bennett, *Reviving Liberty*, 70–71; Coke, *Third Part of the Institutes*, 233.
28. Helmholz, *Roman Canon Law*, 163–64.

against Adam. As Milton himself says in *Doctrine and Discipline of Divorce*, God "binds himself like a just lawgiver to his own prescriptions," and he suggests that, given the highly public nature of Adam's offense, God cannot simply waive the penalties and still maintain the course of justice (*CPW* 2:292).

God's careful attention to motive in *Paradise Lost* also reflects early modern ideas about the proper use of the pardon. While a consideration of motive is indispensable in modern trials and crime dramas, it was only just beginning to have a formal role in sixteenth- and seventeenth-century courts. Trials for homicide illustrate this fact clearly: all killings were technically capital offenses in the eyes of the law, whether the accused was a hired assassin or had killed by accident or in self-defense. But while an assessment of motive had little place at the trial stage, it was crucial at the pardoning stage. The first statutory recognition of mens rea, or malice aforethought, appears in a late-fourteenth-century document barring the king from pardoning those who have killed "of malice prepensed."[29] By the early modern period, it was commonly held that pardons should be calibrated to the degree and nature of the motive present, and Richard Hooker wrote, "Who knoweth not, that harme advisedly done is naturally lesse pardonable, and therefore worthie of the sharper punishment?"[30] Accordingly, early modern acts of grace routinely discriminated on the basis of motive, as when the new James I, in his general pardon issued for York, pointedly excluded "willfull murtherers" from mercy.[31] Milton's God performs a similar calculus of intent when he declares that those who are "self-tempted, self-depraved" cannot find mercy. Although Adam and Eve will commit substantively the same treasonous offense as Satan, they are pardonable because they were seduced by another. In one sixteenth-century pardon document, an anonymous judge recommends that the Crown offer clemency to the accused who,

29. Quoted and discussed in Chesney, "Concept of *Mens Rea*," 635.
30. Hooker, *Laws of Ecclesiastical Polity*, 1:104.
31. T. M., *True Narration*, D4v.

"being young, were persuaded by others to commit the offenses whereof they stand indicted."[32] By showing God granting a pardon in *Paradise Lost* for a similar reason, Milton suggests that a sober assessment of motive is an important part of mercy both in Heaven and on Earth. He also seems aware that, for hardened offenders, pardons just paved the way to renewed crimes. In *The Tenure of Kings and Magistrates*, Milton argues that mercy, if extended to one who has shown himself to be a tyrant, is really just a form of cruelty, particularly since such spurious expressions of mercy hazard "the welfare of a whole Nation" in behalf of a few offenders (*CPW* 3:193). Satan effectively admits as much when he allows that even if God were to grant an act of grace, his own nature would lead him to "a worse relapse/And heavier fall," one that would bring renewed disorder and division to the Heavenly commonwealth (4.100–101).

But while Milton establishes points of continuity between the acts of grace in Heaven and those on Earth, he also highlights a crucial difference between the two: God's general pardon does not arise from political considerations, and it is not a "tool of state formation" in the manner of most Stuart pardons.[33] One preliminary qualification is in order here, since Milton shows that God's proclamation of mercy in book 3 works to consolidate the polity of Heaven. In a sense, it even *creates* the polity of Heaven, since Milton first refers to the collective body of angels immediately after his account of God's prophetic proclamation of grace. God declares that "mercy first and last shall brightest shine" and that this edict "in the blessèd spirits elect/Sense of new joy ineffable diffused"—narratively speaking, Milton's first description of the angelic hosts (3.134, 136–37). But although the proclamation of mercy results in increased unity and obedience among the good angels, it is not motivated by political expediency. Under the Tudors and the Stuarts, in contrast, acts of grace often depended on careful assessments of power and advantage.

32. Quoted in Kesselring, *Mercy and Authority*, 108.
33. Kesselring, *Mercy and Authority*, 3.

In his *Eikon basilike*, King Charles frankly admits as much when he comments that while pardons are acts of "Christian charitie and choice," they are also "act[s] of State-policie and necessitie."[34] Charles had issued a series of pardons during the Civil War, as with his 1642 "Proclamation of His Majesties Grace, Favour, and Pardon, to the Inhabitants of His County of Dorsett," which promised a pardon to the men of Dorset provided that they laid down their arms and took certain key offenders into custody. The king's discussion of the death of Sir John Hotham and his son shows a similarly calculated awareness of the advantages of mercy. Although Hotham had initially fought for Parliament and had held Hull, with its valuable munitions depot, against royalist forces, he later conspired with his son to surrender the city to the king. Commenting on Parliament's subsequent execution of the Hothams as traitors, Charles regrets that they were "so unhappie as to fall into the hands of their Justice and not my mercie."[35] Milton takes up this claim in *Eikonoklastes*, asserting that since Charles had not pardoned others who had similarly opposed him, the hypothetical postmortem mercy extended to the Hothams was merely a political gambit intended to refurbish the king's image (*CPW* 3:432).

Indeed, judging from discussions in *Eikonoklastes* and *Observations upon the Articles of Peace*, Milton despised the way in which pardons had become bargaining chips in a larger political game. In *Eikon basilike*, lamenting the armies raised against him, King Charles exclaims, "Is this the reward and thanks that I am to receive for those many acts of Grace I have lately passed?"[36] In response, Milton scoffs, "He twitts them with *his Acts of grace*; proud, and unself-knowing words in the mouth of any King. . . . For if they were unjust acts, why did he grant them as of grace? If just, it was not of grace, but of his duty and his Oath to grant them" (*CPW* 3:435). Milton here argues that by congratulating

34. Charles I, *Eikon basilike*, 244.
35. Ibid., 50.
36. Ibid., 54.

himself on his acts of grace and expecting gratitude for them, the king reveals that he granted pardons merely to consolidate his own hold on power. Similarly, when Charles says that the "tumults" occasioned by Parliament "threatned to abuse all Acts of Grace, and turne them into wantonnesse" (in Miltonic terms, to turn liberty into license), Milton retorts that the king uses the Pauline language of grace to cover his own political use of mercy (*CPW* 3:404).[37] In his *Observations upon the Articles of Peace*, Milton cites item 18 of the Articles of Peace, which was an extensive Act of Oblivion remitting the offenses of the Irish rebels and punishing instead "any person or persons that will not obey and submit unto the peace concluded and agreed on by these Articles."[38] Milton claims that with this politically motivated act of grace, Charles I "sold away that justice so oft demanded" in order "to be aveng'd" on his opponents in England (*CPW* 3:308). In *Paradise Lost*, Milton is careful to show that God, unlike Charles I, practices a disinterested form of mercy. In book 10 the Son promises to "temper so/Justice with mercy" (10.77–78), a phrase that alludes to the English coronation oath in which the monarch swore to "cause Law and Justice, in Mercy, to be executed" in all judgments.[39] But whereas Tudor and Stuart monarchs frequently reaped political and financial rewards from the exercise of mercy, Milton specifies that the Son has nothing to gain.[40] As the Son reminds the Father, "I go to judge/On Earth these thy transgressors, but thou know'st,/Whoever judged, the worst on me must light" (10.71–73).

37. Ibid., 29.

38. Ireland, *Articles of Peace*, 19.

39. Schramm, *History of the English Coronation*, 225.

40. As David Loades demonstrates, when King Philip came to the throne of England through marriage to Mary, he actively awarded pardons to create a clientage network loyal to him. See Loades, "Philip II," 181. Sometimes pardon requests degenerated into purely financial transactions, as when Anthony Bacon frankly asked for £100 and a bond for £500 more in return for his intercession on behalf of Robert Booth. Kesselring, *Mercy and Authority*, 130. See also the discussions in Stain, "'Snared Subject.'"

It is worth pausing here to note a related way in which this scene in *Paradise Lost* mirrors early modern judicial practice, for Adam and Eve actually have time to ask for pardon. In the first part of the judgment scene, Milton stresses the speed of events. Once the Son hears their confessions, "without delay/To judgment he proceeded on th' accused," and he leaves with equal rapidity (10.163–64). But although Adam and Eve are left with judgment ringing in their ears, they see no immediate evidence of their sentence being enacted. Milton even emphasizes the delay. Oppressed by his deferred sentence, Adam laments, "Why delays/His hand to execute what his decree/Fixed on this day?" (10.771–73). While Milton here reflects theological consensus about why Adam and Eve did not die on the day of their sin, he also nods toward contemporary judicial practice. In previous centuries, convicted criminals were taken straight from the courtroom to the scaffold, stocks, or whipping post. The case of Arnold Cosby, convicted in 1591 for the fatal stabbing of Lord Burke, speaks to this common practice. Hearing the pronouncement of his death sentence, Cosby asked that he "might not bee executed that present daie, but that he might have that daies respite, and a Preacher appointed to comfort him," a request that the judge allowed.[41] By Milton's day, this gap between sentencing and punishment had become a matter of course. After the trial, the convict was returned to jail, and penalties were not enacted until the end of the Quarter Sessions or Assizes, a delay that sometimes stretched for weeks. In the words of one historian, "The reason [for the delay] was neither to allow the judge time to reflect nor the prisoner to squirm, but to allow time to secure pardon or prepare a motion in arrest of judgment."[42] This is precisely how the delay works for Adam. He tells Eve, "We expected/Immediate dissolution," but the deferral of sentence and the Son's mildness as a judge embolden Adam to think of begging a pardon (10.1048–49).

41. Hunsdon, *Araignment, Examination, Confession*, B4.
42. Baker, "Criminal Courts and Procedure," 40.

In one important respect, Milton seems intent on correcting rather than simply reflecting early modern pardoning practices. In *Doctrine and Discipline of Divorce*, he expresses his distaste for what he calls the "visibility of Law-witnessing" (*CPW* 2.335), and he takes steps in *Paradise Lost* to show that Adam and Eve's pardon—like their judgment before the Son—is a private one. Indeed, the scene in which the Son brings Adam and Eve's penitent prayers into the throne room of God is arguably the only private conversation that God and the Son have in the epic. Having conceded to his Son's petition for mercy, God then says, "But let us call to synod all the blest/Through Heav'n's wide bounds," and the Son then "gave signal high/To the bright minister that watched" (11.67–68, 72–73). Milton specifies that only this one attendant angel has heard the Son's intercession and the Father's merciful assent. The "bright minister" blows his trumpet, and the hosts of Heaven come flocking in: "the sons of light/Hasted, resorting to the summons high,/And took their seats" (11.80–82). As with the earlier act of grace in book 3, God shares his merciful decree with his angels. He says, "From them I will not hide/My judgments," and he knows that because of this administrative transparency, the good angels "in their state, though firm, stood more confirmed" (11.68–69, 71). But there is a crucial difference between a public pronouncement of pardon and the public theater of pardon. Over and over again under the Tudors and Stuarts, pardons had become forms of state-sanctioned spectacle. For instance, in the aftermath of the 1603 Bye Plot, James I carefully stage-managed the last-minute pardons he dispensed. The accused men were painstakingly put through the preexecution ceremonies on the scaffold, only to be told that the hanging would be delayed several hours, and one observer, noting the king's care "to prevent all . . . colour of suspicion" that a pardon was forthcoming, called the whole affair a "well-acted comedy."[43] Theatrical themselves, pardons also made for good stage material, as

43. Janet Spencer discusses this pardon and provides the quotes in "Staging Pardon Scenes." On the theatricality of pardons, see also Richard Wilson, "Quality of Mercy."

attested by the pardons that Prospero hands out at the end of *The Tempest* and the pardon that Shylock receives in *The Merchant of Venice*. But while both the Globe audience and the onstage audience watched as Shylock was told, "Down, therefore, and beg mercy of the Duke," Milton allows for no such drama.[44] When the good angels arrive in response to the "summons high," Milton specifies that they "took their seats," a detail that suggests a legal arena like Westminster Hall (11.82; 11.81). By invoking the image of a quasi-judicial building, the seats all filled with attentive angels, Milton tacitly draws more attention to the fact that there are no abject pardon petitioners on the arena's floor.

Special Pardons

The collective pardon is not the only form of human mercy that Milton alludes to in *Paradise Lost*, for Satan seems to be considering also the possibility of a special or individual pardon when, having asked, "Is there no place/ . . . for pardon left?," he answers himself, "None left but by submission" (4.79–81). As historian Krista Kesselring notes, the single most important criterion in special pardon petitions was the "simple, abject submission" of the convicted man or woman.[45] The need for unreserved submission is made spectacularly clear in a 1602 letter from Hugh O'Neill, the Earl of Tyrone and the defeated leader of the Irish rebellion, to Lord Mountjoy, who was acting as Queen Elizabeth's proxy in Tyrone's ongoing pardon negotiations. Tyrone laments that Mountjoy has rejected his earlier petition on the grounds that he "did not make therein an absolute submission." Accordingly, Tyrone remedies the lapse: "Without standing upon any terms or conditions I do hereby both simply and absolutely submit myself to her Majesties mercy."[46] Early modern pardoning protocols

44. Shakespeare, *Merchant of Venice*, 4.1.358.
45. Kesselring, *Mercy and Authority*, 116–17.
46. McNeil, *Tanner Letters*, 52.

held that these acts of submission were best performed in person, as Queen Elizabeth stipulated in another letter to Mountjoy: "First, our pleasure is upon no consideration to give him our pardon unless he do come personally where you shall assign him to receive it."[47] Given these contexts, Satan accurately understands that a pardon would require him to come before God and "bow and sue for grace/With suppliant knee" (1.111–12). Although such personal professions of submission might seem the sine qua non of all pardons, this was not uniformly the case. As Davis demonstrates, early modern French offenders had to craft a pardon narrative that made their offense look excusable by law, and while a humble demeanor was certainly helpful, petitioners needed more to make a convincing claim to innocence (or, at least, to strongly mitigating circumstances). Indeed, an overly profuse submission could be counterproductive, since it could verge on an admission of guilt.[48] As a result, Satan reasons specifically like an early modern Englishman when he admits that his only route to clemency would involve coming before God and abjecting himself. Milton invites us to contrast Satan's obduracy with Adam and Eve's willingness to perform all the right gestures of penitence:

> [They] prostrate fell
> Before him reverent and both confessed
> Humbly their faults, and pardon begged, with tears
> Watering the ground, and with their sighs the air
> Frequenting. (10.1099–1103)

While such physical forms of submission were important in early modern special pardons, they needed to be supplemented by the active efforts of an intercessor. In Davis's words, "The obstacle to asking for the king's pardon was not so much poverty by itself, but isolation."[49] Kesselring shows that the phenomenon Davis traces in early modern France applied just as much in England:

47. Ibid., 57.
48. Davis, *Fiction in the Archives*, 60–61, 74–75.
49. Ibid., 10.

"In a polity predicated upon personal relationships and hierarchical ties of obligation, it should come as no surprise that the receipt of a pardon often relied upon the favor and support of those better situated within the social hierarchy." As a result, "mediators were not just important in bringing cases to the Crown's attention—they did not just remedy a gap in bureaucratic procedures. Rather, their intervention and humble requests formed part of the cultural protocol for pardon."[50] Pardoning was not a two-way transaction between the person asking for mercy and the person conferring it. Rather, it was a three-, four-, or five-way transaction that helped repair the kinds of social bonds that the offense had damaged in the first place. To give just one example of many, a late-sixteenth-century man named Michael Shafto, in an attempt to get his brother pardoned, wrote to Sir Henry Percy, who in turn wrote to the Earl of Sussex, who in turn presented Shafto's request to Queen Elizabeth.[51] Milton was clearly no fan of social hierarchies based on traditional claims of blood, and he would have rejected the idea that the ability to intercede on another's behalf was a perquisite of rank. However, he seems to have appreciated the role of influential mediators in the pardoning process, for Milton scholars have long accepted that his own pardon was likely due to the intercession of interested parties who could exert political leverage. In Richardson's words, Milton had "very Powerful Friends at That time."[52] Because effective pardons presumed a network of communal bonds, when Satan wonders if there is room for pardon, seventeenth-century readers would likely have understood that this question raised a related one: who would intercede on his behalf? Satan has isolated himself from all society; as he tells Uriel, he has come "alone thus wand'ring" (3.667). Realistically, the only available intercessor, should he sue for pardon, would be the Son. The

50. Kesselring, *Mercy and Authority*, 120, 133. Douglas Hay traces the way that pardons were part of the eighteenth-century culture of patronage. See his "Property, Authority."

51. Kesselring, *Mercy and Authority*, 124.

52. Darbishire, *Early Lives of Milton*, 271.

fact that Satan speaks to the Sun with "no friendly voice" (4.36) when he should instead be speaking to the Son indicates that he is simultaneously aware of and unwilling to follow the approved channels of intercession. And without such intercession, no pardon can happen.

The Son performs precisely this intercessory function on behalf of Adam and Eve. When he writes in book 3 that the Son will act as a "patron or intercessor" for humanity (3.219), Milton draws on a specifically legal meaning of "patron" as a "defender or advocate before a court of justice."[53] In book 11 the Son's chosen role as the "patron or intercessor" enables the success of Adam and Eve's pardon petition, for the prayers of Adam and Eve fly up "through Heav'nly doors," where they are "clad/With incense" by "their great Intercessor" (11.17–19). The Son then brings these petitions with him into the presence of God: "Before the Father's throne: Them the glad Son/Presenting, thus to intercede began" (11.20–21). In this passage, Milton alludes to Hebrews 7:25–28, where Jesus is the priest of God, offering up sacrifices on behalf of a fallen humanity. However, by showing the Son coming into a throne room and bearing the petitions of those guilty specifically of "treason" (3.207), Milton also echoes contemporary pardon requests. The Son's language recalls that used by early modern patrons as they sought to procure pardons for their clients:

> Now therefore bend thine ear
> To supplication, hear his sighs though mute;
> Unskillful with what words to pray, let me
> Interpret for him. (11.30–33)

According to the unwritten rules of early modern pardoning, the role of the convicted man or woman was humbly to perform an array of sighs, tears, and other postures indicative of sorrow and submission, as when the imprisoned Duke of Norfolk mended

53. "Patron," n., defs. 2b, 4a, *OED Online*.

his own hose as a mute testament to his abjection.[54] The tacit role of the intercessor was to put these penitent gestures into words before the monarch, literally to translate on behalf of the client. Thus the Son acts precisely like a good patron should when he understands that since Adam is "unskillful with what words to pray" and can only heave "mute" sighs, he must "interpret for him."

To some degree, the intercession that the Son performs on behalf of Adam and Eve is enabled by the intercession that Adam and Eve offer to perform for each other. Eve expresses her hope that, if she begs pardon for Adam, "the sentence from thy head removed may light/On me sole cause to thee of all this woe" (10.934–35). Adam replies in kind, imagining himself requesting a pardon for her. He says that he would ask

> that on my head all might be visited,
> Thy frailty and infirmer sex forgiv'n,
> To me committed and by me exposed. (10.955–57)

Milton invites us to contrast such moments of altruism with Satan's self-interested reflections in book 4. When he wonders, "Is there no place/Left for repentance, none for pardon left?," Satan is thinking about a strictly individual form of remission. In effect, he is asking "Am *I* eligible for pardon?" and not "Are *we*?" This focus on his own options conflicts with a whole set of early modern ideas of hierarchy. Particularly in the case of pardons sought after treason and armed insurrections, the paternalistic assumptions of the day held that military leaders should first and foremost seek forgiveness for those who followed them. For example, in another letter to Mountjoy, Queen Elizabeth allows that while Tyrone can negotiate a pardon for himself "and his own natural followers of Tyrone," he may not seek pardon for "all others." These men must "make their own suits for themselves." Elizabeth accepts that in seeking pardon for himself, Tyrone was also duly seeking a pardon for his "natural followers," those Irish-

54. Kesselring, *Mercy and Authority*, 116–17.

men from County Tyrone who owed him loyalty.[55] The fact that Elizabeth so carefully limits the extent of Tyrone's suit for pardon—and accepts automatically that pardoning him entails also pardoning some portion of his followers—indicates the degree to which leaders seeking pardons were assumed to be simultaneously acting on behalf of their subordinates. Since Milton has pointedly said that the rebel angels are not "the fellows of [Satan's] crime" but "the followers rather," Satan should by rights be considering a pardon for all of them (1.606). Indeed Abdiel's reprimand of Satan in book 5 stresses that Satan bears the obligation to intercede on behalf of others. Abdiel tells Satan,

> Cease then this impious rage,
> And tempt not these; but hasten to appease
> Th' incensèd Father, and th' incensèd Son,
> While pardon may be found in time besought. (5.845–48)

The implication is that in abandoning his planned attack and seeking a pardon from God, Satan would be working to protect the angels loyally ranged at his back. But although he earlier wept at the sight of "millions of spirits for his fault amerced," Satan is not considering in his book 4 soliloquy how his own hypothetical plea for pardon might benefit his subordinates (1.609).

When Satan muses, "Say I could repent and could obtain/By act of grace my former state," he is also entertaining a wildly inaccurate idea of the results of a special pardon. In short, virtually none of them came without strings attached or restored the offender to his or her previous position (such unconditional pardons were bestowed only when the accused had clearly been the target of unfair accusation and had powerful friends).[56] For instance, in a letter to a friend about the pardon that the Earl of Somerset (King James's favorite who had been convicted of the Overbury murder) finally received in 1622, John Chamberlain writes, "Somersetts pardon was sealed on Thursday in as ample a manner as

55. McNeil, *Tanner Letters*, 57.
56. Baker, "Criminal Courts and Procedure," 44.

could be devised, and he hath taken a house at Cheswicke, but with promise not to looke towarde the court."[57] Although Somerset's pardon was seen as an "ample" one, there was no question of his resuming his former position at court, and he was confined to a three-mile radius around his Cheswick property.[58] Similarly, after years of negotiations, Lionel Cranfield, the impeached Earl of Middlesex, wrote jubilantly that his impending pardon would finally give him "liberty, *quietus est*, absolute pardon," and that he would be "made a child new born." The irony is that what Middlesex calls an "absolute pardon" entailed the loss of his offices (including surveyor-general of customs, master of the court of wards and liveries, and chief commissioner of the navy) and a ban on ever holding office again.[59] In addition to specific forfeitures and penalties, those who received a pardon understood that they faced generally tighter restrictions than before and that small lapses in loyalty and obedience would result in swift penalties. In *Paradise Lost*, Mammon seems aware of this fact when he rejects the idea of a divine pardon on the grounds that the fallen angels could not bear to "stand in [God's] presence humble, and receive/ Strict laws imposed" (2.240–41). Whereas Mammon understands that a pardon would result in "strict laws" that would bind the pardoned angels more tightly than their unfallen peers, Satan unrealistically imagines himself regaining his "former state" and returning to his wonted "highth" (4.94, 95).

Adam has a better grasp than Satan on the fact that a pardon would not mean the erasure of all penalties, and, unlike Satan, he understands that his "former state" is lost to him. In the discussion leading up to their decision to seek pardon, Adam recalls to Eve the sentence of work laid upon him, and he notes that the Son has already provided them with clothes as a shield against the elements. Adam imagines that penitent prayers might move the Son to further teach them to bear their situation:

57. Chamberlain, *Letters of John Chamberlain*, 2:582.
58. Matthew, *James I*, 218.
59. Prestwich, *Cranfield*, 475.

How much more, if we pray him, will his ear
Be open, and his heart to pity incline,
And teach us further by what means to shun
Th' inclement seasons, rain, ice, hail and snow,
Which now the sky with various face begins
To show us in this mountain, while the winds
Blow moist and keen, shattering the graceful locks
Of these fair spreading trees. (10.1060–67)

Legally speaking, Adam here hopes for a commutation of sentence, in which the offender remains guilty of the crime but the penalty is lessened. Instead of fantasizing a complete release from all punishment, Adam more realistically imagines that they can find means of "remedy or cure/To evils which our own misdeeds have wrought," and he knows that these forms of remission will come from God: "He will instruct us praying" (10.1079–81). Rather than expecting God's pardon to reinstall them in their former life of bliss, Adam holds out the more modest idea that a pardon will allow them to continue residing in the Garden: "here let us live, though in fall'n state, content," and he hopes "to pass commodiously this life" that now lies before them (11.180, 10.1083). Adam's phrasing, however, indicates that he does not fully understand the nature of his crime. When tenants resided temporarily on land that they did not own, they were said to use the land *ad commodum* (to the profit of the owner), and *commodum* was also a term for an easement, a right enjoyed on another's property such as a right of way or a right to pasture cattle.[60] So when Adam imagines that he and Eve might pass "commodiously" their life in Eden, he imagines that he has simply been downgraded to one of the less absolute occupancies that English land law made provision for, such as socage or sergeanty. However, Adam has committed treason, and traitors forfeited all their real and chattel properties. While pardons sometimes spared the offender's life and even remitted part of the forfeiture, they rarely allowed traitors to live as they had before. For instance, although

60. Baker, *Introduction to English Legal History*, 129.

the Earl of Middlesex got his long-sought "absolute pardon," he had to leave his beloved Chelsea House. As a result, Milton's God follows the outlines of English law when he sends Michael down to "seize" (a verb meaning to take formal legal possession of a land holding) a place that he has previously termed Adam's "mansion" (11.221, 8.296). Like the Earl of Middlesex, Adam can be pardoned, but he cannot be pardoned *and* keep his real estate.

Exiled from their homelands because of their crimes, the fallen angels and Adam and Eve are in much the same situation as those many early modern convicts who were transported to work in the colonies. As Evans points out, Hell looks very much like one of the seventeenth-century penal colonies—a place populated by rebellious malcontents who have been banished from their homeland and sent to do forced labor under miserable conditions.[61] Beelzebub suspects that despite their apparent freedom in Hell, the fallen angels remain God's "thralls" and are doomed "here in the heart of Hell to work in fire" (1.149, 152). Adam likewise receives "sad sentence" of "perpetual banishment," and he must go to labor in another land among "thorns also and thistles" (11.109, 108; 10.203). English courts had begun experimenting with transportation near the beginning of the seventeenth century, and by Milton's day transportation was emerging as a viable solution to the nation's growing crime problem.[62] The crucial point is that in early modern England, no one was sentenced to transportation. Rather, those convicted of crimes were sentenced to death, and the sentence was then indefinitely reprieved (a deferral reminiscent of the Son's judgment, which "th' instant stroke of death denounced that day/Removed far off [10.210–11]). In short, those who were transported had received a form of conditional pardon, the condition being their willingness to leave England and to serve

61. Evans, *Milton's Imperial Vision*, 33–40. I am grateful to Mary C. Fenton for suggesting that Adam and Eve were also transported.

62. On the rise of transportation as a judicial option, see Harding et al., *Imprisonment in England and Wales*, 63–65. Beattie demonstrates that the Transportation Act of 1718 was the culmination of decades of thought on and experiment with penal sanctions: Beattie, *Crime and the Courts*, 468–519.

out the stated period of overseas labor.[63] From this standpoint, it is not quite accurate to say that Satan has not received a pardon. Rather, he does not like the kind of pardon he has gotten and instead wants another that offers him more freedom. Indeed, an important difference between Satan and Adam is in how they react to the penalty laid upon them. Whereas Satan repudiates the idea of working as God's thrall, Adam considers his sentence of work and tells Eve, "Idleness had been worse" (10.1055). Because Adam can see and appreciate the mercy extended to him in the midst of justice, he has the chance to create a new inner paradise.

Apocatastasis

Milton's depiction of the pardon as an actively performed set of protocols has important stakes for how he represents God's love. Specifically, it allows him to draw within arm's reach of the doctrine of apocatastasis, or universal salvation. Originating with St. Clement of Alexandria and popularized by Origen, apocatastasis was based on verses such as Acts 3:21 (which refers to the "restitution" of "all things") and Romans 14:11 (which says that "every knee shall bow" to God). It held that all created beings—including the fallen angels—will be reunited with God at the end of time. Although the dominant currents of Protestant theological thinking rejected apocatastasis, the doctrine appealed to many in seventeenth-century England, such as Arminians, who liked its emphasis on the vastness of God's love as opposed to the rigors of his judgment. Milton was conversant with Origen's thinking, and scholars such as Harry Robins and C. A. Patrides have argued that when Satan considers his options for a pardon, Milton alludes to the possibility of universal salvation.[64] But neither critic thinks that Milton was truly interested in this doctrine. Quoting God's claim in *Paradise Lost* that the fallen angels are consigned to Hell "without redemption, without end" (5.615),

63. Herrup, "Punishing Pardon."
64. See Robins, *If This Be Heresy*; Patrides, "Salvation of Satan."

Patrides puts Milton among those who opposed the idea of universal salvation, and he concludes that while Milton nods toward the doctrine of apocatastasis during Satan's soliloquy in book 4, he does so only because the "dramatic context demanded it."[65]

However, Milton seems to be more conflicted about apocatastasis than Patrides allows. From a theological standpoint, Milton seems admittedly reluctant to say that God will simply remit all sins—including Satan's—at the end of time, and so, for example, his vision of Sin and Death being used to "obstruct the mouth of Hell" and "seal up his ravenous jaws" aligns well with orthodox Protestant thinking on the final separation of the damned from the saved (10.635, 636). But Milton's descriptions of pardons in *Paradise Lost* simultaneously point in a different direction, for by depicting Satan's pardon in terms of early modern pardoning protocols, Milton shifts the emphasis from the theological realm (what God will allow) to the social realm (what the pardon seeker does). This depiction accords with his Arminian beliefs, and it de-emphasizes the idea that God's mercy might not be infinite. From the perspective of traditional Protestant theology, for Milton even to raise the question of Satan's pardon is pointless—and arguably cruel—since the fallen angel cannot be pardoned even if he really wanted to be. God's mercy simply does not extend that far. When Patrides claims that Milton alludes to apocatastasis to heighten the dramatic tension in book 4, he ascribes to Milton precisely this kind of pitilessness: Milton cracks opens the door of universal salvation just so that he can have the satisfaction of slamming it shut again in Satan's face. But by representing pardons as more than a theological toggle switch, Milton moves away from the issue of what God will or won't do and invites readers to think also about what Satan will and won't do. Satan cannot be pardoned in part because he refuses to do and say the things that led to successful pardon petitions in the early modern world. Speaking of the traces of ceremonial devotion evident in *Paradise Lost*, Achsah Guibbory argues that while Milton rejected

65. Patrides, "The Salvation of Satan," 472.

the elaborate rituals of the Laudian Church, he also wanted to "engage body as well as soul" in religious devotion.[66] We see a similar effort to involve the whole person—body and soul—in the work of seeking pardon. By showing Satan refusing to perform these actions, Milton shows that Satan will not be the beneficiary of grace primarily because he chooses not to be.

66. Guibbory, *Ceremony and Community*, 205.

9

Conclusion

In book 12 of *Paradise Lost*, Milton shows how the principles of temporal law visible in previous books of the poem first take historical shape in the form of a real legal code that will mitigate the effects of what he calls "sword-law" (11.672). In the process he explores more specifically how God's blessing on a human community relates to its respect for the rule of law. Explaining humanity's future to Adam, the archangel Michael says that the wandering Hebrew exiles in the "wide wilderness" will first set up "their government, and their great senate choose/Through the twelve tribes to rule by laws ordained" (12.224, 225–26). These laws are given to the Israelites by God himself:

> God from the mount of Sinai, whose gray top
> Shall tremble, he descending, will himself
> In thunder, lightning, and loud trumpet's sound
> Ordain them laws; part such as appertain
> To civil justice, part religious rites. (12.227–31)

Milton's vision of the Decalogue as the source of "civil justice" registers the influence of the German Protestant jurist-theologian Philip Melanchthon, a man he praises in *Tetrachordon* as "the third great luminary of reformation" (*CPW* 2:708). Writers before Melanchthon had thought about the Decalogue in the context of each believer's spiritual life, and so the Ten Commandments had appeared most often in penitential literature. However, Melanchthon saw the Decalogue as the basic template for all human legal systems, and as a result of his influence, the Commandments began increasingly to be discussed in works of law.[1] But while Milton echoes Melancthon when he shows God in book 11 handing down "laws" that will foster "civil justice," he differs from Melanchthon about the origin of law. Melanchthon saw the Noachide laws and the Decalogue as the first appearances of the rule of law, but Milton suggests in *Paradise Lost* that law begins to emerge much earlier, in the Garden of Eden. Since law helps to implement God's justice in the social world, and since God's justice is an aspect of his eternal nature, the principles of law are to some degree omnipresent in all human communities, even the first, Edenic one. Thus, the Decalogue is not an unprecedented introduction of law into an erstwhile prelegal world. Rather, it is a gathering together and a reification of legal principles that were there from the beginning.[2]

Adam understands only part of what his vision of the Decalogue means for humanity. He says to Michael, "So many laws argue so many sins/Among them," and he asks the angel, "How can God with such reside?" (12.283–84). The angel answers in the same vein: "Law [was] given them to evince/Their natural pravity, by stirring up/Sin against law to fight," so that the Israelites will learn that "law can discover sin, but not remove" (12.287–90). Adam and Michael make two mistakes here. First, they regard the arrival of law as a distant event and thus neglect the ways in which ideas of law already structure both Heaven and Eden. Second, they look at the Ten Commandments through Pauline lenses, seeing it only in relationship to individual salvation. Throughout his epistles, and

1. On the importance of Melanchthon's jurisprudence, see Berman, *Faith and Order*, 141–85.

2. My claim here is indebted to Rosenblatt's *Torah and Law*, for he argues that if we adopt a Pauline view and regard Mosaic Law only as a symptom of sin, we miss the fact that the principles of Mosaic Law are operative in the prelapsarian books.

especially in the book of Romans, Paul treats the Mosaic Law as a broken bridge. Since it does not provide a pathway to Heaven, the Law's highest function is to draw attention to its own incompleteness and thus to the need for the saving grace of Jesus Christ. For a Reformer like Melanchthon, however, the Mosaic Law also had a socially productive role to play, in that it provided the ultimate model for how a human community should be ordered and governed. Despite his Pauline language, Michael at least partly understands the more positive functions of the law. He tells Adam that once "laws and rites" are "established" among the Israelites, then

> Such delight hath God in men
> Obedient to his will, that he vouchsafes
> Among them to set up his tabernacle,
> The Holy One with mortal men to dwell. (12.245–48)

While Adam sees this as a story about humanity's "natural pravity," it is equally a story about what happens when a people adhere to a righteous rule of law. Because the Israelites are "obedient" to the "laws and rites" that have been given to them, God takes "delight" in them and sends his spirit into the Ark of the Covenant. While from one angle the Law is a foil for sinfulness, from another the establishment of a legal order containing rules about both "civil justice" and "religious rites" is a necessary precondition for the "Holy One" coming to "dwell" "with mortal men."

However, Milton's vision of law as going arm-in-arm with God's favor is a finely balanced one. More than any other early modern writer, Milton was keenly alert to the dangers of idolatry, and so while he suggests that the law is a good thing, it does not deserve civil worship. For Milton, law is like the Ark of the Covenant: its highest function is not to draw attention to itself but rather to that which it contains and expresses: the will of God. Throughout *Paradise Lost*, Milton pairs theology and law not to exalt the law itself but rather to emphasize the way that the law indexes something larger and more important. Sin occurs when people focus on the law and forget what stands behind it. For instance, as I suggested in chapter 6, Adam and Eve fall in part because, faced with a situation in which the voice of the law seems to say "eat" and the voice of God says "do not eat," they choose to listen to the law. As a result, Milton's use of law in the poem is simultaneously a tacit statement about the limits of law.

Milton's reminder that law does not of itself embody truth seems intended to counter an accelerating change in his contemporary world, one that helped to form the conceptual bedrock of the modern understanding of law. During the course of the early modern period, and particularly in the second half of the seventeenth century, the common law in England was seen less as a mere index of the will of God and more as a set of sovereign and self-referential norms. As Goodrich argues, jurisprudential literature in the period increasingly represented the law as "an empire of truth supported by a veridical language or orthodoxy that was peculiar to the law alone."[3] This changing view of the law's status was enabled by contemporary jurisdictional changes. Over the course of the sixteenth and seventeenth centuries, common law jurists such as Coke and Selden worked steadily to erode the independence and authority of England's minor jurisprudences and to engross more and more authority into the common law. For instance, prerogative courts like the Court of Requests and the Star Chamber had traditionally offered swifter and more equitable remedies than common law courts did. In 1641 common lawyers—who made up the majority of the Long Parliament—retaliated by stripping most of the nation's prerogative courts of their compulsive authority, and this same parliamentary ruling also curtailed the jurisdictional reach of the ecclesiastical courts. The result was that matters such as fraud, perjury, forgery, maintenance, slander, libel, divorce, and obscenity that had once fallen within the purview of prerogative courts and ecclesiastical courts were increasingly handled by common law jurists, who scrambled to devise new writs for accommodating them.

3. Goodrich, "Ars bablativa," 44.

Milton was apparently of two minds about these changes. He was certainly no fan of the Star Chamber or of canon law, and in earlier works such as *The Reason of Church Government*, he attacks the ecclesiastical courts as part of his argument that the church had arrogated an authority that did not belong to it. But this does not mean that he wanted the common law to step into the ecclesiastical courts' or the prerogative courts' shoes. Milton was not an Erastian; he believed passionately that certain actions—such as whether or not to tithe and whether or not to divorce—should sit outside the boundary fences of all temporal laws.[4] Moreover, he was also no fan of monopolies. During the seventeenth century, the common law was steadily acquiring one of the most complete monopolies imaginable: it increasingly became "the law" instead of just one of many brands or types of law. Prose works such as *A Readie and Easie Way* and *Proposalls of Certain Expedients* suggest that Milton did not like the common law's spreading sovereignty. In *Proposalls* he calls for the "administration of Civill Justice" to be "in the City or chief towne of every county without appeal, Judges and all such officers by themselves chosen," and in the first edition of *A Readie and Easie Way*, he says that communities should "make their own judicial lawes, and execute them by their own elected judicatures" (*CPW* 7:338, 383). This vision of legal justice being administered flexibly in relation to ground-level realities is diametrically opposed to the common law's representation of itself. In legal historian Nicholas Blomley's words, for Coke and his followers, the common law was "not a variegated and diverse system of localized practices, but a disembedded superstructure," and so the common law should "override the specificities of local legal life."[5] Even as the common law widened its hegemony and became a uniform legal blanket covering the nation, Milton fought back, proposing that the ends of justice were best served when law reflected the patchwork nature of commu-

4. See Gregory, "Did Milton Have Erastian Phase?"

5. Blomley, *Law, Space, and the Geographies*, 76. See also Helgerson, *Forms of Nationhood*, 71.

nities themselves and when it was responsive to and shaped by local needs.

Whereas works such as *A Readie and Easie Way* offer an alternative to the common law's jurisdictional monopoly, *Paradise Lost* resists its growing mystique. The steady consolidation of the various local laws and legal traditions of England into the common law meant that the law acquired not simply an extended range but also what we might think of as a new aura. Common lawyers created an immemorial genealogy for the common law through the myth of the ancient constitution, and so the common law came to seem sempiternal. They were also increasingly likely to present the common law as a "hermetic science," whose truth claims were no longer contingent on other discourses, such as philosophy and ethics.[6] In effect, the law became less an arrow pointing away from itself to God (in the same manner that the natural world or the Bible could be seen as signs that merely directed the viewer toward a higher truth) and more a quasi-sacred thing. Historians have long recognized the growing mystique of the law in late-seventeenth- and early-eighteenth-century England. Historian J. A. Sharpe points out that veneration of the rule of law was one of the most important legacies that the seventeenth century gave the eighteenth, and he claims that by the end of the seventeenth century, "law, it might be argued, was coming to replace religion as the ideological cement which held society together."[7] E. P. Thompson, in his landmark book *Whigs and Hunters*, makes similar points: the social and economic dominance of the eighteenth-century aristocracy and gentry "was expressed, above all, not in military force, not in the mystifications of a priesthood or of the press, not even in economic coercion, but in the rituals of the study of the Justices of the Peace, in the

6. Goodrich, "Ars bablativa," 55. My argument parallels Kneidel's in *John Donne and Early Modern Legal Culture*. Kneidel argues that Donne uses the *Satires* to resist the growing secularization and rationalization of the law. Law is perhaps one of the few issues on which these two poets saw eye to eye.

7. Sharpe, *Crime in Early Modern England*, 12. See also his "People and the Law," where he argues the same point.

quarter-sessions, in the pomp of the Assizes and in the theatre of Tyburn." Moreover, eighteenth-century offenders were more likely to hear about hellfire and salvation from a circuit court judge than from a staid Church of England parish priest.[8]

The danger is that when law acquires a sacral mystique of its own, the claims of law no longer need to be measured against the mandates of conscience and true religion, and lex moves further and further away from jus. We can see this trend in the eighteenth century. Although the period witnessed some notable legal advancements (e.g., the codifications of Blackstone's *Commentaries*, the judicial reforms initiated by Lord Mansfield, and the legislative science of Jeremy Bentham),[9] on balance, the rising tide of late-seventeenth- and eighteenth-century law buoyed up the haves and drowned the have-nots. Discussing the growing use of the law as a means to deny opportunity to the poor and to protect propertied interests, historian Peter Linebaugh refers memorably to the increasing "inexorability of the legal juggernaut . . . [that] ground its victims into finer particles."[10] In *Pilgrim's Progress*, John Bunyan captures what he saw as the growing corruption of the English legal system, for when Christian is put on trial in Vanity Fair, the judge is Lord Hate-Good, and the jury is comprised of Mr. Blind Man, Mr. No-good, Mr. Malice, Mr. Love-lust, Mr. Live-loose, Mr. Heady, Mr. High Mind, Mr. Enmity, Mr. Lyar, Mr. Cruelty, Mr. Hate-light and Mr. Implacable. Bunyan himself was sent to prison for twelve years simply for preaching to those who wanted to hear him talk about God's love, and his wife lamented that he was condemned "because he is a tinker, and a poor man, therefore he is despised, and cannot have justice."[11] We have traveled a long way from Sir John Fortescue's early-fifteenth-century claim in *On the Laws and Governance of England* that "to learn the laws, even

8. Thompson, *Whigs and Hunters*, 262.

9. For a fuller discussion of law and legal theory in the eighteenth century, see Lieberman, *Province of Legislation Determined*.

10. Linebaugh, *London Hanged*, xviii.

11. Quoted in Linebaugh, *London Hanged*, 72.

though human ones, is to learn laws that are sacred and decreed of God."[12] Of course, Fortescue was a jurist writing from within the legal system and seeking to protect it, and Wat Tyler's rebellion in 1381 and Cade's rebellion in 1450 provide ample evidence that a sense of the law's injustice was not unique to Bunyan's world. However, the fact is that there was far more law in Bunyan and Milton's day than there was in Fortescue's. Moreover, this growing corpus of laws had longer and sharper teeth, a fact captured by the nickname for the eighteenth-century criminal justice system: the Bloody Code.

One basic contention of this book is that Milton thought law was a better social cement than religion because it had the potential to help guarantee peace and stability without telling men and women what to believe. But the other basic contention is that Milton would have disagreed strenuously with the increasing English tendency to put the law itself on a pedestal. Law was good only insofar as it pointed to God. This is why Milton relentlessly pairs law and theology in *Paradise Lost*. He is not trying to deify the law itself. To the contrary, his point is that, like theology, law serves to reflect God. The moment that a theological doctrine—such as the Trinity—can be shown to distort God's nature, it must be discarded. Similarly, the moment that a law—such as the Licensing Act—can be shown to violate true justice, it no longer qualifies as a real law, regardless of its real-world juridical standing. But by so pervasively looking at religious matters through a legal lens, Milton may have unintentionally helped pave the way for a rising veneration of the rule of law. As Feisal Mohamed writes, "We hear everywhere in [Milton's] writings the footfalls of those modes of thought predominant in secularism, but these are contained within and measured by a fundamentally non-secular system of belief."[13] Amid what looked like the growing injustice and indifference to liberty in Restoration society, Milton looked for some pipeline

12. Fortescue, *Laws and Governance of England*, 6–7.

13. Mohamed, *Milton and the Post-Secular Present*, 19.

through which the high, pure principles of Heaven might continue to flow down to Earth. The law and the judicial system, despite their manifest failings, had the potential to serve as that pipeline. From his point of view, good laws could provide hospitable conditions under which men and women could cultivate the paradise within. However, there is an inherent risk in calling attention to the continuities between human justice and divine justice: an image in a mirror can be readily confused with the reality it reflects, and the law, which was a mediated expression of God's will much like the Bible, could become the subject of idolatrous veneration. Ultimately, it is one of the great ironies that *Paradise Lost*, which celebrates law and order only insofar as they reflect the will of God, might have contributed to an attitude toward law and the implementation of legal justice that Milton would have deplored.

Bibliography

Achinstein, Sharon. *Milton and the Revolutionary Reader*. Princeton, NJ: Princeton University Press, 1994.

Albyn, Benjamin. *An Appeal to God and the King Together with a True Narrative of Unparallell'd Grievances*. London, 1697.

Almond, Philip C. *Adam and Eve in Seventeenth-Century Thought*. Cambridge: Cambridge University Press, 2008.

Aquinas, Thomas. *Summa theologica*. Translated by Fathers of the English Dominican Province. 5 vols. Westminster, MD: Christian Classics, 1981.

Arnold, Matthew. "The Function of Criticism at the Present Time." In *Essays by Matthew Arnold*, 9–36. London: Humphrey Milford, 1910.

Attie, Katherine Bootle. "Enclosure Polemics and the Garden in the 1650s." *SEL Studies in English Literature 1500–1900* 51 (2011): 135–57.

Aylmer, G. E. "The Meaning and Definition of 'Property' in Seventeenth-Century England." *Past and Present* 86 (1980): 87–97.

Babington, Zachary. *Advice to Grand Jurors in Cases of Blood*. London, 1677.

Bacon, Francis. *The Letters and the Life of Francis Bacon*. Edited by James Spedding. 7 vols. London: Longmans, 1868.

Bailey, Amanda. *Of Bondage: Debt, Property, and Personhood in Early Modern England*. Philadelphia: University of Pennsylvania Press, 2013.

Baker, David Weil. "'Dealt with at His Owne Weapon': Anti-antiquarianism in Milton's Prelacy Tracts." *Studies in Philology* 106 (2009): 207–34.

Baker, J. H. "Criminal Courts and Procedure at Common Law, 1550–1800." In *Crime in England, 1550–1800*, edited by J. S. Cockburn, 15–48. Princeton, NJ: Princeton University Press, 1977.

———. *An Introduction to English Legal History*. London: Butterworths, 1971.

———. "Origins of the 'Doctrine' of Consideration, 1535–85." In *On the Laws and Customs of England: Essays in Honor of Samuel E. Thorne*, edited by Morris S. Arnold, Thomas A. Greene, Sally A. Scully, and Stephen D. White, 336–58. Chapel Hill: University of North Carolina Press, 1981.

Barnes, Thomas G. "The Inns of Court under Elizabeth I and the Early Stuarts, 1590–1640, by Wilfrid R. Prest." *American Historical Review* 78 (1973): 1055–57.

Baxter, Richard. *Three Treatises Tending to Awaken Secure Sinners*. London, 1656.

Beattie, J. M. *Crime and the Courts in England, 1660–1800*. Oxford: Clarendon Press, 1986.

Beaulieu, Luke. *The Terms of Peace and Reconciliation betwixt All Divided Parties*. London, 1684.

Beaver, Daniel C. *Hunting and the Politics of Violence before the English Civil War*. Cambridge: Cambridge University Press, 2008.

Beecher, Donald, Travis Decook, Andrew Wallace, and Grant Williams, eds. *Taking Exception to the Law: Materializing Injustice in Early Modern English Literature*. Toronto: University of Toronto Press, 2015.

Beier, A. L. *Masterless Men: The Vagrancy Problem in England, 1560–1640*. London: Methuen, 1985.

Bellamy, J. G. *The Tudor Law of Treason: An Introduction*. London: Routledge and Kegan Paul, 1979.

Benet, Diana Trevino. "Milton's Toad, or Satan's Dream." *Milton Studies* 45 (2006): 38–53.

Bennett, Joan S. *Reviving Liberty: Radical Christian Humanism in Milton's Great Poems*. Cambridge, MA: Harvard University Press, 1989.

Berman, Harold J. *Faith and Order: The Reconciliation of Law and Religion*. Atlanta: Scholars Press, 1993.

———. *Law and Revolution: The Formation of the Western Legal Tradition*. Cambridge, MA: Harvard University Press, 1985.

———. *Law and Revolution, II: The Impact of the Protestant Reformation on the Western Legal Tradition*. Cambridge, MA: Belknap Press of Harvard University Press, 2003.

———. "The Origins of Historical Jurisprudence: Coke, Selden, Hale." *Yale Law Journal* 103, no. 7 (1994): 1651–1738.

Bernard, Richard. *The Isle of Man: Or, the Legall Proceeding in Man-Shire against Sinne*. London, 1632.

The Bible and Holy Scriptures Conteyned in the Olde and Newe Testament. Geneva, 1560.

Blackstone, William. *Commentaries on the Laws of England*. 4 vols. Oxford, 1766.

Blomley, Nicholas K. *Law, Space, and the Geographies of Power*. New York: Guilford, 1994.

Blount, Thomas. *Nomo-Lexicon, A Law Dictionary*. London, 1670.

Bobbio, Norberto. *Thomas Hobbes and the Natural Law Tradition*. Translated by Daniela Gobetti. Chicago: University of Chicago Press, 1993.

Boswell, Jackson Campbell. *Milton's Library: A Catalogue of the Remains of John Milton's Library and an Annotated Reconstruction of Milton's Library and Ancillary Readings*. New York: Garland, 1975.

Boyer, Allen D. *Sir Edward Coke and the Elizabethan Age*. Stanford, CA: Stanford University Press, 2003.

Bracton, Henri de. *On the Laws and Customs of England*. Edited by Samuel E. Thorne. 2 vols. Cambridge, MA: Belknap Press of Harvard University Press, 1968.

Breight, Curt. "'Treason Doth Never Prosper': The Tempest and the Discourse of Treason." *Shakespeare Quarterly* (1990): 1–28.

A Brief Discourse of the Most Haynous and Traytorlike Fact of Thomas Appeltree. London, 1579.

Briggs, John H. Y. *Crime and Punishment in England: An Introductory History*. New York: St. Martins, 1996.

Brittan, Jillisa, and Richard A. Posner. "Penal Theory in *Paradise Lost*." *Michigan Law Review* 105 (2007): 1049–66.

Brooks, Christopher W. *Law, Politics, and Society in Early Modern England*. Cambridge: Cambridge University Press, 2008.

———. "A Law-Abiding and Litigious Society." In *The Oxford Illustrated History of Tudor and Stuart Britain*, edited by John Morrill, 139–55. Oxford: Oxford University Press, 1996.

———. *Lawyers, Litigation and English Society since 1450*. London: Hambledon Press, 1998.

———. *Pettyfoggers and Vipers of the Commonwealth: The "Lower Branch" of the Legal Profession in Early Modern England*. Cambridge: Cambridge University Press, 1986.

Brownlow, Richard. *Reports: (a Second Part.) of Diverse Famous Cases in Law*. London, 1651.

Brydall, John. *A Compendious Collection of the Laws of England, Touching Matters Criminal*. London, 1675.

Bryson, Michael. *The Tyranny of Heaven: Milton's Rejection of God as King*. Newark: University of Delaware Press, 2004.

Buckle, Stephen. *Natural Law and the Theory of Property: Grotius to Hume*. Oxford: Clarendon Press, 1991.

Burgess, Glenn. *The Politics of the Ancient Constitution: An Introduction to English Political Thought, 1603–1642*. University Park: Pennsylvania State University Press, 1992.

Burroughs, Jeremiah. *Christ Inviting Sinners to Come to Him for Rest*. London, 1659.

Campbell, Gordon. *A Compendium of Roman Law: Founded on the Institutes of Justinian*. London: Stevens and Haynes, 1878.

———. "Milton, Sir Christopher (1615–1693)." In *Oxford Dictionary of National Biography*, edited by H. C. G. Matthew and Brian Harrison. Oxford: Oxford University Press, 2004. Online edition, ed. Lawrence Goldman, January 2008, www.oxforddnb.com/view/article/18798.

Campbell, Gordon, and Thomas N. Corns. *John Milton: Life, Work, and Thought*. Oxford: Oxford University Press, 2008.

The Cavaliers Jubilee: Or, Long Look'd for Come at Last: Viz. The General Pardon. London, 1652.

Chamberlain, John. *The Letters of John Chamberlain*. Edited by Norman Egbert McClure. 2 vols. Philadelphia: American Philosophical Society, 1939.

Chapman, Alison A. "Milton and Legal Reform." *Renaissance Quarterly* 69, no. 2 (Summer 2016): 529–65.

———. "Milton's Captive Audience: Teaching *Paradise Lost* in the Maximum Security Prison." *pms: poemmemoirstory* 9 (2009): 49–61.

Charles I, King of England. *Eikon basilike*. London, 1649.

Charles II, King of England. *A Proclamation for Discovery of Robberies and Burglaries, and for a Reward to the Discoverers*. London, 1661.

Chesney, Eugene J. "Concept of *Mens Rea* in the Criminal Law." *Journal and Criminal Law and Criminology* 29 (1939): 627–44.

Cockburn, J. S. *A History of English Assizes, 1558–1714*. Cambridge: Cambridge University Press, 1972.

Coke, Edward. *The Third Part of the Institutes of the Laws of England*. London, 1644.

Coleman, D. C. "London Scriveners and the Estate Market in the Later Seventeenth Century." *Economic History Review* 4 (1951): 221–30.

Constable, Marianne. *The Law of the Other: The Mixed Jury and Changing Conceptions of Citizenship, Law, and Knowledge*. Chicago: University of Chicago Press, 1994.

Coppe, Abiezer. *A Fiery Flying Roll*. 1650.

Cormack, Bradin. *A Power to Do Justice: Jurisdiction, English Literature, and the Rise of Common Law, 1509–1625*. Chicago: University of Chicago Press, 2007.

Cowell, John. *The Interpreter: Or Booke Containing the Signification of Words*. Cambridge, 1607.

Cunningham, Karen. *Imaginary Betrayals: Subjectivity and the Discourses of Treason in Early Modern England*. Philadelphia: University of Pennsylvania Press, 2002.

Daborne, Robert. *A Sermon Preached in the Cathedrall Church of the Citie of Waterford in Febr. 1617*. London, 1618.

Danielson, Dennis. *Milton's Good God: A Study in Literary Theodicy*. Cambridge: Cambridge University Press, 1982.

Darbishire, Helen, ed. *The Early Lives of Milton*. New York: Barnes and Noble, 1932.

Davis, Natalie Zemon. *Fiction in the Archives: Pardon Tales and Their Tellers in Sixteenth-Century France*. Stanford, CA: Stanford University Press, 1987.

Dean, David. *Law-Making and Society in Late Elizabethan England: The Parliament of England, 1584–1601*. Cambridge: Cambridge University Press, 1996.

Defoe, Daniel. *The Political History of the Devil as Well Ancient as Modern*. London, 1726.

Dekker, Thomas. *The Belman of London Bringing to Light the Most Notorious Villanies That Are Now Practiced in the Kingdome.* London, 1608.

De Laune, Thomas. *Tropologia, Or, A Key to Open Scripture Metaphors.* London, 1681.

Dickinson, H. T. *Liberty and Property: Political Ideology in Eighteenth-Century Britain.* London: Methuen, 1977.

Dobranski, Stephen B. *Milton, Authorship, and the Book Trade.* Cambridge: Cambridge University Press, 1999.

———. *Milton's Visual Imagination: Imagery in "Paradise Lost."* Cambridge: Cambridge University Press, 2015.

Dolan, Frances E. *True Relations: Reading, Literature, and Evidence in Seventeenth-Century England.* Philadelphia: University of Pennsylvania Press, 2014.

Donnelly, Phillip J. *Milton's Scriptural Reasoning: Narrative and Protestant Toleration.* Cambridge: Cambridge University Press, 2009.

Dryden, John. *The State of Innocence, and Fall of Man: An Opera Written in Heroique Verse.* In *The Works of John Dryden*, edited by Vinton A. Dearing, 12:79–146. Berkeley: University of California Press, 1994.

Dugdale, Gilbert. *A True Discourse of the Practices of Elizabeth Caldwell . . on the Parson of Master Thomas Caldwell . . . to Have Murdered and Poysoned Him.* London, 1604.

Dyson, Jessica. *Staging Authority in Caroline England: Prerogative, Law and Order in Drama, 1625–1642.* Burlington, VT: Ashgate, 2013.

Dyzenhaus, David. "Hobbes on the Authority of Law." In *Hobbes and the Law*, edited by David Dyzenhaus and Thomas Poole, 186–209. Cambridge: Cambridge University Press, 2012.

Dzelzainis, Martin. "'In These Western Parts of the Empire': Milton and Roman Law." In *Milton and the Terms of Liberty*, edited by Graham Parry and Joad Raymond, 57–68. Cambridge, UK: D. S. Brewer, 2002.

———. "Liberty and the Law." In *Milton, Rights, and Liberties*, edited by Christophe Tournu and Neil Forsyth, 57–67. Bern, Switzerland: Peter Lang, 2007.

Edgar, Thomas. *The Lawes Resolutions of Womens Rights: Or, The Lawes Provisions for Woemen.* London, 1632.

Edwards, Karen L. *Milton and the Natural World: Science and Poetry in "Paradise Lost."* Cambridge: Cambridge University Press, 1999.

———. "Milton's Reformed Animals: An Early Modern Bestiary T–Z." *Milton Quarterly* 43 (2009): 247–51.

Egerton, Thomas. *A Discourse upon the Exposicion and Understandinge of Statutes*. Edited by Samuel E. Thorne. San Marino, CA: Huntington Library, 1942.

Ellwood, Thomas. *The History of the Life of Thomas Ellwood*. London, 1714.

Empson, William. *Milton's God*. London: Chatto and Windus, 1961.

Epstein, Richard. "Unconscionability: A Critical Reappraisal." In *Foundations of Contract Law*, edited by Richard Craswell and Alan Schwartz, 288–95. New York: Oxford University Press, 1994.

Erickson, Amy Louise. *Women and Property in Early Modern England*. New York: Routledge, 1993.

Est, William. *The Judges and Juries Instruction*. London, 1614.

Evans, J. Martin. *Milton's Imperial Vision: "Paradise Lost" and the Discourses of Colonialism*. Ithaca, NY: Cornell University Press, 1996.

———. *"Paradise Lost" and the Genesis Tradition*. Oxford: Clarendon Press, 1968.

The Execution of the 11 Prisoners That Suffer'd at Tyburn, and One in Little-Brittain, on Wednesday the 22th of This Instant January, 1679. London, 1679.

Faller, Lincoln B. *Crime and Defoe: A New Kind of Writing*. Cambridge: Cambridge University Press, 1993.

———. *Turned to Account: The Forms and Functions of Criminal Biography in Late Seventeenth- and Early Eighteenth-Century England*. Cambridge: Cambridge University Press, 1987.

Fallon, Robert Thomas. *Milton in Government*. University Park: Pennsylvania State University Press, 1993.

Fallon, Stephen M. "Milton's Arminianism and the Authorship of *De Doctrina Christiana*." *Texas Studies in Literature and Language* 41 (1999): 103–27.

———. *Milton's Peculiar Grace: Self-Representation and Authority*. Ithaca, NY: Cornell University Press, 2007.Fenton, Mary C. *Milton's Places of Hope: Spiritual and Political Connections of Hope with Land*. Burlington, VT: Ashgate, 2006.

Fielding, Henry. *The Life of Mr. Jonathan Wild the Great*. Dublin, 1754.

———. *The True Patriot*. In *The Works of Henry Fielding*, vol. 14. New York: Barnes and Noble, 1967.

Filmer, Robert. *Patriarcha*. London, 1680.

Fish, Stanley. *Doing What Comes Naturally: Change, Rhetoric and the Practice of Theory in Literary and Legal Studies*. Durham, NC: Duke University Press, 1989.

———. *How Milton Works*. Cambridge, MA: Belknap Press of Harvard University Press, 2001.

———. "The Law Wishes to Have a Formal Existence." In *There's No Such Thing as Free Speech, and It's a Good Thing*, 141–79. New York: Oxford University Press, 1994.

———. *Surprised by Sin: The Reader in "Paradise Lost."* New York: St. Martins, 1967.

Flannagan, Roy, ed. *Paradise Lost*. In *The Riverside Milton*. Boston: Houghton Mifflin, 1998.

Fletcher, H. F. *The Intellectual Development of John Milton*. 2 vols. Urbana: University of Illinois Press, 1956.

Ford, Richard T. "Law's Territory (A History of Jurisdiction)." *Michigan Law Review* 97 (1999): 843–930.

Forsyth, Neil. *The Satanic Epic*. Princeton, NJ: Princeton University Press, 2003.

Fortescue, John. *On the Laws and Governance of England*. Edited by Shelley Lockwood. Cambridge: Cambridge University Press, 1997.

Fortier, Mark. *The Culture of Equity in Early Modern England*. Burlington, VT: Ashgate, 2005.

Foucault, Michel. *Discipline and Punish: The Birth of the Prison*. London: Allen Lane, 1977.

Fowler, Alastair, ed. *Paradise Lost*. In *The Poems of John Milton*. London: Longman, 1980.

Fox, John C. *A History of Contempt of Court, the Form of Trial and the Mode of Punishment*. Oxford: Clarendon Press, 1927.

Freeman, James A. *Milton and the Martial Muse: "Paradise Lost" and European Traditions of War*. Princeton, NJ: Princeton University Press, 1980.

French, Joseph Milton. *Milton in Chancery: New Chapters in the Lives of the Poet and His Father*. New York: Modern Language Association, 1939.

Fulton, Thomas. *Historical Milton: Manuscript, Print, and Political Culture in Revolutionary England*. Amherst: University of Massachusetts Press, 2010.

Fumerton, Patricia. "London's Vagrant Economy: Making Space for 'Low' Subjectivity." In *Material London, ca. 1600*, edited by Lena

Cowen Orlin, 206–26. Philadelphia: University of Pennsylvania Press, 2000.

Gardiner, Samuel Rawson, ed. *The Constitutional Documents of the Puritan Revolution*. 3rd ed. Oxford: Clarendon Press, 1906.

Gaskill, Malcolm. *Crime and Mentalities in Early Modern England*. Cambridge: Cambridge University Press, 2000.

"God, Law, and Alabama." *People*, September 8, 2003.

Goodrich, Peter. "*Amici curiae*: Lawful Manhood and Other Juristic Practices in Renaissance England." In *Literature, Politics and Law in Renaissance England*, edited by Erica Sheen and Lorna Hutson, 23–49. Houndsmill, Basingstoke: Palgrave, 2005.

———. "Ars bablativa: Ramism, Rhetoric, and the Genealogy of English Jurisprudence." In *Legal Hermeneutics: History, Theory, and Practice*, edited by Gregory Leyh, 43–82. Berkeley: University of California Press, 1992.

———. *Law in the Courts of Love: Literature and Other Minor Jurisprudences*. London: Routledge, 1996.

———. *Reading the Law: A Critical Introduction to Legal Method and Techniques*. Oxford: Blackwell, 1986.

Gray, Charles M. *The Writ of Prohibition: Jurisdiction in Early Modern English Law*. 2 vols. New York: Oceana, 1994.

Green, Richard Firth. *A Crisis of Truth: Literature and Law in Ricardian England*. Philadelphia: University of Pennsylvania Press, 1999.

Green, Thomas Andrew. *Verdict according to Conscience: Perspectives on the English Criminal Trial Jury, 1200–1800*. Chicago: University of Chicago Press, 1985.

Greenberg, Lynne. "Dalila's 'Feminine Assaults': The Gendering and Engendering of Crime in *Samson Agonistes*." In *Altering Eyes: New Perspectives on Samson Agonistes*, edited by Mark R. Kelley and Joseph Wittreich, 192–218. Newark: University of Delaware Press, 2002.

———. "Law." In *Milton in Context*, edited by Stephen B. Dobranski, 328–37. Cambridge: Cambridge University Press, 2010.

———, ed. *Legal Treatises*. 3 vols. The Early Modern Englishwoman: A Facsimile Library of Essential Works. Burlington, VT: Ashgate, 2005.

———. "Paradise Enclosed and the Feme Covert." In *Milton and the Grounds of Contention*, edited by Mark R. Kelley, Michael Lieb, and John Shawcross, 150–73. Pittsburgh: Duquesne University Press, 2003.

———. "'A Peal of Words': Criminal Speech in *Samson Agonistes*." In *Reassembling Truth: Twenty-First-Century Milton*, edited by Charles W. Durham and Kristin Pruitt, 189–200. Selinsgrove, PA: Susquehanna University Press, 2003.

———. "A Preliminary Study of Informed Consent and Free Will in the Garden of Eden: John Milton's Social Contract." In *Living Texts: Interpreting Milton*, edited by Charles W. Durham and Kristin Pruitt, 99–117. Selinsgrove, PA: Susquehanna University Press, 2000.

Gregory, Tobias. "Did Milton Have an Erastian Phase?" *Milton Quarterly* 49 (2015): 159–66.

Grotius, Hugo. *Adamus xul.* In *The Celestial Cycle: The Theme of "Paradise Lost" in World Literature with Translations of the Major Analogues*, edited by Watson Kirkconnell, 96–219. New York: Gordian Press, 1967.

———. *The Rights of War and Peace*. Edited by Richard Tuck. 3 vols. Indianapolis: Liberty Fund, 2005.

Guibbory, Achsah. *Ceremony and Community from Herbert to Milton: Literature, Religion, and Cultural Conflict in Seventeenth-Century England.* Cambridge: Cambridge University Press, 1998.

Hale, Matthew. *The History of the Common Law of England.* Edited by Charles M. Gray. Chicago: University of Chicago Press, 1971.

———. *Pleas of the Crown*. London, 1678.

Halkett, John. *Milton and the Idea of Matrimony: A Study of the Divorce Tracts and "Paradise Lost."* New Haven, CT: Yale University Press, 1970.

Hall, John. *Memoirs of the Right Villainous John Hall, the Late Famous and Notorious Robber*. London, 1714.

Hanford, James Holly, ed. *The Poems of John Milton*. 2nd ed. New York: Ronald, 1953.

Harding, Christopher, Bill Hines, Richard Ireland, and Philip Rawlings. *Imprisonment in England and Wales: A Concise History*. London: Croom Helm, 1985.

Hawkes, David. *John Milton: A Hero of Our Time*. Berkeley: Counterpoint, 2009.

———. "Milton and Usury." *English Literary Renaissance* 41 (2011): 503–28.

Hay, Douglas. "Property, Authority, and the Criminal Law." In *Albion's Fatal Tree: Crime and Society in Eighteenth-Century England*, edited by Douglas Hay, 17–63. New York: Pantheon, 1976.

Hayward, Arthur L. *Lives of the Most Remarkable Criminals*. New York: Dodd, Mead, 1927. Originally published 1735 in three separate volumes.

Helgerson, Richard. *Forms of Nationhood: The Elizabethan Writing of England*. Chicago: University of Chicago Press, 1992.

Helmholz, R. H. *The Canon Law and Ecclesiastical Jurisdiction from 591 to the 1640s*. Vol. 1 of *The Oxford History of the Laws of England*. Oxford: Oxford University Press, 2004.

———. *Roman Canon Law in Reformation England*. Cambridge: Cambridge University Press, 1990.

Herbert, George. *The Works of George Herbert*. Edited by F. E. Hutchinson. Oxford: Clarendon Press, 1945.

Herman, Peter C. *Destabilizing Milton: "Paradise Lost" and the Poetics of Incertitude*. New York: Palgrave, 2005.

———. "'Whose Fault, Whose but His Own?' *Paradise Lost*, Contributory Negligence, and the Problem of Cause." In Herman and Sauer, *New Milton Criticism*, 49–67.

Herman, Peter C., and Elizabeth Sauer, eds. *The New Milton Criticism*. Cambridge: Cambridge University Press, 2012.

Herrup, Cynthia. *The Common Peace: Participation and the Criminal Law in Seventeenth-Century England*. Cambridge: Cambridge University Press, 1987.

———. "Punishing Pardon: Some Thoughts on the Origins of Transportation." In *Penal Practice and Culture, 1500–1900: Punishing the English*, edited by Simon Devereaux and Paul Griffiths, 121–37. New York: Palgrave, 2004.

Hiltner, Ken. *Milton and Ecology*. Cambridge: Cambridge University Press, 2010.

Hobbes, Thomas. *A Dialogue between a Philosopher and a Student of the Common Laws of England*. Edited by Joseph Cropsey. Chicago: University of Chicago Press, 1971.

———. *Leviathan*. Edited by Richard Tuck. Cambridge: Cambridge University Press, 1991.

Hooker, Richard. *Of the Laws of Ecclesiastical Polity*. Edited by Georges Edelen. Cambridge, MA: Belknap Press of Harvard University Press, 1977.

Hoxby, Blair. "*Areopagitica* and Liberty." In *The Oxford Handbook of Milton*, edited by Nicholas McDowell and Nigel Smith, 218–40. Oxford: Oxford University Press, 2009.

———. *Mammon's Music: Literature and Economics in the Age of Milton*. New Haven, CT: Yale University Press, 2002.

Hume, Patrick. *Annotations on Milton's "Paradise Lost."* London, 1695.

Hunsdon, Henry Carey Baron. *The Araignment, Examination, Confession and Judgement of Arnold Cosbye: Who Wilfully Murdered the Lord Burke, Neere the Towne of Wanswoorth*. London, 1591.

Hutson, Lorna. *The Invention of Suspicion: Law and Mimesis in Shakespeare and Renaissance Drama*. Oxford: Oxford University Press, 2007.

Ireland, Lord Lieutenant. *Articles of Peace Made and Concluded with the Irish Rebels and Papists by James Earle of Ormond*. London, 1649.

James I of England. *We Had Hoped, Seeing It Is Notorious to All Our Subjects, How Greatly We Delight in the Exercise of Hunting, as Well for Our Recreations*. London, 1609.

Johnson, Samuel. *The Rambler: In Four Volumes*. London, 1767.

Jones, Edward. "The Itinerant Sibling: Christopher Milton in London and Suffolk." In *A Concise Companion to the Study of Manuscripts, Printed Books, and the Production of Early Modern Texts*, edited by Edward Jones, 87–105. Chichester, West Sussex: Wiley Blackwell, 2015.

Jones, W. J. *The Elizabethan Court of Chancery*. Oxford: Clarendon Press, 1967.

Jordan, Constance. "Interpreting Statute in *Measure for Measure*." In *Shakespeare and the Law: A Conversation among Disciplines and Professions*, edited by Bradin Cormack, Martha C. Nussbaum, and Richard Strier, 101–20. Chicago: University of Chicago Press, 2013.

Kahn, Victoria. *Wayward Contracts: The Crisis of Political Obligation in England, 1640–1670*. Princeton, NJ: Princeton University Press, 2004.

Kahn, Victoria, and Lorna Hutson, eds. *Rhetoric and Law in Early Modern Europe*. New Haven, CT: Yale University Press, 2001.

Kantorowicz, Ernst. *The King's Two Bodies: A Study in Mediaeval Political Theology*. Princeton, NJ: Princeton University Press, 1957.

Kelley, Maurice. *This Great Argument: A Study of Milton's "De Doctrina Christiana" as a Gloss upon "Paradise Lost."* Princeton, NJ: Princeton University Press, 1941.

Kerrigan, William, John P. Rumrich, and Stephen M. Fallon, eds. *Paradise Lost*. In *The Complete Poetry and Essential Prose of John Milton*. New York: Modern Library, 2007.

Kesselring, Krista J. *Mercy and Authority in the Tudor State*. Cambridge: Cambridge University Press, 2003.

Kezar, Dennis, ed. *Solon and Thespis: Law and Theater in the English Renaissance*. Notre Dame, IN: Notre Dame University Press, 2007.

Knafla, Louis A. *Law and Politics in Jacobean England: The Tracts of Lord Chancellor Ellesmere*. Cambridge: Cambridge University Press, 1977.

Kneidel, Gregory. *John Donne and Early Modern Legal Culture: The End of Equity in the "Satyres."* Pittsburgh, PA: Duquesne University Press, 2015.

Knoppers, Laura Lunger. *Historicizing Milton: Spectacle, Power, and Pageantry in Restoration England*. Athens: University of Georgia Press, 1994.

Komorowski, Michael. "Milton's Natural Law: Divorce and Individual Property." *Milton Studies* 53 (2012): 69–99.

Koziol, Geoffrey. *Begging Pardon and Favor: Ritual and Political Order in Early Medieval France*. Ithaca, NY: Cornell University Press, 1992.

The Lady's Law: Or, A Treatise of Feme Coverts: Containing All the Laws and Statutes Relating to Women. London, 1737.

Lambarde, William. *William Lambarde and Local Government: His "Ephemeris" and Twenty-Nine Charges to Juries and Commissions*. Edited by Conyers Read. Ithaca, NY: Cornell University Press for the Folger Shakespeare Library, 1962.

Lawson, P. G. "Lawless Juries: The Composition and Behavior of Hertfordshire Juries, 1573–1624." In *Twelve Good Men and True: The Criminal Trial Jury in England, 1200–1800*, edited by J. S. Cockburn and Thomas A. Green, 117–57. Princeton, NJ: Princeton University Press, 1988.

Lehnhof, Kent. "'Impregn'd with Reason': Eve's Aural Conception in *Paradise Lost*." *Milton Studies* 41 (2002): 38–75.

Lemon, Rebecca. *Treason by Words: Literature, Law, and Rebellion in Shakespeare's England*. Ithaca, NY: Cornell University Press, 2006.

Leonard, John. "Satan as Con Man: A Handbook for Suckers." Paper presented at the Eleventh International Milton Symposium, University of Exeter (UK), July 22, 2015.

Lieb, Michael. "*Paradise Lost* and the Myth of Prohibition." *Milton Studies* 7 (1975): 233–65.

———. *Poetics of the Holy: A Reading of "Paradise Lost."* Chapel Hill: University of North Carolina Press, 1981.

Lieberman, David. *The Province of Legislation Determined: Legal Theory in Eighteenth-Century Britain*. Cambridge: Cambridge University Press, 2002.

Linebaugh, Peter. *The London Hanged: Crime and Civil Society in the Eighteenth Century*. Cambridge: Cambridge University Press, 1992.

Loades, David. "Philip II and the Government of England." In *Law and Government under the Tudors*, edited by Claire Cross, David Loades, and J. J. Scarisbrick, 177–94. Cambridge: Cambridge University Press, 1988.

Lobban, Michael. "Thomas Hobbes and the Common Law." In *Hobbes and the Law*, edited by David Dyzenhaus and Thomas Poole, 39–67. Cambridge: Cambridge University Press, 2012.

Locke, John. *Second Treatise of Government*. Edited by C. B. Macpherson. Indianapolis: Hackett, 1980.

Loewenstein, David. *Representing Revolution in Milton and His Contemporaries: Religion, Politics, and Polemics in Radical Puritanism*. Cambridge: Cambridge University Press, 2001.

Maclean, Ian. *Interpretation and Meaning in the Renaissance: The Case of Law*. Cambridge: Cambridge University Press, 1992.

Maine, Henry Sumner. *Ancient Law: Its Connection with the Early History of Society, and Its Relation to Modern Idea*. New York: Dorset, 1986.

Majeske, Andrew J. *Equity in English Renaissance Literature: Thomas More and Edmund Spenser*. New York: Routledge, 2006.

Manning, Roger B. *Hunters and Poachers: A Social and Cultural History of Unlawful Hunting in England, 1485–1640*. Oxford: Clarendon Press, 1993.

———. *Village Revolts: Social Protests and Popular Disturbances in England, 1509–1640*. Oxford: Clarendon Press, 1988.

Manwood, John. *A Brefe Collection of the Lawes of the Forest*. London, 1592.

———. *A Treatise and Discourse of the Lawes of the Forrest*. London, 1598.

Marcus, Leah S. "Justice for Margery Evans: A 'Local' Reading of *Comus*." In *Milton and the Idea of Woman*, edited by Julia M. Walker, 66–85. Urbana: University of Illinois Press, 1988.

———. *Politics of Mirth: Jonson, Herrick, Milton, Marvell, and the Defense of Old Holiday Pastimes*. Chicago: University of Chicago Press, 1986.

Marjara, Harinder Singh. *Contemplation of Created Things: Science in "Paradise Lost."* Toronto: University of Toronto Press, 1992.

Marlowe, Christopher. *Edward II*. Vol. 3 of *The Complete Works of Christopher Marlowe*, edited by Richard Rowland. Oxford: Clarendon Press, 1987.

Martin, Randall. *Women, Murder, and Equity in Early Modern England*. New York: Routledge, 2008.

Matthew, David. *James I*. Tuscaloosa: University of Alabama Press, 1968.

Maus, Katherine Eisaman. *Being and Having in Shakespeare*. Oxford: Oxford University Press, 2013.

McIlwain, Charles Howard. *The High Court of Parliament and Its Supremacy: An Historical Essay on the Boundaries between Legislation and Adjudication in England*. New Haven, CT: Yale University Press, 1910.

McNeil, Charles, ed. *The Tanner Letters: Original Documents and Notices of Irish Affairs in the Sixteenth and Seventeenth Centuries*. Dublin: Stationery Office, 1943.

Milbank, John. *Theology and Social Theory*. Oxford: Blackwell, 2006.

Miller, Leo. *John Milton's Writings in the Anglo-Dutch Negotiations, 1651–1654*. Pittsburgh: Duquesne University Press, 1992.

Miller, Shannon. *Engendering the Fall: John Milton and Seventeenth-Century Women Writers*. Philadelphia: University of Pennsylvania Press, 2008.

Mohamed, Feisal G. *Milton and the Post-Secular Present: Ethics, Politics, Toleration*. Stanford, CA: Stanford University Press, 2011.

Mohl, Ruth. *John Milton and His "Commonplace Book."* New York: Frederick Ungar, 1969.

Mollenauer, Lynn Wood. *Strange Revelations: Magic, Poison, and Sacrilege in Louis XIV's France*. University Park: Pennsylvania State University Press, 2007.

Muldrew, Craig. *The Economy of Obligation: The Culture of Credit and Social Relations in Early Modern England.* New York: St. Martin's Press, 1998.

Munsche, P. B. *Gentlemen and Poachers: The English Game Laws, 1671–1831.* Cambridge: Cambridge University Press, 1981.

A New Canting Dictionary: Comprehending All the Terms, Antient and Modern, Used in the Several Tribes of Gypsies, Beggars, Shoplifters, Highwaymen, Foot-Pads and All Other Clans of Cheates and Villains. London, 1725.

Nyquist, Mary. *Arbitrary Rule: Slavery, Tyranny, and the Power of Life and Death.* Chicago: University of Chicago Press, 2013.

Oakley, Francis. *Natural Law, Laws of Nature, Natural Rights.* New York: Continuum, 2005.

Ogilvie, Charles. *The King's Government and the Common Law, 1471–1641.* Westport, CT: Greenwood Press, 1958.

Orgel, Stephen, and Jonathan Goldberg, eds. *John Milton.* Oxford: Oxford University Press, 1991.

Orr, D. Alan. *Treason and the State: Law, Politics, and Ideology in the English Civil War.* Cambridge: Cambridge University Press, 2002.

Pagitt, Ephraim. *Heresiography: Or, A Description of the Heretickes and Sectaries of These Latter Times.* London, 1645.

Patrides, C. A. "Milton and the Protestant Theory of the Atonement." *PMLA* 74, no. 1 (1959): 7–13.

———. "The Salvation of Satan." *Journal of the History of Ideas* 28 (1967): 467–78.

Pendry, E. D. *Elizabethan Prisons and Prison Scenes.* 2 vols. Salzburg, Austria: Institut Für Englische Sprache und Literature Universität Salzburg, 1974.

Pepys, Samuel. *The Diary of Samuel Pepys.* Edited by Robert Latham and William Matthews. 11 vols. Berkeley: University of California Press, 1971.

Peters, Julie Stone. "A 'Bridge over Chaos': *De jure belli, Paradise Lost,* Terror, Sovereignty, Globalism, and the Modern Law of Nations." *Comparative Literature* 57 (2005): 273–93.

Picciotto, Joanna. *Labors of Innocence in Early Modern England.* Cambridge, MA: Harvard University Press, 2010.

———. "Reforming the Garden: The Experimentalist Eden and *Paradise Lost.*" *English Literary History* 72 (2005): 23–78.

Plucknett, Theodore F. T. *A Concise History of the Common Law*. 5th ed. Boston: Little, Brown, 1956.

Pocock, J. G. A. *The Ancient Constitution and the Feudal Law: A Study of English Historical Thought in the Seventeenth Century*. Cambridge: Cambridge University Press, 1987.

Pollard, Tanya. *Drugs and Theater in Early Modern England*. Oxford: Oxford University Press, 2005.

Poole, William. *Milton and the Idea of the Fall*. Cambridge: Cambridge University Press, 2005.

Potter, Harry. *Hanging in Judgment: Religion and the Death Penalty in England*. New York: Continuum, 1993.

Prall, Stuart E. *The Agitation for Law Reform during the Puritan Revolution, 1640–1660*. The Hague: Martinus Nijhoff, 1966.

Prestwich, Menna. *Cranfield: Politics and Profits under the Early Stuarts: The Career of Lionel Cranfield, Earl of Middlesex*. Oxford: Clarendon Press, 1966.

Pym, John. *The Declaration of John Pym Esquire upon the Whole Matter of the Charge of High Treason against Thomas Earle of Strafford*. 1641.

Rajan, Balachandra. *"Paradise Lost" and the Seventeenth Century Reader*. Ann Arbor: University of Michigan Press, 1967.

Ramesey, William. *De Venenis, Or, A Discourse of Poysons Their Names, Natures and Vertues*. London, 1663.

Rastell, John. *An Exposition of Certaine Difficult and Obscure Words, and Termes of The Lawes of This Realme*. London, 1595.

Reid, Rachel R. *The King's Council in the North*. Totowa, NJ: Rowman and Littlefield, 1975.

Renfrow, Jacquelyn Janelle. "Tudor and Stuart Theories of Kingship: The Dispensing Power and the Royal Discretionary Authority in Sixteenth and Seventeenth Century England." PhD diss., University of Michigan, 1970.

Revard, Stella P. *The War in Heaven: "Paradise Lost" and the Tradition of Satan's Rebellion*. Ithaca, NY: Cornell University Press, 1980.

Ricks, Christopher. *Milton's Grand Style*. Oxford: Clarendon Press, 1963.

Robins, Harry F. *If This Be Heresy: A Study of Milton and Origen*. Urbana: University of Illinois Press, 1963.

Rogers, John. *The Matter of Revolution: Science, Poetry, and Politics in the Age of Milton*. Ithaca, NY: Cornell University Press, 1996.

Rosenberg, Phillippe. "Sanctifying the Robe: Punitive Violence and the English Press, 1650–1700." In *Penal Practice and Culture,*

1500–1900: Punishing the English, edited by Simon Devereaux and Paul Griffiths, 157–82. New York: Palgrave, 2004.

Rosenblatt, Jason P. "The Law in Adam's Soliloquy." In *Literary Milton: Text, Pretext, Context*, edited by Diana Trevino Benet and Michael Lieb, 180–201. Pittsburgh: Duquesne University Press, 1994.

———. *Renaissance England's Chief Rabbi: John Selden*. Oxford: Oxford University Press, 2006.

———. *Torah and Law in "Paradise Lost."* Princeton, NJ: Princeton University Press, 1994.

Rumrich, John P. *Milton Unbound: Controversy and Reinterpretation*. Cambridge: Cambridge University Press, 1996.

Russell, Conrad. "The Theory of Treason in the Trial of Strafford." *English Historical Review* 80 (1965): 30–50.

Sacks, David Harris. "The Promise and the Contract in Early Modern England: Slade's Case in Perspective." In Kahn and Hutson, *Rhetoric and Law in Early Modern Europe*, 28–53.

Salgado, Gamini. *The Elizabethan Underworld*. New York: St. Martins, 1992.

Saltern, George. *Of The Antient Lawes of Great Britaine*. London, 1605.

Sauer, Elizabeth. *Milton, Toleration, and Nationhood*. Cambridge: Cambridge University Press, 2014.

———. *"Paper Contestations" and Textual Communities in England, 1640–1675*. Toronto: University of Toronto Press, 2005.

Schiavone, Aldo. *The Invention of Law in the West*. Translated by Jeremy Carden and Anthony Shugaar. Cambridge, MA: Belknap Press of Harvard University Press, 2012.

Schramm, Percy. *A History of the English Coronation*. Translated by Leopold Legg. Oxford: Clarendon Press, 1937.

Seipp, David J. "Concept of Property in the Early Common Law." *Law and History Review* 12 (1994): 29–91.

Selden, John. *Of the Dominion, or Ownership, of the Sea*. London, 1652.

Shakespeare, William. *The Merchant of Venice*. In *The Norton Shakespeare Based on the Oxford Edition*, edited by Stephen Greenblatt, Walter Cohen, Jean E. Howard, Katharine Eisaman Maus, and Andrew Gurr, 1081–1124. New York: W. W. Norton, 1997.

Shapiro, Barbara J. *A Culture of Fact: England, 1550–1720*. Ithaca, NY: Cornell University Press, 2000.

———. "Law and Science in Seventeenth-Century England." *Stanford Law Review* 21 (1969): 727–66.

Sharp, Buchanan. *In Contempt of All Authority: Rural Artisans and Riot in the West of England, 1586–1660*. Berkeley: University of California Press, 1980.

Sharpe, James A. *Crime in Early Modern England, 1550–1750*. London: Longman, 1984.

———. *Crime in Seventeenth-Century England: A County Study*. Cambridge: Cambridge University Press, 1983.

———. "The People and the Law." In *Popular Culture in Seventeenth-Century England*, edited by Barry Reay, 244–70. London: Croom Helm, 1985.

Sharpe, Kevin. *The Personal Rule of Charles I*. New Haven, CT: Yale University Press, 1992.

Shawcross, John. *The Arms of the Family: The Significance of John Milton's Relatives and Associates*. Lexington: University Press of Kentucky, 2004.

———. *The Development of Milton's Thought: Law, Government, and Religion*. Pittsburgh: Duquesne University Press, 2008.

———. *John Milton: The Self and the World*. Lexington: University Press of Kentucky, 1993.

Sheppard, William. *Actions upon the Case for Deeds*. London, 1663.

———. *An Epitome of All the Common and Statute Laws of This Nation Now in Force*. London, 1656.

Shuger, Debora. *Censorship and Cultural Sensibility: The Regulation of Language in Tudor-Stuart England*. Philadelphia: University of Pennsylvania Press, 2006.

———. "The Prison Diaries of Archbishop Laud." In Beecher et al., *Taking Exception to the Law*, 120–36.

———. *The Renaissance Bible: Scholarship, Sacrifice and Subjectivity*. Berkeley: University of California Press, 1994.

Silver, Victoria. *Imperfect Sense: The Predicament of Milton's Irony*. Princeton, NJ: Princeton University Press, 2001.

———. "'A Taken Scandal Not a Given': Milton's Equitable Grounds of Toleration." In *Milton and Toleration*, edited by Sharon Achinstein and Elizabeth Sauer, 203–23. Oxford: Oxford University Press, 2007.

Simpson, A. W. B. *A History of the Common Law of Contract: The Rise of the Action of Assumpsit*. Oxford: Clarendon Press, 1975.

———. *Legal Theory and Legal History: Essays on the Common Law.* London: Hambledon Press, 1987.

Sirluck, Ernest. Introduction to *Complete Prose Works of John Milton*, edited by Don M. Wolfe. Vol. 2. New Haven, CT: Yale University Press, 1953.

Skinner, Quentin. "Milton and the Politics of Slavery." In *Milton and the Terms of Liberty*, edited by Graham Parry and Joad Raymond, 1–22. Cambridge: D. S. Brewer, 2002.

Smith, Nigel. "*Areopagitica*: Voicing Contexts, 1643–5." In *Politics, Poetics, and Hermeneutics in Milton's Prose*, edited by David Loewenstein and James Grantham Turner, 103–22. Cambridge: Cambridge University Press, 1990.

———. *Literature and Revolution in England, 1640–1660*. New Haven, CT: Yale University Press, 1994.

Smith, Thomas. *De republica anglorum: A Discourse on the Commonwealth of England.* Edited by L. Alston. Shannon, Ireland: Irish University Press, 1972.

Sokol, B. J., and Mary Sokol. *Shakespeare, Law, and Marriage.* Cambridge: Cambridge University Press, 2003.

Sommerville, J. P. "History and Theory: The Norman Conquest in Early Stuart Political Thought." *Political Studies* 34 (1986): 249–61.

———. *Politics and Ideology in England, 1603–1640*. London: Longman, 1986.

Spencer, Janet. "Staging Pardon Scenes: Variations of Tragicomedy." *Renaissance Drama* 21 (1990): 55–89.

Spenser, Edmund. *The Faerie Queene*. In *Edmund Spenser's Poetry*, edited by Hugh Maclean. New York: Norton, 1968.

Spring, Eileen. *Law, Land, and Family: Aristocratic Inheritance in England, 1300–1800*. Chapel Hill: University of North Carolina Press, 1993.

Stachniewski, John. *The Persecutory Imagination: English Puritanism and the Literature of Religious Despair.* Oxford: Oxford University Press, 1991.

Stain, Virginia Lee. "The 'Snared Subject' and the General Pardon Statute in Late Elizabethan Coterie Literature." In Beecher et al., *Taking Exception to the Law*, 100–119.

Stein, Arnold. *Answerable Style: Essays on "Paradise Lost."* Minneapolis: University of Minnesota Press, 1953.

Stevens, Paul. "The Pre-Secular Politics of *Paradise Lost*." In *The Cambridge Companion to "Paradise Lost,"* edited by Louis Schwartz, 94–108. Cambridge: Cambridge University Press, 2014.

St. German, Christopher. *The Dialogue in English between a Doctor of Divinity and a Student in the Laws of England*. London, 1660.

———. *An Exact Abridgement of That Excellent Treatise Called Doctor and Student*. London, 1658.

Stoljar, S. J. *A History of Contract at Common Law*. Canberra: Australian National University Press, 1975.

Stoner, James R. *Common Law and Liberal Theory: Coke, Hobbes, and the Origins of American Constitutionalism*. Lawrence: University of Kansas Press, 1992.

Stretton, Tim. *Women Waging Law in Elizabethan England*. Cambridge: Cambridge University Press, 1998.

Stymeist, David. "Criminal Biography in Early Modern News Pamphlets." In *Taking Exception to the Law: Materializing Injustice in Early Modern English Literature*, edited by Donald Beecher, Travis Decook, Andrew Wallace, and Grant Williams, 137–61. Toronto: University of Toronto Press, 2015.

T.M. *The True Narration of the Entertainment of His Royall Majestie, From the Time of His Departure from Edenbrough; Till His Receiving at London*. London, 1603.

Teeven, Kevin M. *A History of the Anglo-American Common Law of Contract*. New York: Greenwood Press, 1990.

Theis, Jeffrey S. "The 'Ill Kill'd' Deer: Poaching and the Social Order in the Merry Wives of Windsor." *Texas Studies in Literature and Language* 43 (2001): 46–73.

———. *Writing the Forest in Early Modern England: A Sylvan Pastoral Nation*. Pittsburgh: Duquesne University Press, 2009.

Thompson, E. P. *Whigs and Hunters: The Origin of the Black Act*. New York: Pantheon, 1975.

Thorne, Samuel E. Introduction to *A Discourse upon the Exposicion and Understandinge of Statutes*, by Thomas Egerton. San Marino, CA: Huntington Library, 1942.

Tubbs, J. W. *The Common Law Mind: Medieval and Early Modern Conceptions*. Baltimore: Johns Hopkins University Press, 2000.

Tuck, Richard. *Natural Rights Theories: Their Origin and Development*. Cambridge: Cambridge University Press, 1979.

———. *The Rights of War and Peace: Political Thought and the International Order from Grotius to Kant*. Oxford: Oxford University Press, 1999.

Turner, James Grantham. *One Flesh: Paradisal Marriage and Sexual Relations in the Age of Milton*. Oxford: Clarendon Press, 1987.

Veall, Donald. *The Popular Movement for Law Reform, 1640–1660*. Oxford: Clarendon Press, 1970.

Visconsi, Elliott. *Lines of Equity: Literature and the Origins of Law in Later Stuart England*. Ithaca, NY: Cornell University Press, 2008.

Von Maltzahn, Nicholas. "The First Reception of *Paradise Lost* (1667)." *Review of English Studies* 47 (1996): 479–99.

———. "Making Use of the Jews: Milton and Philo-Semitism." In *Milton and the Jews*, edited by Douglas Bush, 57–82. Cambridge: Cambridge University Press, 2008.

Walsham, Alexandra. *Providence in Early Modern England*. Oxford: Oxford University Press, 1999.

Walter, John. *Crowds and Popular Politics in Early Modern England*. Manchester, UK: Manchester University Press, 2006.

Warren, Christopher N. "Milton and the Epochs of International Law." *European Journal of International Law* 24 (2013): 557–81.

Weber, Max. *Economy and Society: An Outline of Interpretive Sociology*. Edited by Guenther Roth and Claus Wittich. New York: Bedminster Press, 1968.

White, R. S. *Natural Law in English Renaissance Literature*. Cambridge: Cambridge University Press, 1996.

Wilson, Luke. "Ben Jonson and the Law of Contract." In Kahn and Hutson, *Rhetoric and Law in Early Modern Europe*, 143–65.

———. *Theaters of Intention: Drama and the Law in Early Modern England*. Stanford, CA: Stanford University Press, 2000.

Wilson, Richard. "The Quality of Mercy: Discipline and Punishment in Shakespearean Comedy." *Seventeenth Century* 5 (1990): 1–42.

Winstanley, Gerrard. *The Works of Gerrard Winstanley*. Edited by George H. Sabine. Ithaca, NY: Cornell University Press, 1941.

Witte, John. *From Sacrament to Contract: Marriage, Religion, and Law in the Western Tradition*. Louisville, KY: Westminster John Knox Press, 1997.

———. *God's Joust, God's Justice: Law and Religion in the Western Tradition*. Grand Rapids, MI: William B. Eerdmans, 2006.

———. *Law and Protestantism: The Legal Teachings of the Lutheran Reformation*. Cambridge: Cambridge University Press, 2002.

———. *The Reformation of Rights: Law, Religion, and Human Rights in Early Modern Calvinism*. Cambridge: Cambridge University Press, 2008.

Wittreich, Joseph. "Milton's Transgressive Maneuvers: Receptions (Then and Now) and the Sexual Politics of *Paradise Lost*." In *Milton and Heresy*, edited by Stephen B. Dobranski and John P. Rumrich, 244–66. Cambridge: Cambridge University Press, 1998.

Wolfe, Don M., ed. *Leveller Manifestoes of the Puritan Revolution*. New York: Thomas Nelson, 1944.

Woodbridge, Linda. *Vagrancy, Homelessness, and English Renaissance Literature*. Urbana: University of Illinois Press, 2001.

Worden, Blair. *Literature and Politics in Cromwellian England: John Milton, Andrew Marvell, Marchamont Nedham*. Oxford: Oxford University Press, 2007.

Wyville, Christopher. *Of Christian Magistracy*. London, 1697.

Zurcher, Andrew. *Spenser's Legal Language: Law and Poetry in Early Modern England*. Cambridge: D. S. Brewer, 2007.

Index

Abdiel, 69, 89; Satan confrontation with, 70–71, 75–76, 86–87, 91–93, 102–3
absentia, 197–98
accessories, 3–4
accusations, 28, 98, 202
Achinstein, Sharon, 27
Act of Indemnity and Oblivion (1660), 219, 221, 222, 223, 224, 229
Adam: as defendant, 186–87, 195–200, 202–3; and divine dispensation, 81–82, 83; fall of, 100, 116, 154, 209–10, 240, 247; God's judgment of, 7, 99–100, 187, 194; as informant in Eve, 200–202; legal soliloquy by, 161–63, 171–72; marriage to Eve, 129, 130, 132–36, 140–41, 143–47, 164–65; pardon request by, 14, 214, 216–17, 225–27, 230, 231, 235, 236, 238–39; penitence by, 216, 233; and property ownership, 126, 127, 128–29, 132–38, 164; Satan's entry into Bower of, 117–18, 119; and Son, 131–32, 139–41, 144, 145, 186, 202; treason by, 13, 65–66, 68–69, 78–79, 80–83
Admiralty court, 162
Ad patrem (Milton), 18
Aeneid, 94
Agar, Thomas, 18
Agreement of the People, An, 82n25
Albyn, Benjamin, *An Appeal to God and the King*, 185
Alfred, King, 107
allocution, 198
American Civil Liberties Union, 184
Animadversions (Milton), 30, 46, 109
animals, 104, 133n12
"Another on the Same" (Milton), 199
apocatastasis, 241–43
Apology against a Pamphlet, An (Milton), 23, 30–31, 44, 221n17
Appletree, Thomas, 216n4
Aquinas, Thomas, 49; *Summa*, 20–21, 52
Archaeion (Lambarde), 21
Arden of Faversham, 29
Areopagitica (Milton), 9, 10–11, 20, 101; reader as juror in, 27–28, 31–32
Ariosto, Ludovico, 52
Aristotle, 10, 20, 132, 153, 155
Ark of the Covenant, 246

Arminianism, 241; Milton's, 212, 215, 242
Arnold, Matthew, 1
arraignment, 198–99
Ashworth v. Milton, 145
Assizes, 187–89, 192–93, 230, 250
Attie, Katherine Bootle, 111
Attorneys Academy, The (Powell), 21
audience: "fit audience," 25, 32–33, 34, 212; as legal term, 32–33
Austin, John, 38, 155

Babington, Zachary, *Advice to Grand Jurors in Cases of Blood*, 212–13
Bacon, Sir Francis, 56, 62–63, 107n19, 193
Bailey, Amanda, 146
Baker, David, 58n43
Bartholomew Fair (Jonson), 29
Baxter, Richard, 137
Beattie, J. M., 99n4, 217, 240n62
Beaulieu, Luke, 15–16
Belial, 89, 223
Bennett, Joan, 84–85, 88, 224
Bentham, Jeremy, 38, 135, 250
Berman, Harold J., 40
Bernard, Richard, 63–64
Beza, Theodore, 45
biblical law, 43, 155, 237
Blackstone, Sir William, 134, 147–48, 250
Blomley, Nicholas, 248
bonds, 145–46; sealed, 5
Bownd, Jefferie, 118
Bracton, Henri de, 10, 21, 72
Bradshaw, John, 20
Brief Notes upon a Late Sermon (Milton), 20, 66–67, 68
Brittan, Jillisa, 60–61
Brooks, Christopher W., 24
Brownlow, Richard, *Reports of Diverse Choice Cases in Law*, 182
Brydall, John, 3, 4
Bunyan, John, 250
Burgess, Glenn, 52–53n34
burglary: Coke's definition of, 110; in London, 106–7, 109–10; by Satan, 108, 109, 110, 111
Burroughs, Jeremiah, *Christ Inviting Sinners to Come to Him for Rest*, 188

Cade's rebellion (1450), 251
Caldwell, Elizabeth, 118
calumny, 26–27
Calvin, John, 49
Calvinism, 8
Campbell, Gordon, 220n13
capital punishment, 120, 125
Castlehaven, Earl of, 105–6n16
Catholics, 51, 71
censorship, 39–40
Chamberlain, John, 237–38
Chancery Court, 18; Milton's dealings with, 19, 20, 49, 55, 145; powers and functioning of, 54–55, 162, 163
character, defendant's, 98–99
Character of the Long Parliament, The (Milton), 47
Charles I, 86, 121; and courts, 52–53, 192n17; *Eikon basilike* by, 220, 228; Milton criticisms of, 44, 56, 74, 79–80, 101; pardon issued by, 228–29; trial and execution of, 45, 66–67, 72, 74, 75, 80, 199, 224
Charles II, 121, 219, 223
chattels, 175–76, 182–83
Cicero, 10, 38; *De officiis*, 20, 56
circuit courts, 188, 189, 190, 192
civil law, 5, 10, 28–29, 50–51n29, 125
Civil War, English, 1, 25, 45, 217–18, 228
Clement of Alexandria, St., 241

Coke, Sir Edward, 19, 54, 114, 225; on burglary and larceny, 108, 110; common law promoted by, 53, 56–57, 248; influence on Milton of, 20, 21, 52; on legal jurisdictions in England, 48, 247; on ownership, 125–26; on treason, 67, 70, 77, 83, 103
Colasterion (Milton), 21, 22–23
collateral, 141–42
Commentaries on the Laws of England (Blackstone), 134, 147–48, 250
common law, English, 3, 67, 160, 162, 204–5; betraying one's lord in, 5, 103; Coke on, 53, 56–57, 248; components of, 52–53; contracts in, 170–71; evolution of, 51–53, 248–49; jurisdictional monopoly of, 249; Milton's view of, 55, 56–57, 58; participatory nature of, 24, 29–30, 210; on property and ownership, 125–26, 131; as set of legal norms, 14–15, 53–54, 247
Commonplace Book (Milton), 22, 24n47, 35–36, 52, 118; "Of Laws, Dispensations from Them, and Indulgences" entry in, 81; "Of Navigation and Shipwrecks" entry in, 112; "Of Theft and Highway Robbery" entry in, 107
Common Pleas, Court of, 17, 158, 162
communities, local, 193–94
complaints, legal, 202
Complete Memoirs of the Life of That Notorious Imposter, William Morrell, The, 120
Concilia ecclesiastica (Spelman), 21
consideration, doctrine of, 168
Considerations Touching the Likeliest Means to Remove Hirelings Out of the Church (Milton), 9
Constable, Marianne, 40n13
Contemplations, Moral and Divine (Hale), 63
contempt, 101
contracts, 14, 151–52, 164–73; and commercial exchange, 173–74; in common law, 170–71; evolution of, 37–38, 164, 167; between humanity and nature, 166–67; marriages as, 164–65; Satan and, 178–79; social contract, 37, 164, 170; strict liability concept in, 170, 171–72
Cope, Sir John, 19, 145
Coppe, Abiezer, *Fiery Flying Roll*, 126–27
1 Corinthians 6:3, 185
Cormack, Bradin, 37, 53
Corns, Thomas N., 220n13
Cosby, Arnold, 230
Council of the North, 75
Council of Wales and the Marches, 51, 53n35
counterfeiting, 67
Country Justice, The (Dalton), 29
Court of Requests, 101, 160, 247
courts: Admiralty, 162; Assizes, 187–89, 192–93, 230, 250; Chancery, 18, 19, 20, 49, 54–55, 145, 162, 163; circuit, 188, 189, 190, 192; Common Pleas, 17, 158, 162; ecclesiastical, 22, 51, 75, 109, 160, 248; forest, 48, 116; Palatinates, 48; prerogative, 48, 51, 53, 75, 192n17, 247–48; of Requests, 101, 160, 247; Star Chamber, 51, 216n4, 247, 248
coverture, 147–49
Cowell, John, 71–72, 130–31
crime: burglary and larceny, 5, 106–7, 108, 109–10, 159, 217; popular fascination with, 120, 211–12; and punishment, 81, 86, 159, 226; rate in England, 106–7, 125, 222; Satan and, 74–75, 97–98, 100–104, 116–18,

crime (*cont.*)
121–22, 124; social, 112–13; trespassing, 100–102, 158–59, 174; violent, 116–20, 226. *See also* treason
criminal biography, 120–24
Croke, Sir John, 118
Cromwell, Oliver, 22, 47, 121
Culture of Fact (Shapiro), 208

Daborne, Robert, 188
Dalton, Michael, 29
Danby, Earl of, 218n5
Dante Alighieri, 140
David and Goliath, 91
Davis, Natalie Zemon, 233
Death, 4, 34, 78, 122, 242; on Satan as "traitor angel," 6, 65, 105; as Satan's child, 103, 116–17
debt bondage, 146–47
Decalogue, 9, 185; Milton's vision of, 244–45
defamation, 26–27
defendants, 98, 172, 187–88; Adam and Eve as, 186, 196, 198–99, 202–3, 206; books as, 32; character of, 98–99; judges' kindness toward, 190–91; in lawsuits, 26, 27, 30, 55; plea entering by, 40–41. *See also* trials
defense counsel, 38, 191
Defense of Himself (Milton), 22, 25–26, 106
Defense of the English People, A (Milton), 21, 22, 25–26, 58–59, 74; on English common law, 56–57; fusion of law and religion in, 38, 45; on treason, 72, 225
Defoe, Daniel, 121, 122
De jure belli ac pacis (Grotius), 19, 21, 90, 91, 133n12
De jure naturali et gentium (Selden), 20, 21
Dekker, Thomas, *The Belman of London*, 109
De Laune, Thomas, *Tropologia, or, A Key to Open Scripture Metaphors*, 189
De republica anglorum (Smith), 21
Desborough, John, 20
detection, 203
de Veil, Sir Thomas, 191
devolving, 200, 203–4
Diggers, 126, 175
Diodati, Charles, 18
dispensations, 81–82, 83
Dobranski, Stephen, 95
Doctor and Student (St. German), 41
Doctrine and Discipline of Divorce (Milton), 10–11, 17, 19, 20, 26, 46, 231; on divine law and religion, 6, 8, 9, 42, 43, 44–45, 47, 62, 88, 96, 154–55, 226; on law's goal, 43; readership of, 30, 33
Donne, John, 1, 249n6
dowry, 138–39
Dryden, John, 175
Duck, Arthur, 55
Dyson, Jessica, 37n9
Dzelzainis, Martin, 44, 51

ecclesiastical courts, 51, 75, 109, 160; Milton and, 22, 248
Edenic Law, 61–62
Edgar, King, 107, 188, 194
Edgar, Thomas, 204–5
Edward III, 56
Edwards, Karen L., 89n33
Eikon basilike (Charles I), 220, 228
Eikonoklastes (Milton), 45–46, 82, 107, 220; on Charles I, 44, 56, 74, 75, 79–80, 228; on common law's authority, 58; on legal penalties, 81, 86; on Parliament and statutory law, 59–60, 76; on treason, 68, 72, 74, 84

Elements of the Common Law of England (Bacon), 63
Elizabeth I, 218, 219, 232–33, 234, 236
Ellwood, Thomas, 28
empiricism, 37, 206–7
Empson, William, 7
enclosure, 174–75
England: Civil War in, 1, 25, 45, 217–18, 228; crime rate in, 106–7, 125, 222; judicial and legislative powers in, 33; law reform in, 37, 100, 173–74; legal jurisdictions in, 48–49, 152, 163, 187–88, 247; participatory judicial system in, 29–30; Restoration in, 16, 60, 121, 131, 218, 251. *See also* Charles I; Parliament
English Rogue Described in the Life of Meriton Latroon, The, 120
Epicurus, 10
Epitome of All the Common and Statute Laws of This Nation Now in Force (Sheppard), 104, 131, 148
equity, 155–56, 163; as English legal system, 54–55; legal importance of, 161–62
Est, William, 82, 195
Eustachio, Bartolomeo, 119
Evans, Anne, 211–12
Evans, J. Martin, 127–28, 178n50, 240
Eve: Adam as informant on, 200–202; as adversary of law, 68–69, 209; dispensation for, 81–82; fall of, 116, 165, 209–10, 240, 247; as feme covert, 147, 148–50; God's judgment of, 99–100, 194; intentions and justifications by, 99–100, 152; marriage to Adam, 129, 130, 132–36, 140–41, 143–47, 164–65; pardon request by, 14, 214, 216–17, 226–27, 230, 231, 235, 236; penitence by, 216, 233; and property ownership, 126, 127, 128–29, 132–38, 164, 180–81; Satan's entry into Bower of, 117–18, 119; Satan's tempting of, 101, 152–53, 157–61, 167–70, 174, 175–80, 183; Son's judgment of, 195–200. *See also* Adam
evidence, 38, 98–99; and fact, 208–9, 210–11, 212–13; as term, 207
exile, 205, 240–41
experimentalism, 11, 142
Eyre, Adam, 29
Ezekiel 46:17, 103

"Fable of the Peasant and the Landlord, The" (Milton), 181
fact (term), 208–9, 210–11
Faerie Queene, The (Spenser), 119
Faller, Lincoln, 117
felony, 40n15, 93, 105–6
feme covert, 147–51, 204
Fenton, Mary C., 131, 180n56
Fielding, Henry, 122–23, 124
Filmer, Robert, 88, 127, 128, 170
Fish, Stanley, 36, 38, 62; *How Milton Works*, 7, 173; *Surprised by Sin*, 63, 64
"fit audience," 25, 32–33, 34, 212
Fitzherbert, Anthony, 21
Fleta, 21, 72
Fletcher, H. F., 18, 23
forest rights, 112–13
forfeiture, 40, 66, 146, 199, 204; betraying one's lord as cause for, 5, 103; and pardons, 238, 239–40
Forsyth, Neil, 98
Fortescue, Sir John, 21, 41, 250–51
Fortier, Mark, 161
Foucault, Michel, 29–30
Fowler, Alastair, 129
France, 24, 30, 222, 233–34
Francis II, 119
fraud, 169–70

French, James, 19, 55
fundamental law, 66, 156

Gabriel, 94–95, 101–2
Gay, John, 122; *Beggar's Opera*, 121
Genesis, Book of, 165, 194, 195, 197
Germany, 22
Glanville, Ranulf de, 21, 73
God's Judgment. *See* justice (divine); law (divine)
Goldberg, Jonathan, 129
Goodrich, Peter, 35, 38, 40, 41, 247
grand larceny, 5, 108, 159
Gratian, 50; *Decretum*, 21
Green, Richard Firth, 67n3
Greenberg, Lynne, 53, 127n4, 164–65
Grotius, Hugo: *Adamus exul*, 178; *De jure belli ac pacis*, 19, 21, 90, 91, 133n12; influence on Milton of, 19, 21, 90, 133n14
Guibbory, Achsah, 242–43
guilt, 196–97, 209–10, 220–21
guilty verdicts, 217

Hale, Sir Matthew, 56–57, 62, 63; *Pleas of the Crown*, 73–74, 199, 210
Halkett, John, 132
Hall, John, 109, 218–19
Hanford, James Holly, 129
Harald, King, 107
Hart, H. L. A., 38, 155
Headley, Thomas, 138
Hebrews 7:25-28, 235
Henry VIII, 218
Herbert, George, *Country Parson*, 41
Heresiography (Pagitt), 203
Herman, Peter C., 6n15, 8n18
Herrup, Cynthia, 28, 217
History of Britain (Milton), 107, 194, 208
History of the Common Law of England, A (Hale), 63
Hobart, Sir John, 123
Hobbes, Thomas, 39, 168; *Leviathan*, 172
Hobson, Thomas, 199
homicide, 117–18, 226
Hooker, Richard, 56, 62, 226; *Laws of Ecclesiastical Polity*, 20–21, 63
Horn, Andrew, 21
Hotham, Sir John, 228
How Milton Works (Fish), 7, 173
Hoxby, Blair, 140n25
Hume, Patrick, 109, 115
hunting, 113, 114–15, 116
Hutson, Lorna, 29, 30, 37
Hyde, Judge, 149, 156

identification, formal, 196
Iliad (Homer), 94
impartiality, 34, 36, 82, 95, 186, 188, 211
injunctions, 13, 163
Institutes (Justinian), 21, 36, 51, 52, 58
Institutes of the Laws of England (Coke), 21, 52; importance of, 54, 125–26; third part of, 67, 70, 77, 83, 225
intent, 69n6, 99–100, 156–57, 206
interdicts, 163–64
interest charging, 140
Interpreter, The (Cowell), 71–72, 130–31
Invention of Law in the West (Schiavone), 36
Ireland, 71
Isle of Man (Bernard), 63–64

James I, 68, 116, 193; pardons issued by, 222, 224, 226, 231
James II, 218
Jermyn, Judge, 42, 53–54
Jesus Christ, 188–89, 235, 246. *See also* Son
Johann of Schwarzenberg, 51

John, Book of: 1 verse 3:12, 117; verse 8:44, 117
Johnson, Samuel, 15
Jonson, Ben, 1, 217
judges, 188–89, 190, 202–3; in ecclesiastical courts, 109; kindness toward defendants by, 190–92; legal determinations by, 153, 155–56, 157; and local communities, 194
Judgment of Martin Bucer, The (Milton), 10
juries, 28, 206, 217; readers as, 30–31; weighing of evidence by, 210–11, 212–13
jurisdictions, legal, 152, 187–88, 247; rivalries and conflicts of, 48–49, 163
justice (divine), 64, 84–96, 97, 205; Assizes and, 188; and dispensations, 81–82, 83; and God's pardon, 4–5, 214–15, 223–24, 226–27, 229; and God's punishment, 4, 40, 45; and human justice, 7, 88–89, 190, 252; law embedded in, 6, 42, 47–48, 95, 96, 152, 163; publicly explaining, 6–7, 9, 96; and redemption, 99–100. *See also* law (divine)
justice (human): and animal kingdom, 133n12; Aristotle on, 132; divine justice linked to, 7, 88–89, 190, 252; and equity, 155–56; and holy war, 92; as independent from state, 192–93; law linked to, 42, 56, 155–56; local communities as source of, 193–94; and religion, 9; scales of, 94–96. *See also* common law, English; courts
justices of the peace, 28n56, 29, 98, 249
justify (term), 5–6
Justinian, 22, 56; *Corpus juris civilis*, 50; *Institutes*, 21, 36, 51, 52, 58
Kahn, Victoria, 37n9
Kesselring, Krista J., 224n23, 232, 233–34
King's Bench, 118, 158, 160, 172
Knafla, Louis A., 163n18
Kneidel, Gregory, 249n6
Komorowski, Michael, 129–30, 143

Labors of Innocence (Picciotto), 142, 210
laesa maiestas, 71
Lambarde, William, 21, 219
landed property, 175–76, 182–83
larceny, 174; petty vs. grand, 5, 22, 108, 159
Laud, William, 72, 75
law (divine), 8, 21–22, 61, 84–96, 163; judicial interpretation of, 154–55; Satan's treason against, 75–77; temporal law linked to, 6, 8, 12, 42, 43–46, 49, 62, 88, 95, 184–85
law (human): and cultural change, 37–38; disciplinary estrangement of, 35, 36–38; divine justice and, 6, 42, 95, 96, 152, 163; early attitudes about, 14–15, 40–42; as expression of God's will, 47, 87, 126, 186, 190, 252; Foucault on, 30; Milton's view of, 8, 10–11, 15, 35–36, 43–46, 47, 61, 84, 155, 246, 247; mystique of, 249–50; nonnegotiable character of, 165, 173; of obedience, 76–77, 85, 87; origins of modern, 38–42, 244; popular knowledge about, 29–30; and religion, 9–10, 38, 42, 45, 62–63, 249, 251; and rhetoric, 33, 207–8; and theology, 15, 36, 246, 251; as tool of wealthy, 250. *See also* justice (human)
law (types): biblical, 43, 155, 237; canon, 22, 50–51, 53, 56, 210; civil, 5, 10, 28–29, 50–51n29, 125; contract, 14,

law (types) (*cont.*)
37–38, 151–52, 166–67, 173–74; divine, 6, 8, 12, 21–22, 42, 43–46, 49, 61, 75–77, 84–96, 163, 184–85; Edenic, 61–62; fundamental, 66, 156; Mosaic, 43–44, 46, 61–62, 154–55, 246; Natural, 8, 10, 12, 40, 46, 49–50, 57–58, 61, 73, 84, 155, 170–71; real estate, 126; Roman, 3, 43–44, 52, 71, 131, 164; statutory, 48–49, 51, 59–60, 73, 76, 156. *See also* common law, English
Lawes Resolutions of Womens Rights, The (Edgar), 204–5
Laws of Ecclesiastical Polity (Hooker), 20–21, 63
lawyers, 3n6, 27n52, 51n29, 71, 130, 247; and common law, 53, 58, 247, 249; as defense counsels, 38, 191; law seen as linked to, 37, 41; Milton's relatives and friends as, 18–20; in trials, 191
legal books and textbooks, 20–22, 29, 41, 54
Leges Edwardi Confessori, 46
Leighton, Alexander, 221
Letter to a Friend, A (Milton), 193
Levelers, 86, 127
lex iniusta non est lex, 46, 170–71
Ley, Sir James, 20
license, 26, 27, 229
Licensing Act (1662), 251
Licensing Order of 1643, 48
Lieb, Michael, 91, 165–66
Life and Death of Major Clancie, the Grandest Cheat of This Age, The, 120
Life of Mr. Jonathan Wild the Great, The (Fielding), 122–23
Lilburne, John, 42, 53
Linebaugh, Peter, 250
Littleton, Thomas, 21, 54, 125–26
Lives of the Most Remarkable Criminals (Hayward), 105
Loades, David, 229n40
loans, 140, 146
Locke, John, 133n14; *Second Treatise of Government*, 86
London, 176, 187–88; crime in, 106–7, 222; public executions in, 120
Long Parliament, 247

Magna Carta, 24, 46
Maine, Sir Henry Sumner, 167
Manby v. Scott, 149, 156
Mansfield, Lord, 250
Manwood, John, *Treatise of the Lawes of the Forest*, 113, 115, 116
Marcus, Leah S., 48, 53
marriage: of Adam and Eve, 129, 130, 132–36, 140–41, 143–47, 164–65; as bond of nature, 142–43, 144–46; as contract, 164–65; and dowry exchange, 138–40; England's canon laws on, 48; and female coverture, 147–50; and property ownership, 129–30, 143–44; sole propriety model of, 6, 14, 126, 128–38, 143, 146–47, 150; women's responsibilities in, 204–5
Marten, Henry, 20
Masque Performed at Ludlow Castle, A (Milton), 161, 166–67
Maus, Katherine Eisaman, 176
Maynard, Sir John, 75
Melanchthon, Philip, 51, 244–45, 246
mercy. *See* pardons
Middlesex, Earl of (Lionel Cranfield), 238, 239–40
Militia Ordinance, 25
Milton, Anne (sister), 18
Milton, Christopher (brother), 17–18

Milton, John, Sr. (father), 16–17
Milton, John — biographical: Arminian theology of, 212, 215, 242; Chancery Court dealings, 19, 20, 49, 55, 145; commitment to Parliamentary side, 45, 123; family, 15–18; Grotius influence on, 19, 21, 90, 133n14; in hiding and prison, 219–20; Justinian influence on, 21, 52, 58; legal reading and familiarity, 20–24; litigation experiences, 19, 55; Natural Law advocate, 8, 12, 46, 49–50, 57–58, 61, 73, 155; pardoning of, 215, 219–21, 234; possible legal career, 18–19; reading audience of, 25–34; renting houses in London, 176; Selden influence on, 19–20, 21; translation of Psalms, 84–85; writing style, 123–24
Milton, John — works: *Ad patrem*, 18; *Animadversions*, 30, 46, 109; "Another on the Same," 199; *An Apology against a Pamphlet*, 23, 30–31, 44, 221n17; *Areopagitica*, 9, 10–11, 20, 27–28, 31–32, 101; *Brief Notes upon a Late Sermon*, 20, 66–67, 68; *The Character of the Long Parliament*, 47; *On Christian Doctrine*, 67n2, 165, 171; *Colasterion*, 21, 22–23; *Commonplace Book*, 22, 24n47, 35–36, 52, 81, 107, 112, 118; *Considerations Touching the Likeliest Means to Remove Hirelings Out of the Church*, 9; *Defense of Himself*, 22, 25–26, 106; *A Defense of the English People*, 21, 22, 25–26, 38, 45, 56–57, 58–59, 72, 74, 225; *Doctrine and Discipline of Divorce*, 6, 8, 9, 10–11, 17, 19, 20, 26, 30, 33, 42, 43, 44–45, 46, 47, 62, 88, 96, 154–55, 226, 231; *Of Education*, 19; *Eikonoklastes*, 44, 45–46, 56, 58, 59–60, 68, 72, 74, 75, 76, 79–80, 81, 82, 84, 86, 107, 220, 228; "The Fable of the Peasant and the Landlord," 181; *History of Britain*, 107, 194, 208; *The Judgment of Martin Bucer*, 10; *A Letter to a Friend*, 193; *A Masque Performed at Ludlow Castle*, 161, 166–67; *Observations Upon the Articles of Peace* (Milton), 83, 228–29; *Prolusion 7*, 9, 10; *Proposalls of Certaine Expedients*, 162, 193, 194, 248; *A Readie and Easie Way*, 60, 111–12, 193–94, 248, 249; *The Reason of Church Government*, 23–24, 248; *Of Reformation*, 59; *Samson Agonistes*, 206; *A Second Defense of the English People*, 9, 11, 20, 24, 25–26, 47–48; *The Tenure of Kings and Magistrates*, 9, 10, 22, 56, 58, 59, 68, 74, 82, 90, 101, 159, 227; *Tetrachordon*, 19, 23, 26–27, 45, 56, 128, 142–43, 154, 168, 244–45; *A Treatise of Civil Power*, 9, 10; *Of True Religion*, 185. See also *Paradise Lost*
Milton, Richard (grandfather), 112
"Milton and Legal Matters" (Shawcross), 48–49
Milton in Chancery (French), 19, 55
"Milton's Natural Law: Divorce and Individual Property" (Komorowski), 129–30, 143
Milton vs. Duck, 55
Mirror for Justice, The, 56
Mirror for Justices (Horn), 21
misdemeanors, 100–104
Mohamed, Feisal, 251
Mohl, Ruth, 24n47
Moore, Roy, 184–85
More, Alexander, 106

More, Sir Thomas, 1
Mosaic Law, 43–44, 46, 61–62, 154–55, 246
Moses, 24, 43, 205
motive, 206, 226
Mountjoy, Lord, 232–33

Natural Law: and jurisprudence, 40, 57, 84; Milton's support for, 8, 12, 46, 49–50, 57–58, 61, 73, 155; principles of, 10, 46, 170–71
New Milton Criticism (Herman and Sauer, eds.), 8n18
Norfolk, Duke of, 235–36
La nouvelle natura brevium (Fitzherbert), 21

obedience, 220, 238; to God and Son, 76–77, 82, 86, 87, 88, 167, 227; Milton on importance of, 173
Observations upon the Articles of Peace (Milton), 83, 228–29
Of Dominion, or Ownership of the Sea (Selden), 127
Of Education (Milton), 19
Of Reformation (Milton), 59
Of True Religion (Milton), 185
On Christian Doctrine (Milton), 67n2, 165, 171
O'Neil, Shane, 79, 83
On the Laws and Customs of England (Bracton), 21
On the Laws and Governance of England (Fortescue), 21, 41, 250–51
Orgel, Stephen, 129
Origen, 241
original sin, 67n2, 148
Orlando Furioso (Ariosto), 52
ownership. *See* property and ownership

Pagitt, Justinian, 18
Palmer, Herbert, 26
Paradine v. Jane, 171–72
Paradise Lost (Milton): Abdiel-Satan confrontation in, 70–71, 75–76, 86–87, 91–93, 102–3; Adam and Eve marriage in, 129, 130, 132–36, 139–41, 143–47, 164–65; Adam's legal soliloquy in, 161–63, 171–72; and apocatastasis, 242; audience reference in, 32, 33–34, 212; divine justice and law in, 7–8, 9, 11, 16, 85–96, 134, 186, 189–90, 192, 226, 244, 251; God's pardoning in, 14, 214–15, 216–17, 225–27, 229, 231, 232, 235, 236, 238–39; on holy war, 91–92; language of bonds in, 144–47; legal reasoning by Satan in, 152, 153, 154, 155, 156, 157–61, 167–70, 174; on legal rights, 179–80; and modern assumptions of law, 60–64, 252; property and possession in, 102–4, 128–32, 133–38, 139–42, 180–81; Satan's link to crime in, 74–75, 97–98, 100–104, 106, 107–8, 113–18, 121–22, 124; Satan's request for pardoning and grace in, 221–22, 223–24, 234–35, 237, 241, 242; Satan's tempting of Eve in, 101, 152–53, 157–61, 167–70, 174, 175–80, 183; stated goal of, 5; treason theme in, 65–66, 68–71, 74–75, 79–83, 84; trial and judgment of Adam and Eve in, 186–87, 194, 195–209, 210; trial of the angels in, 187; use of legal terminology in, 2–3
pardons, 14, 214–43; as admission of guilt, 220–21; and apocatastasis, 241–43; collective, 218, 221–32; conditional, 240–41; by English monarchs, 7, 222–23, 224–25, 226,

227–29, 231–33, 237–38; by God, 4–5, 214–15, 223–24, 226–27, 229; individual and special, 218, 232–41; and motive, 226; opportunity for, 230; and penitence, 235–36; Satan's begging of, 214–15, 216, 221–22, 223–24, 232, 233, 234–35, 237, 241, 242; in seventeenth century, 215, 217–18; theological virtue of, 4–5

Paré, Ambroise, 119

Parliament, 33, 153; Charles I struggle against, 45, 75n16, 80, 199; determination of treason by, 73, 77n18, 83–84, 228; Long Parliament, 247; pardoning by, 218, 222–23; statutory laws of, 59–60, 76, 156

partner (term), 150, 182

Patriarcha (Filmer), 88, 170

Patrides, C. A., 224n26, 241–42

peers, 30, 105–6n16

peine fort et dure, 199–200

"Penal Theory in *Paradise Lost*" (Brittan and Posner), 60–61

penitence, 216, 233, 235–36

Pepys, Samuel, 109–10

Percy, Henry, 234

Peters, Julie Stone, 4n10, 90–91

Petition of 11 September 1648, 86

Petition of January 1648, 86

Petition of Right, 19, 86

petty larceny, 5, 22, 108, 159, 217

Phillip II, 229n40

Phillips, Edward, 18, 219

philosophy, 37, 208, 249; and law, 38

Picciotto, Joanna, 11–12, 142, 210

Pilgrim's Progress (Bunyan), 250

Plato, 10; *Laws*, 20, 56

plea bargains, 203–4

plea entering, 40–41, 198–99

Pleas of the Crown (Hale), 73–74, 199, 210

Plucknett, Theodore, 174

poaching, 113–16

Pocock, J. G. A., 52–53n34

poisoning, 118–19

positivism, 38–39, 155

Posner, Richard, 60–61

possession. *See* property and ownership

Powell, Richard (Milton's brother-in-law), 18

Powell, Richard (Milton's nephew), 18

Powell, Thomas, 21

prerogative courts, 48, 51, 53, 75, 192n17, 247–48

private property. *See* property and ownership

processional pageants, 190

Proclamation for Discovery of Robberies and Burglaries, and for a Reward to the Discoverers, A, 107, 201

Proclamation for the Better Discovery and Prevention of Burglaries, Robberies, and Other Frauds and Abuses, A, 106–7

prohibition: God's, 165–66; as legal term, 160–61; writs of, 192n17

Prolusion 7 (Milton), 9, 10

proof, 207. *See also* evidence

property and ownership, 13–14, 125–50; Adam and Eve and, 131–32, 164, 176–77, 181–82; and bonds, 145–46; changing historical view of, 134–35; chattels as, 175–76, 182–83; common law's concern with, 125–26; contracts and, 174; feme covert as, 147–51; forfeiture of, 5, 40, 66, 103, 146, 199, 204, 239–40; history of concept, 100, 126–28; landed, 175–76, 182–83; Milton concern about protection of, 111–

property and ownership (*cont.*)
12; in paradise, 173–83; possessory property, 104; rights and, 179; roman law vs. common law on, 131; sacramental property, 183; Satan and, 102–4, 152–53, 174–78; Sheppard on, 104, 131; sole propriety model of marriage, 6, 14, 126, 128–38, 139–40, 143, 146–47, 150; trespassing offense against, 100
Proposalls of Certaine Expedients (Milton), 162, 193, 194, 248
Protestantism, 42, 63, 224, 242
Psalms, 84, 190
public policy, 170
punishment: and crime, 81, 86, 159, 226; gap between sentencing and, 230; God's, 4, 40, 45; *peine fort et dure*, 199–200; transportation and exile, 205, 240–41
Puritans, 49, 171
purlieu, 114–15
Pye, Sir Robert, 20
Pym, John, 73

Quick, John, *Hell Open'd, or, The Infernal Sin of Murther Punished*, 211–12

Rajan, Balachandra, 111n32
Ramesey, William, *De venenis, or, A Discourse of Poysons*, 118–19
Ranters, 126–27
Raphael, 81, 87, 92, 123
Rastell, John, *An Exposition of Certaine Difficult and Obscure Words, and Termes of the Lawes of This Realme*, 105
Readie and Easie Way, A (Milton), 60, 111–12, 193–94, 248, 249
Reading the Law (Goodrich), 38
real estate law, 126
Reason of Church Government, The (Milton), 23–24, 248
religion, and law, 9–10, 38, 42, 45, 62–63, 249, 251. *See also* ecclesiastical courts; theology
Restoration, 16, 60, 121, 131, 218, 251
Reviving Liberty (Bennett), 84–85, 88
Rex v. Williams, 77
rhetoric, 33, 207–8
Richardson, Jonathan, 219, 234
Ricks, Christopher, 135
right, legal, 179
riot, 3–4
Robins, Harry, 241
Rogers, John, 12n23
Roman law, 3, 52, 131, 164; *laesa maiestas* in, 71; and Mosaic law, 43–44
Romano-canon law, 22, 50–51, 53, 56, 210
Romans, Book of, 246
Rosenberg, Phillippe, 192–93
Rosenblatt, Jason, 61–62, 151, 171n35
Russell, Conrad, 75n16
Rutherford, Samuel, *Lex Rex*, 193

sacramental property, 183
Sacred Meditations (Bacon), 63
Salmasius, Claudius, 21, 72, 225
Saltern, George, 127, 128
Samson Agonistes (Milton), 206
1 Samuel 17, 92
Satan: Abdiel confrontation with, 70–71, 75–76, 86–87, 91–93, 102–3; as arch-felon, 105–6, 107–8; burglary by, 108, 109, 110, 111; complaints about God's laws by, 86–87, 89; and crime, 74–75, 97–98, 100–104, 116–18, 121–22, 124; Gabriel's debate with, 94–95, 101–2; language of possession by, 102–4, 174–80, 183; legal reasoning by, 152, 153, 154, 155, 156, 157–61, 167–70,

174; as Lucifer, 102–3; pardon request by, 214–15, 216, 221–22, 223–24, 232, 233, 234–35, 237, 241, 242; as poacher, 113–16; and poisoning, 118; Sin and Death's collaboration with, 3–4; temptation of Eve by, 101, 152–53, 157–61, 167–70, 174, 175–80, 183; as traitor, 6, 13, 65–66, 69–71, 74–76, 78; as trespasser, 100–102, 158–59, 174; trial of, 92–95
Sauer, Elizabeth, 8n18
scales of justice, 94–96
Schiavone, Aldo, 36
sealed bonds, 5
Second Defense of the English People, A (Milton), 9, 20, 24, 25–26, 47–48, 111
Seipp, David J., 133n14, 134, 175n44
Selden, John, 53, 56, 247; influence on Milton of, 19–20, 21; on property, 127, 128
Shafto, Michael, 234
Shakespeare, William, 1, 37; *Hamlet*, 29, 119; *The Merchant of Venice*, 146–47, 232; *Othello*, 29; *The Tempest*, 232
Shapiro, Barbara J., 37, 208
Sharpe, J. A., 249
Shawcross, John, 48–49, 165
Sheppard, Jack, 120
Sheppard, William: *Actions on the Case for Deeds*, 171; *Epitome of All the Common and Statue Laws of This Nation Now in Force*, 104, 131, 148; on property, 104, 131
shipwrecks, 112
Shuger, Debora, 1, 39–40, 62–63, 98n2
silence, 26
Silver, Victoria, 7, 48, 55
Simpson, A. W. B., 2–3n3
sin, 48, 81, 144; by Adam and Eve, 79, 80, 130, 144, 162–63, 171, 183, 200, 204, 207, 209, 230; and law, 11–12, 45, 63, 151–53, 183, 245; original, 67n2, 148; property and, 126, 143; trespass as, 158, 159, 160; what it is, 246–47
Sin, 4, 34, 84, 103, 207, 242; opens gates of Hell, 69, 122
Skinner, Cyriack, 220
Skinner, Quentin, 51
slavery, 138, 146
Smith, Sir Thomas, 21, 191
smuggling, 112
social contract, 37, 164, 170
social crimes, 112–13
soliciting, 162–63
Somerset, Earl of, 237–38
Sommerville, J. P., 52–53n34
Son: Adam and, 131–32, 139–41, 144, 145, 186, 202; as judge, 95–96, 150, 157, 186, 187, 189, 190–98, 202–4, 206, 229–30; law of obedience to, 76, 77, 85, 87; and mercy, 4–5, 231–32, 234–36; rebellion quelled by, 223–24; Satan's animus against, 70–71; work with Father by, 163, 231. *See also* Jesus Christ
Southern Poverty Law Center, 184
Spelman, Sir Henry, 21
Spencer, Janet, 231n43
Spenser, Edmund, 1, 119
Stachniewski, John, 8–19n19
standing mute, 199–200
Star Chamber, 51, 216n4, 247, 248
State of Innocence, The (Dryden), 175
statutory law, 54, 61, 156; Milton's support for, 48–49, 59–60, 73
Stein, Arnold, 135
Stevens, Paul, 15
St. German, Christopher, 41, 156–57
Strafford, Earl of (Thomas Wentworth), 72, 74, 75, 103

Stretton, Tim, 99n4, 148n38
strict liability, 170, 171–72
Stuarts, 113; pardons by, 218, 227–28, 231–32
Surprised by Sin (Fish), 63, 64
Sussex, Earl of, 234

Ten Commandments, 184, 245
Tenure of Kings and Magistrates, The (Milton), 58, 59, 90, 227; anti-monarchical arguments in, 68, 74, 101; on constitutional law, 22, 56; on punishment, 82, 159; on religion and justice, 9, 10
Tenures (Littleton), 21, 54, 125–26
Tetrachordon (Milton), 19, 23, 45, 56, 154, 244–45; on bonds of nature, 142–43; on calumny, 26–27; on doctrine of consideration, 168; on property, 128
Theis, Jeffrey, 115
Theodosius, 56
theology, 52, 242; and law, 15, 36, 246, 251; Milton's Arminian, 212, 215, 242. *See also* religion
Thompson, E. P., 249
Thorne, Samuel E., 155
toads, 118–19
Torah and Law in "Paradise Lost" (Rosenblatt), 61–62, 151
transportation (punishment), 240–41
treason, 65–96; by Adam, 13, 65–66, 68–69, 78–79, 80–83; as attack on law itself, 73–74, 77; Coke on, 67, 70, 77, 83, 103; definitions of, 67–68, 71–72, 80; felony compared to, 105–6; and forfeiture of property, 40n15; impersonal, 71–84; intent in, 69n6; against kings, 66–68; Milton's shifting view of, 67–69; pardoning of, 218n6, 225, 236; Parliament determination of, 73, 77n18, 83–84, 228; by Satan, 6, 13, 65–66, 69–71, 74–76, 78; two types of, 66–71
Treason Act of 1351, 67, 68, 69
Treatise of Civil Power, A (Milton), 9, 10
Treatise on the Laws and Customs of the Kingdom of England (Glanville), 21
trespassing, 100n5, 158; Satan and, 100–102, 158–59, 174
trial by combat, 92–94
trials: arraignment and plea entering in, 40–41, 198–99; defense counsel in, 38, 191; establishing motive in, 206, 226; formal identification in, 196; presentation of accusations in, 28, 202; role of lawyers in, 191; weighing of facts and evidence in, 210–11, 212–13. *See also* defendants
Trinity, 251
True Patriot, The (Fielding), 124
Tubbs, J. W., 52–53n34, 156
Tudors, 53, 227–28, 231
Tyler's rebellion, Wat (1381), 251
Tyrone, Earl of (Hugh O'Neill), 232, 236–37

Urbino, Duke of, 119
use right, 133
usury, 17, 49, 140n23, 141

Valentinian, 56
Veall, Donald, 105–6n16
verdict: God's, 92–95; guilty, 217; as term, 213
violent crime, 116–20
Visconsi, Elliott, 163

war: in Heaven, 90–91, 95–96; holy, 91–94
Weber, Max, 39

weighing, act of, 94–95
Wentworth, Thomas. *See* Strafford, Earl of
Whigs and Hunters (Thompson), 249
Whitelocke, Bulstrode, 20
William the Conquerer, 107
Wilson, Luke, 21, 37, 167
Winstanley, Gerrard, 174–75
Witte, John, Jr., 40
wrecking (practice), 112
Wyville, Christopher, 185

Yelverton, Henry, 77